New
THOROUGHBRED
OWNERS *Handbook*

New
THOROUGHBRED
OWNERS *Handbook*

AN ESSENTIAL GUIDE TO THOROUGHBRED OWNERSHIP

Edited by Laura Proctor

ECLIPSE
PRESS

Lexington, Kentucky

Library of Congress Control Number: 2002114042

ISBN 1-58150-097-1

Printed in The United States
First Edition: May 2003

Distributed to the trade by
National Book Network
4720-A Boston Way
Lanham, MD 20706
1.800.462.6420

a division of
Blood-Horse Publications
PUBLISHERS SINCE 1916

Contents

Preface

We are owners of the most expensive, most pampered, and arguably the most beautiful domesticated creature the world has ever known: the Thoroughbred racehorse. Owning one brings unparalleled excitement.

What thrill can match the sight of your horse, bearing a jockey in the colors and design you have chosen, blazing through the last furlong of a race and snatching victory at the finish line? Life doesn't get much better.

Our attachment to the horses we own is so deep that some of us are willing to lose money each year in order to maintain our horses. When one veteran owner was asked, "Do you stay in because you can't resist the challenge?" he replied, "No...because I can't resist the dream."

Owners, along with the people who wager on races, are the sole support for the entire racing industry. In the aggregate, owners have poured the ransom of many kingdoms into the support of their horses. Owners are tied emotionally and economically to the sport of racing, to the business of breeding, and to buying crop after crop of these beautiful animals.

Do we have to lose money in order to stay in the game? Possibly.

But the combination of proper management and the careful acquisition of durable horses can go a long way toward cutting potential losses and can turn a stable "bought for pleasure" from a losing proposition into an economically viable – even very profitable – operation.

There is no guarantee that durable, winning horses can be found. On the other hand, every owner can become a knowledgeable and successful manager if he or she is willing to take the time to learn how to do something more with Thoroughbred ownership than write the monthly support check.

In general, most of us pursue careers outside racing so that we can provide the economic support demanded by our stables. We rarely have the opportunity to share our knowledge with other owners. Informal interviews with many owners yielded a persistent answer to questions about the manner in which their Thoroughbred business is run: "Well, that's just the way we've always done it..."

Racing is perhaps the only sport that seems to treat its devotees as "outsiders." The language of racing can be intimidating, even to experienced owners. In some cases, it stymies the impulse to become involved in the day-to-day operation of the stable's business. The more owners can familiarize themselves with the arcane vocabulary of the sport, the more confident they are in the hands-on running of their horse business.

It doesn't matter how much of any single horse you own or how many you have committed to support, you are operating a stable. Whether you are already a veteran owner, or whether you are simply wondering about becoming involved in the ownership of Thoroughbred racehorses, there are matters of sound management that deserve consideration. Many are outlined or suggested in this primer.

Owning a racehorse is not for everyone. The experience is an emotional and financial roller coaster. There are no guarantees – indeed, there will be more disappointments than successes. (A vivid reminder is that there is only one winner in every race; the rest are "also-rans" that may or may not share in the earnings and that achieve only "small glory.")

However, no matter what the "business" outcome may be, one thing is certain: If you love the beauty and spectacle of Thoroughbred racing, if you love the idea of stabling and owning a gifted – and perhaps one day fabled – equine athlete, and if you love the combination of challenge, chance, and skill, you will not be disappointed.

There is a world of practical knowledge you can acquire once you plunge into the management of your Thoroughbred business, while your chance for profit will greatly increase by exploring the directions opened in this book.

Introduction

This book is dedicated to outlining the unparalleled joys, as well as the hazards, of Thoroughbred racehorse ownership. We hope it will serve as an important resource for the experienced owner and a primer for those who always dreamed of owning a Thoroughbred but were daunted by the problems and mysteries of getting started.

The business of racing Thoroughbreds is more of an art than an economic science. It involves a deep emotional attachment to the horses, a zest for challenge, and steady shoulders. As a result the owner occupies a unique niche in the world of horse racing. The goal of this book is to view racing solely from the owners' perspective, which may bring it occasionally into conflicts with other points of view. If you find opinions contrary to those registered in the following pages, the authors suggest you consider their source and examine the motivation of those who disagree.

In short, we welcome you to the wondrous world of owning, and we trust you have found, or will find, Thoroughbred racehorse ownership one of the most rewarding experiences of your life.

Thoroughbred ownership can bring unparalleled joy.

1

Before You Start...

While the thrills of Thoroughbred racehorse ownership are unparalleled, they do come at a cost. For most investors, those costs aren't insignificant. Racing is a speculative venture, and not everyone can handle the emotional highs and lows that inevitably come with owning racehorses.

Horses are not machines. They cannot be programmed, nor do they always perform on command. They are often unpredictable, at times temperamental, and are surprisingly fragile creatures. Like children, they don't always live up to your hopes and dreams. Successful owners, like good parents, are prepared to deal with the ups and downs, both emotional and financial, that overseeing a living being entails.

How does one increase his or her chance of becoming a successful owner? Through thorough preparation and continuing education, not to mention a healthy dose of common sense. So, if you are serious about investing in Thoroughbreds and becoming an owner, consider these suggestions:

Familiarize Yourself with the Thoroughbred Industry

Read industry publications such as *The Blood-Horse*, *Daily Racing Form*, *Owners' Circle*, and *Thoroughbred Times*.

Attend your nearby races and auctions and visit a local Thoroughbred farm. Observe owners, trainers, consignors, buyers, veterinarians, and other professionals in action.

Network through the owner or breeder association in your state (see Appendix) and nationally through TOBA. Inquire about the services offered and membership benefits. Become involved with the organizations and use them to make personal contacts with local horsemen and women.

Ask respected owners, trainers, and other industry insiders if you may speak with them about how you might get involved in the business. We bet you'll be pleasantly surprised by the number of insiders who are willing to assist prospective owners, regardless of the investment level.

Consult a more experienced owner or consultant who is willing to serve as a mentor. But be discriminating and ask for and check references in the case of a professional consultant. The objective here is to find someone you can trust. Listen to the advice given but don't feel obligated to follow it, as ultimately every decision you make should be your own.

Participate in industry-sponsored events and educational programs. TOBA sponsors numerous educational opportunities throughout the year, as does the Thoroughbred Owners of California and various state owner and breeder organizations around the country.

Define Reasonable Goals and Objectives

Before you take the plunge, start to outline what you'd like to accomplish as an owner. In other words, what's your plan? Answering these questions will help you devise your road map.

How much money can I afford to allocate to this business?

Generally speaking, the level of investment is the primary consideration in determining the most appropriate means of becoming an

Do your homework before you invest in a Thoroughbred.

owner. Determine the total amount of money that you are willing to allocate to this investment. Develop a budget, identifying the amount to be used for the initial purchase of racing stock and obtain realistic estimates of daily expenditures. This handbook will help you develop those estimates.

How much time do I intend to devote to my equine activities?

To answer this question, you will need to ask yourself: How involved do I intend to be? Will my schedule permit me to spend time monitoring my equine investments? For example, do you have the time to talk with your trainer or visit the stable area on a daily or weekly basis?

Do I prefer to invest as an individual or in a partnership?

The level of investment and amount of time you have to spend on your equine activities should guide you in determining the appropriate form of ownership. However, your personal preferences and past experiences may be equally as important. What level of control do you wish to maintain? Are you the type of individual who must call all the shots, assume all the risks, and have all the glory? Or do you prefer to spread the risks and share the rewards?

Before deciding, read "Public Partnerships" in the chapter on purchase options and also "Types of Entities" in the business issues chapter to gain a deeper understanding of the pros and cons of sole ownership.

What are my short-term and long-term goals?

How long are you willing to wait for a return on your investment? Are you looking for the immediate action offered by racing or for the long-term challenge of breeding and developing young horses?

What type of equine investment should I make?

If you want immediate action, then your investment strategy will be quite different from those interested in breeding and developing young stock. However, the opportunities are not mutually exclusive. You may consider diversifying your investment by purchasing a filly as a broodmare prospect, breeding her, and selling the resulting offspring; acquiring a stallion share; and/or owning horses of racing age.

Where should I race?

While most likely you want to be able to see your horse as often as possible, it may not fit in with your goals as a racehorse owner. If having convenient access to your horse is imperative, then you must think and act regionally. On the other hand, given that some states offer lucrative racing and breeding programs, you may want to consider how these programs could impact your investment. See Chapter 14 for information on state-bred programs.

At what level am I looking to participate?

Everyone wants to own a classic winner. Unfortunately, not all horses have the ability to compete and win at the top level. You have a variety of levels at which to compete, either claiming, allowance, or stakes levels, which vary depending on region. Your financial resources will ultimately dictate the level at which you compete.

If action is what you want, your strategy will be different than someone seeking the classic horse. You will more likely spread your money out over a larger stable, with more horses racing on regional circuits. If your goal is to find the "big horse," you might have fewer horses that race less often.

Commercial breeding presents a similar scenario. Not everyone can participate at the top level. However, there are ample opportunities, especially in the middle markets, where breeders can sell and buyers can purchase a useful horse.

Remember, the thrills of owning a claiming horse or breeding a maiden winner often match those experienced by owners of more accomplished horses.

What type of tax treatment do I seek for my equine business activities?

Regardless of which form of ownership you choose, be sure your equine investment activity is clearly structured and treated as a business. A detailed analysis of business structure options and related tax and liability options can be found in Chapter 4, The Business of Racing.

What can I expect from my experience as a Thoroughbred owner?

How about a wonderful network of new friends, endless social activities, a sense of significant achievement, and hours of unsurpassed entertainment? But don't forget, the objective of most owners is to realize meaningful financial gains. That's not easy to do, but it's part of the lure.

Remember, Ownership Has Its Perks, Too!

There are many non-monetary perks associated with Thoroughbred ownership. Psychological income, as some have termed it, may be one of the most influential factors in making the decision to invest in the Thoroughbred industry.

Make the most of being a Thoroughbred owner. Take advantage of all the game has to offer, including the following:

owners' pass: A credential granting free admission to the racetrack and access to the paddock and stable area. Free parking is usually included, too.

hospitality services: Services vary from track to track but generally include assisting with seating and complimentary meals on race day, use of the horsemen's lounge, and assistance with hotel and dining reservations, winner's trophies, etc.

name recognition: Your name or stable name will appear in the racing program, *Daily Racing Form*, and perhaps the local newspaper. As an owner, you have the opportunity to be profiled in many industry and trade publications. TOBA and other state organizations are at work enhancing the exposure and recognition of the contribution and achievements of owners.

social networking: Become involved. As a Thoroughbred owner, you are part of a diverse and distinguished group sharing the rewards and challenges inherent in the industry. Take time to cultivate friendships. These relationships can provide much insight and valuable information and may aid the overall success of your business. Regardless of their business value, they will unquestionably enhance your overall enjoyment of the Thoroughbred industry. Make the most of them!

2

Developing a Business Plan

Business plans are like works of art — no two are exactly alike. Unlike business plans written in the corporate world to attract investors and raise capital, a plan written for your Thoroughbred business might be read only by you. So personalize it. Make it reflect what you intend to accomplish and how you intend to go about it. Have some fun when writing it — you probably won't be using it to impress a venture capitalist or banker. Instead, use it as your road map for reaching success.

Advantages to a Plan

It's important that you take the time to develop a plan, if for no other reason than to show the Internal Revenue Service that, in the event of an audit, you're in business. In March 2001 the IRS published a guide to train its examiners in auditing horse operations to determine whether they satisfy the Section 183 hobby loss provisions. One of the first things the guide instructs examiners to do is ask the taxpayer to present and explain his or her business plan. The examiner will look to see if the

A business plan will help you determine how actively you plan to be involved in your Thoroughbred activities.

owner has developed a valid, thorough, and realistic business plan as a tool for making his or her horse business profitable and uses the plan as an operating guide.

The process of writing a plan will also help clarify your thoughts and intentions, reveal just how much cash flow your Thoroughbred business will require, and help you to avoid getting in over your head. For example, having four horses at the track might be more than your bank account can handle in your first few years; perhaps your budget dictates that you scale down to two. Preparing a business plan will allow you to forecast your expenses and determine just how deeply you can become involved.

When creating a business plan, think it through before you are tempted by the excitement of the sale or want to claim a promising horse. Focus on what you want to accomplish, be it winning a graded stakes, breeding your own racehorse, or simply having a stable that runs in the black. Then use your plan as a tool to help manage your business as you work toward your goal.

Items to Include

A sound business plan need not be elaborate. However, it should be put in writing. Follow these steps to outline your plan:

1) Define the type of business. Is it a sole proprietorship, a corporation, a limited liability company, or a general or limited partnership? If you opt for the latter, enlist the partners when developing the plan. Each form of business entity has specific economic and income attributes that should be considered when selecting the form of business for your particular circumstances (refer to Forming Your Business, Chapter 4).

2) Identify goals and objectives. Is the business geared toward breeding to race, racing to develop breeding stock, racing to make a profit and then selling, or breeding to sell commercially?

3) Specify the type of consultants to be used. Depending upon the circumstances, it may be appropriate to identify the professionals you consulted and outline their credentials.

4) Outline how you will acquire horses. Will the horses be acquired through auction, claims, or private purchase?

5) Establish a timeline. Forecast when you will acquire horses, hire employees, expect income, and have large cash outlays.

6) Indicate location and scope of activity. Will the business operate on a regional or national basis? How large do you envision it to become? At what level will it operate (at the major-league tracks or regional ones?).

7) Project expenditures and revenues. Create a preliminary budget with reasonable projections. Budget line items should include (at the minimum) purchase price, depreciation, typical operating expenses such as training fees, commissions, and lay-up costs, breeding fees, transportation invoices, veterinary and blacksmith charges, stakes fees (nomination, entry, and starting fees), administrative expenses, insurance, professional services, travel, and entertainment, etc.

8) Provide for appropriate insurance. Depending upon the type of equine investment, you should consider obtaining insurance coverage for the risks inherent with that investment. For example, would commercial general liability, mortality, live foal, or transportation insurance be appropriate?

9) Articulate the activity's term. Do you intend to remain in the business indefinitely or are you limiting the term of your equine business activities? For example, if your goal is to race, you may want to state that you intend to review each horse's performance at the end of each year and then decide whether to continue to race the horse, retire it for breeding purposes, or sell it.

Review Regularly

Referring to your business plan will help you stay focused and operate within your budget. Review your business plan regularly, about once a month or so, to see if you are "on track." Then make adjustments to your plan according to how your business is progressing, especially when you are first starting out. When reviewing, remember to continually evaluate each horse economically — and be prepared to sell the unprofitable ones. A business plan should not be etched in stone but should be flexible to incorporate changes that arise during the course of business, such as a different method of acquiring horses than planned, an unforeseen setback (from injury or illness), or an unexpected windfall in purses.

Forecasting income is probably the most difficult part of the plan to develop. One simple way is to try and build upon the income generated in the first year — making more in subsequent years. Or if you are operating a racing stable, you could predict the number of times each horse will start in a year (the national average is seven), and then figure how many times you think a horse will finish in the money. Or, you may want to outline how much it will cost to get each horse to the races and then determine how much that horse must earn to become profitable. Whichever method you choose, try and set some financial goals, and then streamline your business as you gain experience to increase its efficiency.

Is developing a business plan hard work? Yes. But taking the time and making the effort to devise a good plan will help you enjoy your Thoroughbred activities and satisfy the IRS.

Helpful Resources

A sample plan outline and on-line resources are listed here:

Bplans.com – Shows sample business plans, has business plan software, etc.

www.SBA.gov – The Small Business Administration's website. Visit the "Starting Your Business" section, then click on "Business Plans" to view step-by-step instructions for developing a business plan.

Morebusiness.com – Lists more plans, templates, etc.

Sample Business Plan Outline

Name of Business:

Goals/Objectives: *Operate at a profit within x years? Win a classic race? Develop stakes winners? Raise quality racehorses?*

Location: *Where will you be headquartered?*

Scope: *In which states will you operate? At what level do you wish to operate – stakes horses, a claiming stable, etc.*

Business Structure: *Do you want to operate as a sole proprietor, partnership, or corporation?*

Consultants: *Who will advise you?*

Trainer: *May want to list background, achievements, etc.*

Bloodstock Agent: *ditto*

Veterinarian: *Educational background, experience, etc.*

Accountant: *ditto*

Equine Assets:

Method of Acquisition:

Horse	When Acquired	When Sold or Bred
Auction		

Claiming

Private Purchase

Breeding

HORSE #1: *This may be done on a horse-by-horse basis if desired.*

Projected Annual Expenditures:

Acquisition Cost:

Training Fees:

Trainer Commissions:

(Jockey commissions are not listed as they are usually automatically deducted from the purse.)

Other Commissions: *i.e., a bloodstock agent's 5% commission on a private purchase.*

Veterinary Expenses:

Farrier Expenses:

Equine Dentistry Expenses:

Insurance:

Stakes Fees: *Nomination, entry, and starting fees.*

Other Nominations: *Breeders' Cup, state-bred incentive programs.*

Equine Transportation: *Vanning or flying to and from races or to and from farms, etc.*

Other Race Day Costs: *Pony to post, mount fees, etc.*

Board: *Farm lay-up.*

   Depreciation:

   Travel:

   Entertainment:

   Professional Services: *Accountant, attorney, etc.*

   Administrative:

   Other:

Total Projected Annual Expenses: $

   Projected Annual Revenue:

Purses:

Horse Sales:

Total Projected Annual Revenues: $

   Estimated Profit/Loss $

Use Sound Business Judgment

Remember to exercise sound business judgment when becoming involved in Thoroughbreds. Some pointers include these ideas:

- Open a separate bank account for your Thoroughbred business.
- Maintain complete and accurate financial records.
- Employ professional consultants when necessary.
- Document the number of hours spent on your equine business activities, including all meetings, telephone calls, stable visits, sales attended, inspections, farm visits, travel time, and industry-related reading and studies, etc. Note as much as possible the time, place, and purpose of such activities.

3

Selecting Trainers and Other Advisers

Every new owner has the urge to develop a stable on his or her own, especially when it comes to selecting the horses. But novice owners who go it alone risk setbacks and even failure.

Thoroughbred racing and breeding should be approached as a team sport. Success depends on more than the natural talent of its athletes. In addition to outstanding athletes, a good team must have a good coach, astute scouts, a capable physician, satisfactory support personnel, and a savvy owner.

Recognize early on that the success of your racing operation will depend, significantly, on the makeup of the team. Exercise as much, if not more, care in selecting a team of consultants as you would in selecting your first horse.

The size of your investment and your general objectives should dictate the types of advisers you retain. For many owners, a trainer may be all that he or she needs to enjoy many years of Thoroughbred racing. Others may want to include a bloodstock agent, pedigree adviser, veterinarian, and more experienced owners for advice.

Decide how your team will assist you. Will they merely participate in the selection and evaluation of potential purchases or will they help refine and execute your business plan? When making this decision, remember to use sound business judgment, and keep in mind the following thoughts:

1) Thoroughbred racing and breeding are businesses; treat them as such. Be rational, not emotional.

2) Disclose your objectives and business plan from the start.

3) Determine whether the consultants considered have expertise in these areas.

4) Stay within the budget you created. Realistically evaluate your ability to invest in the industry at the level you have selected, and scale down

your level of participation if necessary. Remember, it can be just as much fun to own part of a horse as it is to own the entire animal.

5) Once your consultants have been selected, let them do their jobs. Stay involved, but allow the professionals to do what you have hired them to do, which is provide advice in areas in which you have little knowledge or expertise.

Trainers

Like the owners who hire them, trainers tend to be rugged individualists – strong-minded men and women who, in most cases, are self-made. Many started out as hotwalkers or exercise riders and managed to pull

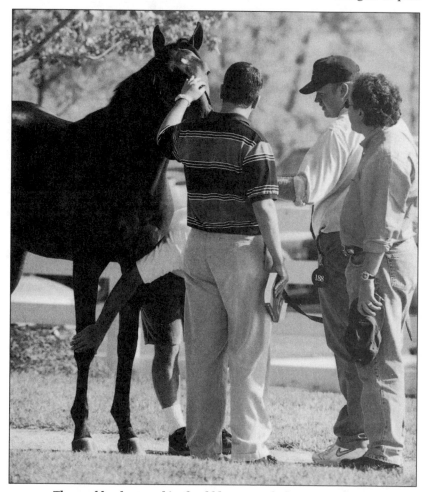

Thoroughbred ownership should be approached as a team sport.

away from the "pack" by sheer hard work and smarts. Competitive with one another, and secretive, they keep to themselves and run their barns like principalities.

Trainers regard themselves as professionals – experts for hire – and not as "employees" in the common sense. There was a time when a saying on the backside went something like, "owners should be treated like mushrooms: kept in the dark and fed bull..." Well, you get the idea. Fortunately, increased involvement by knowledgeable owners and a new breed of modern, businesslike trainers have combined to change that attitude.

Those who still don't know a horse's hock from his stifle tend to look upon a trainer in the same manner as we view our medical doctors. We take their statements on faith and pray that they make wise decisions. In most cases, we don't even know which questions to ask, much less the course of action to take.

"Training" horses is not an exact science. It consists largely of instinct, a trained eye, a smartly run barn, the ability to maintain relationships with volatile people over the long term, and above all, hands-on, in-the-trenches experience. A trainer is most akin to an athletic coach. The trainer will help spot and "recruit" talented horses for the owner and take responsibility for the horses' health and their individual conditioning programs. This includes feed and feed supplements, any needed "sports-type" treatments such as poultices and bandaging, and veterinary care. They keep an eye out for injuries or developing problems, monitor each horse's mood and psychology, and give their judgment on the best workout and racing schedule for each horse. Unlike athletic coaches, however, the racehorse trainer never has an "off season." They work seven days a week, every week of the year, and nightlife is a long-forgotten memory. Many successful trainers rise at 3:30 a.m. and often put in 16-hour days. Clearly, their careers as trainers are looked on far more as a calling than as a "job."

Choosing a Trainer

Finding the right trainer is probably your most important decision as an owner.

Once the emotional and financial commitments of owning a horse have been made, the process of selecting a trainer becomes crucial. Experienced owners and neophytes alike can become a cropper at this point. How do you determine which trainer fits your needs as well as those of your horses? The answer lies in asking the right questions. The first set of questions are the ones you must ask yourself.

Horse ownership is a gamble. How much are you prepared to gamble for the thrill of owning your own sports franchise? What level of risk are you comfortable with? It will come down to a combination of passion and pocketbook and, depending on the level at which you wish to participate, you may need both in abundance. The money you spend as an owner of racehorses is money you must be prepared to kiss goodbye. Bad breaks and good ones, faith, slumps, hunches, and especially luck are the ultimate rulers in this sport, so it takes the right trainer to make the experience worthwhile.

In selecting a trainer (or, eventually, trainers), there are three basic questions you will need to ask yourself. 1) How much can you afford to spend? (A trainer's success and location raises or lowers his "price.") 2) How active do you wish to be in the management of your horse(s)? 3) Which trainer best suits your personality and philosophy?

For example, a successful trainer will command a higher price and has the option — if it's in his or her makeup — of taking more control of your horse's career with less involvement from you than you might like. In this case, you must weigh the value of his or her "win average" against your desire to be a hands-on owner. In the extreme, a very successful trainer with an autocratic bent is likely to prefer making most of the decisions, from choosing the date when the horse will race and the level at which it will run to which jockey will ride it. The trainer may also prefer to determine the extent of veterinary care needed, which vet will treat the horse, and what treatments will be administered. On the other hand, the top trainer may have a garrulous personality, enjoy talking to you and conferring with you fairly often, and even relish the process of educating you about Thoroughbred horses.

The point is: determine your priorities and find a trainer who will be comfortable with them. The top trainers generally don't need your business (unless you're bringing a lot of it), so if you want a high level of involvement and participation, you may have to drop down the "win ladder" a little to find it. But don't mistake the willingness to listen as a sign of insecurity or weakness. It takes a very well-schooled and sure-handed trainer to be willing to listen and, in fact, teach an owner what must be learned to make the right choices. And no matter how willing or "democratic" the trainer, remember to respect the fact that he or she has more experience with horses and with racing than you do. (As one amiable veteran trainer likes to put it: "If you know so much about these horses, then what are you paying me for?").

It is best to explain your expected involvementduring the initial interviews with trainers. This will help you find a trainer who will accept your involvement and avoid any misunderstandings later.

There are several ways to seek out the names of trainers. First, you might spend time at the track asking "veteran" racetrackers which trainers they most admire, talking to other owners, and getting recommendations. Trainers are frequent visitors to the owners' boxes, so you might

Selecting a trainer will be one of the most important decisions you make.

make initial contact there and get a feel for the chemistry between you. Trainers' telephone numbers can usually be obtained through the track's racing office, although such progressive organizations as the Thoroughbred Owners of California have produced a trainers directory with contact and biographical information.

You can feel free to call most trainers and ask for an appointment to talk. The best hours to call are usually between 9 a.m. and 11 a.m. — before and after that, their days are generally busy. Be aware that if you are calling a top trainer, he or she may not be taking new clients or horses (unless your pockets have no bottom and your ambitions no ceiling or unless you are offering horses of top stakes class, which no trainer can resist). Though you may be most comfortable inviting the trainer to lunch (or a very early dinner) to talk, it would be far more enlightening to arrange a meeting at his or her barn, where you can see the staff and horses and get a feel of how the barn is run. The barn should be orderly, and the horses exercised, bathed, hot-walked, and bandaged. The trainer and assistant trainer, if it's a very big operation, should have seen every horse that morning and be familiar with the physical and emotional condition of each. No matter how "important" the trainer, he or she should know every horse by name and sight, and the good ones will be proud to show that they do.

Once your interview is set, be ready with your questions; trainers usually have very little spare time.

Suggested questions include:

What is your philosophy of training? (Listen well.)

How much contact do you think is appropriate between an owner and trainer? (i.e., how much and how often if I have one horse with you, or three, or 10?)

Is it preferable for me to call you or vice versa? If you'd rather I call, what times of day are best?

Will you automatically call me if my horse is going to work, if it is sick, or if something is developing with its physical condition or training program? Are you likely to consult me on the selection of races for my horse? (The answers to these questions will give you an insight into the depth to which you will be invited to participate in your horse's care.)

What is your "day rate" per horse? The range can vary widely depending on the trainer's reputation, "batting average," and location. For example, in California day rates vary greatly within the state and racing circuit. On the southern California circuit, day rates range from $65 to $90, with the top trainers commanding $90. In northern California, the day rates range from $50 to $60. The day rate is a necessity. Every sound or reasonably sound horse requires hours of daily attention. It must be exercised in some manner, whether that consists of walking, jogging, galloping, breezing, or actually working. It must be taken from its stall, bathed, and groomed. Its stall must be cleaned and its food prepared and served. The "day rate" and what services are incorporated in it are somewhat negotiable.

Though "stars" in any field can and usually will command "star fees," a trainer's day rate is rarely set by caprice or ego. With a higher day rate, you are also likely to find a higher employee-to-horse ratio, better feed supplements, hand-walking (as opposed to machine-walking), and generally more attentive care of the horses in that barn. Most trainers will insist that they break even or actually lose money on their day rates. Why would they be willing to lose money? Because, like you, they only make "real money" on their percentages of winnings. If they see a promising horse, they may go into day-rate deficit to turn that horse into a winner, because that's where the profit is. On the other hand, there are smaller, fledgling trainers who make their living on their day rate because they have fewer horses. An interesting fact to keep in mind when considering day rates is this: it costs as much, if not more, to condition and train a "cheap" horse as it does an expensive one.

What does your day rate include? The items usually covered are feed, grooming, exercise riders, ponies for workout, paddock and gate schooling, hotwalking, vitamins, bandages, and similar "supplies," the assistant trainer's fee, and your share of worker's compensation insurance for every employee of the barn. Some common additional expenses in the day rate are (though not limited to): 1) farrier (shoeing expenses), 2) veterinary costs (X-rays, medications, also dental care), and 3) transportation costs.

Is your worker's compensation insurance current, and what is its rate? Who is responsible if an employee gets hurt?

What is your average vet bill per horse per month? Some trainers use vets almost compulsively and with good results, while others use them sparingly and with equally good results. It depends on the trainer and, to some extent, the quality of horses under his care. Ask if it is the trainer's practice to call you, warn you, or consult with you on major veterinary expenses. Does the trainer check the vet bill before forwarding it to you? (see Chapter 9 on Veterinary and Farrier Care).

What are your views on the use of medication? Some trainers use medication more sparingly than others, preferring to let nature take its course by giving the horse time to heal. Such patience is usually rewarded by increased longevity in a horse's racing career.

What is your background; how much hands-on experience have you had; and who "taught" you? On average, the more years of firsthand experience trainers have had and the more years in the business, the better "bets" they are.

What percentage do you charge on winning horses? The trainer's share is usually 10% of earned purses (although some only charge for first- through third-place finishes), plus a 1% to 3% share for the "barn" — i.e., all personnel from the assistant trainer down to the grooms — or a flat 12% to 13% on wins, which includes everyone (except the jockey). By the way, this figure is usually more negotiable than any other, including the trainer's day rate.

Am I invited to visit the barn and see my horse (perhaps even feed it a carrot), or am I restricted? This facet of being an owner may or may not be important to you, but it's worth getting the answer now.

Good Communication is Key

The sport of horse racing is one of the few business situations left in which management (owner) and contractor (trainer) generally operate on a handshake, which makes communication — including the full discussion and understanding beforehand of what you're shaking on — even more crucial than in ordinary enterprises. As uncommon as it is to sign contracts with trainers, some owners will insist on getting certain details in writing, such as the amount of trainer's commissions on purses and the sale of horses, and a list of expenses not covered by the daily training fee.

The key to everything, however, is good communication from the outset. How do you lay the groundwork for mutual respect and trust, for a relationship that invites candid exchange and avoids rancor? Brand yourself into an appropriate level of expectation. For example, only two out of three young

Thoroughbreds ever get to a race, and few of those "survivors" ever get to the top level. This is rarely the trainer's fault and should not be assumed to be. Horses behave with what one observer called "an awesome randomness" when they race. Somewhere inside, all hot bloods still possess a wildness that a trainer can't always predict and a jockey can't always control. Most horses, for whatever reason, lose. If your horse loses, ask questions first, and only "shoot" much, much later, and never in the heat of disappointment.

Finally, no matter who you choose, it still behooves you to carry into the relationship as much knowledge about training and racing operations as you can possibly absorb...but keep close at hand a reasonable amount of humility.

There are questions that you will be dying to ask, and often, such as "when will my horse be ready to run?" This is a world of guessing and tip-toeing. There are times when getting a horse ready to race seems to proceed at the speed which grass grows. Progress takes weeks. The bills mount. Patience wears thin.

If the horse's progress is excruciatingly slow, it might make some sense to send the horse to a training facility where the costs are almost half of what they are at a racetrack. If this is done, the trainer loses his daily fee. (While trainers do not seek to "lumber" owners with costs, some may resent losing control of the horse's training and the daily fee attached. This should be open to discussion in any ongoing, forthright owner-trainer dialogue.) The fact is, your horse will be ready when it's ready, and no amount of pressure from you or your trainer will change that very much. All you can do is be tuned to pick the right moment.

Finally, there are a few simple "wisdoms" that will help in your all-important relationship with your trainer. 1) Be honest to the point of bluntness. 2) Remember "luck" and avoid the temptation to blame. 3) When in doubt, don't "suspect"; ask. 4) When you ask, listen. 5) Be open about your intentions — for example, if you plan on using more than one trainer for your racing operation, say so.

Your trainer, ideally, should be as close and as trusted as family. The racing world is a small world. Relationships last a long time and bad blood will eventually come around to bite you where it hurts. Finally, if at any point you find you don't trust your trainer, you should, both for the trainer's sake and yours, get another.

Bloodstock Agents

Bloodstock agents primarily assist owners in the evaluation of horses based upon their pedigree and conformation for the purpose of buying and selling at auction or privately. Generally speaking, they may also facilitate the purchase process, from establishing credit with the sales company to finding an equine veterinarian to selecting an appropriate boarding facility, etc.

It should come as no surprise that selecting the right bloodstock agent is not as easy as it seems. Unlike trainers, bloodstock agents need not be licensed to conduct business, and anyone who cares to call themselves an agent can do so. So just like any other business decision, exercise good judgment, sound reasoning, and, above all, trust your instincts.

And consider these tips when making your selection.

1) Consult industry-accepted reference materials. Both the TOBA Membership Directory and *The Source* for North American Racing and Breeding, published by Blood-Horse Publications, provides names and contact information for many bloodstock agents.

2) Solicit recommendations from reputable industry leaders. Ask others in the industry, sales company executives, owners, trainers, etc., their recommendations and endorsements.

3) Contact local horsemen's organizations for recommendations of reputable agents. Ask others within the industry about the reputation and character of your candidates. Remember, there will be a reluctance on the part of many to make less than complimentary remarks about an individual. Instead, they may refer you to someone else or offer an evasive answer, which can provide you some clues.

4) Interview candidates. Evaluate the candidates as you would any other financial adviser.

5) Discuss compensation. Agents typically charge a small commission, (usually 5%) for the purchase or sale of a horse at auction and 10% for those bought or sold privately. Obtain assurances that your agent will fully disclose all commissions for every transaction. Determine if the agent regularly buys from the same consignor. This may evidence a good working relationship, and it should be discussed openly and frankly.

6) Request references, then check them.

7) Review their past purchases with their references. Have the horses been successful? Does this agent have experience buying within your price range?

8) Establish guidelines to resolve potential disagreements.

Above all, recognize that it's your investment, your money, and, ultimately, your horse. Retain the final say.

Veterinarians

While a veterinarian may play a significant role in keeping your horse healthy, you may not consider one an "adviser" until you decide to plunge into the auction world, and then you may find yourself lining up the services of one, fast.

When searching through a slew of yearlings at the sales for sound, durable horses with a potentially quick turn of foot, you may need a veterinarian to "scope" and X-ray horses for you. Veterinarians can quickly perform endoscopic exams ("scope") and take X-rays of individuals you like (see Chapter 5, Acquiring a Thoroughbred), and those that don't pass these exams can quickly be culled from your list. Better yet, many sales have implemented repositories that contain X-rays and "scoping" results on many of the horses in the sale, but you will need your vet to read and interpret these reports for you. When you buy a two-year-old at a training sale, the vet's role can become critical in determining whether a horse has withstood the training pressures placed on it to work fast on preview day.

Veterinarians play a role in private sales transactions, too, X-raying, scoping, and giving a horse a general going over to determine its health and fitness for racing. But they normally will not pass or fail a horse; instead they will give you their opinion of a horse's physical state, sometimes in quite technical or conservative terms. It's your job (and your trainer's) to interpret the vet's findings to determine if you want the horse.

If you have a trainer, let him or her suggest which vet to use, as they probably already have a good working relationship with one. If you are attending a sale without your trainer (or if you have yet to select one), ask the sales company to recommend a veterinarian. Most sales have a good number of vets working their grounds, and the sales staff can quickly put you in touch with one.

Farms and Boarding Facilities

If your preference is to invest first in the breeding side of the industry either by owning a broodmare or young stock, one of your first decisions will be selecting a farm or boarding facility. Owners, trainers, bloodstock agents, and state breeder's organizations can assist you in locating reputable farms.

Again, as with selecting other advisers, you should follow the same sound business principles and pose the same type of questions. While the circumstances may be a bit different, the issues are essentially identical. Consider the following:

What are the costs, and what do they cover?

What type of services does the farm offer?

What facilities does the farm offer? Are the barns in good shape? Is there a training track?

Will the farm represent you at the sales?

Is there a veterinarian on staff?

What is the employee/horse ratio?

Is the farm in good condition? Does it appear to be well kept? How do the horses look? Do they seem well cared for?

Will they call if your horse has a problem or gets injured?

Will your trainer periodically check on your horse if he is laid up there?

Review your concerns, goals, and objectives to make sure they are compatible with those of the farm. Remember, your horses are ultimately your responsibility. Consequently, you should routinely visit the farm to ensure that your animals are receiving proper care.

4

The Business of Racing

Forming Your Business

Before making the transition from racing fan to owner, before claiming that horse you've been eyeing, before you even fill out the form to obtain your owner's license, there are questions to ask yourself. You are entering a whole new world of business, one that will easily and seductively consume as much time, energy, and money as you care to give it. To be an effective player, you will need to devote considerable time to managing, decision-making, tracking, and learning about your new vocation. Can your bank account, friendships, other businesses, and most important, the well-being of your family afford this new commitment?

Once you decide to become a horse owner, you can choose from several styles or forms of doing business:

sole proprietorship

general partnership (public or private)

limited partnership

limited liability partnership

C corporation/S corporation/limited liability company

syndicate

leasing

Regardless of which entity you choose, heed this advice from veteran owners: Start small and go slowly at first. Before you make too costly or permanent a commitment, take time to find out if you have the time for this undertaking, to discover whether you enjoy the art and challenge of owning a racing stable, and to see if you're comfortable with the ongoing costs that are inevitably involved.

Lastly, before making the decision on how you are going to "do business," obtain professional advice (perhaps from your accountant) that takes into consideration both your personal assets and your personal goals. For a list of tax consultants, lawyers, and insurance agents visit www.toba.org.

Different business entities offer different advantages and disadvantages. Here's an overview.

Sole proprietorship: As the sole owner of your racing stable, you can make all the decisions, put your name by the horse's in the racing program, and keep all the glory (not to mention the purses). On the other hand, you (and your estate) will be personally responsible for paying all the bills and defending yourself from (or else absorbing) any liability your stable incurs. Revenues and expenses are reported on your individual tax return. A sole proprietorship is the simplest form of doing business.

General partnership (public or private): In a partnership you will operate under a "stable name" or other agreed-upon and registered grouping of names rather than your own name. Generally, most state racing commissions require partnerships to register, especially when using an assumed name, such as a "stable name."

In any version of partnership, your horse will race under silks jointly selected by you and your partners. The silks selected — and the order of the names appearing on the program — cannot be changed on a race-by-race basis. Both your trainer and the clerk of the course (see Chapter 12, The Races) must have an accurate record of each horse's silks and ownership roster in order for that horse to be entered in any race.

Partnership is quite a popular form of ownership as it allows participation in the thrills and inside experiences of ownership without a drastic individual investment. Although each member of a general partnership (in most racing states) must obtain and maintain an owner's license, this form of business allows you and your partners to reduce the individual risks and costs by splitting them. And you can split them according to whatever percentages you and your partners desire.

However, there is always the chance that one or more partners will either 1) default on their share of the bills, or 2) incur a debt by some action taken in the "ordinary course of the partnership's business." In these cases, each of the remaining partners may be held individually liable for those debts to the full extent of their assets, regardless of agreed-upon ownership percentages. This bears repeating: In a general partnership, all personal assets of each partner, *including non-partnership assets*, are exposed in the off chance your partnership incurs liabilities that must be satisfied. Over time you and your partners may also develop irreconcilable differences with regard to the training or racing schedule of your horse(s). If that happens, you may end up going through a fairly laborious, often costly, and usually acrimonious separation of assets — sometimes even requiring a dissolution or sale of all the horses in which you share an interest. So even if you form a private partnership with friends — say a group that has long enjoyed going to the races together — be prepared for almost anything. A pal is one thing: a partner, with trustworthy business practices and the financial resources to fulfill his or her obligations, is another. To minimize the chance of future problems, it would be wise (though you will find most partners don't bother) to have a clearly defined, written agreement in place before going into the horse business together. And make sure you know your partners well.

Limited partnership: In the case of a limited partnership — a very strictly prescribed form of business that must comply with a number of state rules — there will likely be at least one general partner and one or more limited partners. Only a general partner may be licensed as an owner and actually participate in the management of the stable and partnership. The partnership must appoint one or more managing partners who have a primary management responsibility and are accountable to the state racing commission. A limited partner contributes capital and shares in the purses (or profits, depending upon how the partnership is written), but is not actually bound by the obligations or liabilities of the partnership. In other words, the partners' liability is limited to those assets contributed to the partnership, with the exception of the general partner, whose liability is not limited. However, be careful of this form of business if you are trying to prove to the IRS that you are an active partner (see "Ownership and the IRS" below), as limited partners are generally (but not always) considered passive participants. However, limited partners' losses can be used to offset future income or can offset any income during the year the limited partnership ceases operation.

Typically, lawyers formally spell out the terms and time limits of "limited" partnerships.

Limited liability partnership (LLP): Although similar to general partnerships, LLPs limit the liability of a partner for the wrongful acts of another — a major advantage if you are contemplating forming a partnership with people you don't know. As an LLP partner, you are allowed to participate actively in decision making if you so choose and your income is taxed only once, on your individual tax return. Disadvantages include an LLP's administrative requirements and related expenses. Also, as this form of business may not be recognized by all states, its liability limitations may not apply when the partnership is operating outside the state in which it is created — cause for consideration if you anticipate running your horse out of state.

C corporation: For those of you with significant assets and who fear exposing your assets to a lawsuit, you may wish to consider using the corporate form of ownership for your racing operation. No doubt you have heard of C corporations and S corporations. For legal purposes, they are of the same breed. However, from an income tax standpoint they are horses of a different color. A C corporation files its own income tax return and pays its own tax. The shareholders of a C corporation do not get to use any of the corporation's losses on their own returns. Without delving into the arcane intricacies of our income tax statutes, let us just follow the general rule that C corporations are not recommended for horse operations.

S corporation: Legally, an S corporation is the same type of business structure as described above. However, the shareholder or shareholders in an S corporation have elected to be treated similarly to a partnership for tax purposes, with the profits and losses of the S corporation being passed through to the shareholders. Although the S corporation files its own income tax return, the shareholders pay any income taxes.

Limited liability company (LLC): A creation of the roaring 1990s, limited liability companies (LLCs) are rapidly becoming the favorite form of doing business in this country. An LLC typically has the same legal immunities of a corporation, as well as the ability to be taxed as a sole proprietorship, a partnership, a C corporation, or an S corporation, depending on how the owner(s) wishes to organize his or her business. Our federal income tax statutes do not recognize LLCs; they are disregarded entities. Therefore, an LLC may be taxed as a sole proprietorship if it has only one owner or it may elect to be taxed as a C corporation or an S corporation. If the LLC has more than one owner, it may be taxed as a partnership, C corporation, or S corporation.

LLCs, like corporations and limited partnerships, are inventions of state statutes. Although most of our states have similar statutes regarding

LLCs, there are some quirks. If you choose this type of entity, be sure to engage a knowledgeable attorney. Also, even if an LLC is recognized as a sole proprietorship, it must be treated as a separate entity with its own checking account and books.

Most attorneys and CPAs will urge prospective horse owners to consider this form of business.

Racing syndicate: Racing syndicates operate much like partnerships, but there are key qualitative differences between the two. First, the members of a syndicate are rarely racetrack buddies or even acquainted; they are usually strangers brought together, sometimes from all over the world, by a professional syndicator (you will see advertisements by such individuals in the *Daily Racing Form*, *The Blood-Horse*, *Thoroughbred Times*, and sometimes even in the track's official program). Second, a syndicate is usually formed to buy a horse of stakes quality — a horse so valuable that not many individuals could afford to buy it outright on their own. In other words, most participants in a syndicate are people willing to invest a great deal of money (but not an outrageous sum) to own a share of a horse sufficiently well bred enough to win a world class stakes race. Note that syndicates can own one horse or several; in the case where there are multiple horses in a syndicate, the members' sights may not be set as high as say, the Triple Crown, but the horses are expected to win stakes races or otherwise pay off as breeding animals for the top dollars it cost to buy them.

Generally, but not always, the horse or horses will race under the name and colors of the syndicate manager, who serves as a managing partner. The syndicate manager generally does the paperwork, as well as making the purchasing and racing decisions for the horse or horses owned by the syndicate. In addition, the syndicate manager will ensure that a partnership return is filed and that each syndicate member receives a K1 that he or she must use to complete individual income tax returns. Under common law, syndicates are considered partnerships unless they are structured differently, i.e., as a corporation. Thus, syndicate members are considered partners by the government and should file the K1, which can be likened to a W2. Filing a K1 is often ignored in the horse business, but do so at your own risk.

Although it is impossible to know whether a given syndicate is a good bet (except in the unlikely event you are able to buy into an already existing syndicate with proven horses and proven profits), there are certain measures you can take to reduce your chances of being led down the proverbial garden path. First, do the homework. All Thoroughbreds' bloodlines and racing records, plus records of their sires, dams, their half brothers, half sisters, and every other close relative for that matter, are readily available. Such records and pedigrees may easily be obtained (for a small fee) over the web through such sites as The Jockey Club's www.equineline.com, Bloodstock Research's www.brisnet.com, and others. Or contact your state breeders' association, as many can download pedigrees and forward them to you for a small fee. Such information will offer up the hard facts on a horse's potential...but only if you dig for them. Second, the syndicator will publish or give you an account of his or her experience, credentials, and past performance and will often include references. Check them. Another point of caveat emptor, or let the buyer beware, strongly suggests that you call your local racing commission for assurance that the syndicator's license is current and in good standing. Third, find out who formerly trained the horse(s) and who will be training it for the syndicate. A simple difference in feed or veterinary care can make a real monetary difference in a horse's future. Fourth, if the horse proposed for syndication is foreign born — which many are — you need to check its record carefully (again, via the sources mentioned above) and find out whether its winning races (or its star sire's or dam's) were run under conditions that will not apply in the United States or in the state in which you will be racing. Likewise, you may want to consider that a foreign-born horse may not have been racing on medications that are allowed here (i.e., Lasix) — a fact that may work in your favor.

Finally, in terms of a syndicate, keep in mind that the syndicator — once she or he has recouped from syndicate investors the capital laid out for the purchase of the horse — has nothing to lose. As soon as the horse or horses are fully syndicated, they have been fully paid for by the investors (and perhaps to the profit of the syndicator, since you may have no way of knowing how much the product cost). Whether the syndicator retains a share or percentage is immaterial; whether the members in a syndicate win or lose on the syndicated horses' performances, the syndicator is, most likely, already in profit.

Be careful to note that in most syndicates, investors may assume unlimited liability and each syndicate member is responsible for his or her tax consequences.

Leasing: The hands-off advantages to racehorse leasing are very similar to those involved in the leasing of a car or any other piece of property. Of course, the big disadvantage of leasing is the inability to build up equity. And the lessee must still qualify for and pay for an owner's license.

Leasing is more commonly used in the breeding business. Oftentimes, an individual may have the opportunity to breed to a top stallion but does not desire to or cannot expend the capital to purchase a mare worthy of such a mating. Leasing a top mare is an attractive option, as the owner will obtain a well-bred foal without having to expend a significant sum to purchase the mare.

Are You Active or Passive?

And we're not talking about your workout routine. Being considered an "active" or "passive" participant in your horse business may have significant tax consequences and directly affect your operation's bottom line.

Our income tax statutes place taxable income into three categories:

Portfolio (dividends, interest, and other investment income)

Material participation (wages, active business, or sweat income)

Passive (rents, inactive investment-type business)

Furthermore, these statutes generally dictate that losses from passive activities can only offset income from passive activities. In other words, a $50,000 loss from a passive activity cannot offset your $100,000 salary or your $10,000 dividend income. If you don't use passive losses, they will be suspended and carried forward until you either have passive income, dispose of the passive activity, or die.

Obviously, you should try to be a material participant or active investor in your racing enterprise, which would allow you to offset any losses against other income.

What makes a person an active investor? First, he or she should spend at least 500 hours a year in the activity. Fortunately, a spouse can share these 500 hours. Since the horse business takes many forms, these hours may be spread over a racehorse solely owned by you, a breeding stallion share that you own, and/or an interest in one or more broodmare syndications. You may count hours used in conferring with syndicate managers, trainers, and partners, as well as research, studying the trade magazines, and attending your horses' races.

Sure, the type of ownership you select for your racing business is an indicator of your level of activity, but it is not controlling. A limited partnership interest indicates a passive activity, but the income tax regulations expressly state that a limited partnership interest may be considered an active interest. Again, the level and amount of activity are important.

There are other criteria for meeting the material participation or active requirements, but they are generally applicable only to a small number of horsemen. A spouse who inherits a non-passive activity can still be considered active for several years regardless of whether he or she individually meets the 500-hour standard. Similarly, a retiring material participant can be considered active although he or she may not reach the 500-hour threshold.

IRS "Hobby Loss Rules"

Most horsemen believe that the IRS requires a horse operation to show a profit two out of every seven years in order to qualify as a business rather than a hobby. Although this guideline is considered evidence of a profit motive, it is not a controlling factor.

If you declare losses year after year on your tax return — meaning you write off expenses in excess of your gross income as a racehorse owner — the IRS is liable to decide that your business is *not* a business but a hobby and disallow all deductions. (In fact, in a given year, you might opt to sell a perfectly good horse just to achieve that second profit-making year out of seven. Though emotionally costly, this may end up being a financially sensible move.)

Notwithstanding the fact that the horse racing industry is legitimate, and despite the fact that other highly risky businesses such as mining, filmmaking, oil and gas development, and securities trading are just as likely to lose money, racehorse ownership is one of the businesses most likely to be downgraded to a hobby by the IRS.

Fortunately, Congress has created a safe harbor provision that includes racehorse owners. The provision states that any business established for the breeding, training, showing, or racing of horses that shows a profit in two out of seven years should not be presumed to be a hobby, but should be considered engaged in for profit. Current losses, therefore, may be deducted. The very real problem is that owners, even when trying by every means possible, may be unable to show a profit in one, let alone two, out of seven years, especially if the years in question are the first seven. This makes maintaining your IRS status as a business more difficult — but certainly not impossible. In simple terms, you need to show that your actions and expenditures are founded in a good-faith profit motive.

There are nine factors the IRS must consider in determining whether an activity is a hobby or a legitimate business. These are as follows:

1) The manner in which the taxpayer carries on the activity (the key words here being in a businesslike fashion).

2) The expertise of the taxpayer or his advisers (i.e., you must be hiring people who know what they're doing and paying them accordingly).

3) The time and effort the taxpayer expends in carrying on the activity.

4) The expectation that assets used in the activity may appreciate in time.

5) The taxpayer's success in carrying on other similar or dissimilar (i.e., equally risky) activities.

6) The taxpayer's history of income or losses with respect to the activity (meaning the two out of seven years formula).

Reading industry trade publications is considered "active" participation in your horse business.

7) The amount of occasional profits, if any, that are earned.

8) The taxpayer's financial status.

9) The elements of personal pleasure and recreation (might they be a stronger motive than profit?).

Your best answer to this daunting checklist is to keep records assiduously. Keep a business diary, noting every time you talk to your trainer, veterinarian, or accountant on horse-related business. Keep an accounting of miles traveled to and from the track and record your visits. Keep all receipts for box seats and note when you purchased a *Daily Racing Form* or gave a gratuity. In other words, keep a record of proof that you are seriously engaging in Thoroughbred ownership, hopefully as a profit-making venture.

An important note: Taxation in the horse industry is a specialty. At the very least, you should closely consult with your accountant or financial adviser before forming your business…and your adviser, in turn, may do well to consult with a specialist in accounting for the Thoroughbred industry.

Depreciation Considerations

Thankfully, our income tax statutes allow Thoroughbred owners to deduct depreciation on their racing and breeding stock. Racehorses over two years old and breeding horses over 12 are generally (some exceptions can be made for foreign horses) considered "three-year class" property, with depreciation taking place over four years, as follows:

Racehorses: Three-Year Class Property Depreciation Schedule

Year	% of Original Cost to be Depreciated
1	25%
2	37.5%
3	25%
4	12.5%

For racehorses, a sizeable chunk of a horse's original cost can be depreciated annually, a small positive considering, on average, their relatively short racing careers. Like most other tax deductions, the depreciation deduction directly reduces your gross income from racing or breeding.

Racehorses under two and breeding stock (mares and stallions) that are age 12 or under are depreciated on a seven-year schedule. Owners of breeding stock must wait longer to depreciate their equine investments, but this stands to reason as mares and stallions usually have longer careers on the breeding farms than at the track and young horses have a lifetime of earning power ahead of them.

Breeding Stock

Year	% of Original Cost to be Depreciated
1	10.715%
2	19.134%
3	15.033%
4	12.248%
5	12.248%
6	12.248%
7	12.248%
8	6.126%

A fact not known even by many tax technicians is that racing and breeding horses may qualify for the "first year expensing allowance." This tax rule allows the horse person to expense up to $24,000 of the cost of a racehorse or breeding stock in the year of purchase. This "expensing" is elective and contains several limitations.

Depreciation considerations should also be considered when switching a horse from racing to breeding stock, as the equations can become tricky and the figures involved could have a bearing on when to retire your racehorse from the track and take him or her to the breeding shed.

When switching a horse from racing to breeding, the percentage of the horse yet to be depreciated is shifted from the three-year to the seven-year schedule in a rather complex manner that is best illustrated through example.

Let's say that after two hard-knocking years at the track, you retire your favorite race filly in your third year of owning her. So far, you have claimed 62.5% of the filly's cost as depreciation (25% + 37.5%). What happens to the remaining unclaimed 37.5%? The federal government stipulates that you must establish a new depreciation schedule for it using the seven-year class property schedule.

As you have already taken 62.5% of the filly's cost under the three-year class schedule (which actually depreciates horses over four years), you now have six years left when you switch the filly to a seven-year class schedule (which really depreciates horses over eight years), as you have already depreciated her first two years. The remaining 37.5% of the filly's cost is now spread over the remaining years in a rather complex manner, as follows:

Year	Adjusted %		Unrecovered % of Cost		% to be Depreciated
3	(15.033% / 70.151%*)	=	21.43% x 37.5%	=	8.03%
4	(12.248% / 70.151%)	=	17.46% x 37.5%	=	6.55%
5	(12.248% / 70.151%)	=	17.46% x 37.5%	=	6.55%
6	(12.248% / 70.151%)	=	17.46% x 37.5%	=	6.55%
7	(12.248% / 70.151%)	=	17.46% x 37.5%	=	6.55%
8	(6.126% / 70.151%)	=	8.73% x 37.5%	=	3.27%

* The 70.151% denominator is the remaining percentage had the filly been depreciated the first two years under the seven-year class property schedule instead of the three-year schedule. It is calculated by adding the percentages in years one and two under the seven-year schedule (10.715% + 19.134% = 29.849%) and subtracting the sum from 100% to arrive at 70.151%.

An important note: The IRS uses the actual age (foaling date) of the horse, and not January 1, when determining age. The IRS also discourages large depreciation deductions at the end of the year. Taxpayers enjoy fewer depreciation advantages if they make more than 40% of the their purchases during the fourth quarter.

While depreciation can be somewhat complex, it is a tool that if wisely used can help show "profit" years and also help to reduce your tax burden.

The Capital Gains Spread

Prior to 1994 there was little difference between ordinary income tax rates and long-term capital gains rates on sales of horses for profit. Now the maximum federal income tax rate on long-term taxable gains is 20%, while maximum ordinary income tax rates are approximately 40%. For certain taxpayers, the difference is made even greater by the effect of state taxes.

The holding period to obtain the favorable long-term capital gains treatment on the sale of your horse(s) is two years. If this holding period is met, it is possible for those of you in the higher tax brackets to receive a federal tax savings of approximately 20% or more on your horse sale transactions.

Thus, timing the sale of a horse can affect both its depreciation rates and the way your proceeds will be taxed. Carefully consider the ramifications when selling — and consult your accountant.

Helpful Resources from the American Horse Council

For further information on tax issues, be sure to consult the American Horse Council (AHC). This organization publishes the hefty *Horse Owners and Breeders Tax Handbook* ($60) and a condensed version, *Tax Tips for Horse Owners* ($10). To obtain either of these invaluable resources, contact the American Horse Council at 202-296-4031, e-mail them at ahc@horsecouncil.org, or visit their website, www.horsecouncil.org.

Insurance Concerns & Coverages

After spending a significant sum on your Thoroughbred, you probably should consider insuring your equine investment. Equine insurance coverage does exist that will allow you to recoup some of your financial outlay if your horse dies.

Should you insure? Would your dollars devoted to insurance premiums make financial sense?

That's a question only you can answer. If you own a racing stable with a barn full of horses, the premiums charged to insure all of them could become staggering. However, if you are an owner with one or two horses and if your investment represents a significant portion of your net worth, then it might make sense to purchase a policy on them.

Significant differences exist between the types of insurance coverage available for owners of racing stock and those who own breeding stock. As racehorses in training are somewhat fragile creatures, the equine insurance industry offers only mortality insurance for horses at the track or at a training center. Loss-of-use insurance is not available nor is insurance to cover the cost of colic surgery. This bears repeating: If you are an owner of a horse in training, understand that you can only buy insurance that will protect you in the event a catastrophic injury or illness befalls your horse.

That said, let's take a closer look at equine insurance.

Mortality insurance: Mortality insurance is the only type of coverage available to owners of horses in training. It covers your horse in the event it is lost, killed, or has to be destroyed for any reason, such as in transport, as a result of poisoning or kidnapping (remember Shergar?), or from severe injury or disease. However, before you can collect on this type of policy, you must have done everything possible — regardless of cost — to save the horse's life. Read the terms of your policy carefully. If there is anything mystifying to you, have it explained to your complete satisfaction by your broker and negotiate an adjustment if you feel the policy is inadequate for your peace of mind.

As a rule, the premium for mortality insurance on racehorses, except geldings, is about 4.25% of the value of your horse. Geldings cost a tick or two more as insurance companies realize that, due to their lack of residual breeding value, geldings tend to race more often. If you are paying the appropriate amount in premium, you can be assured of recouping at least the market value of the animal in the event of its death or necessary destruction.

However, any mortality that is inexplicable or could conceivably be "malicious or willful injury caused by the insured" — i.e., a slaughter for economic motives — will be heavily investigated and the claim likely denied.

Post-mortems are de rigueur in mortality claims. They must be ordered by you in a timely fashion (as soon as possible) and be performed by a private vet at your expense. Also "necessary destruction," whether on the track or in the barn, is not a matter you or your trainer can decide. You must have a licensed racing veterinarian vouch — either before or after the horse's destruction — that your animal could not have survived its injuries or was in a state of suffering that could not be relieved.

Insured Value Can Fluctuate

Most insurance companies will assess the market value of your horse at the time of its death and may adjust your reimbursement down accordingly, even if you are paying a premium that insures it at a higher value. The insurance company will not, however, adjust reimbursement up if you have been paying the premium on a lower dollar amount than your horse was worth. A good equine insurance agent can help you determine the amount your horse can and should be insured for and will help you adjust your horse's insured value as its racing career develops. Adjusting the amount insured for is a relatively easy process, although the insurance carrier will require a veterinary certificate showing the horse to be in good health.

For example: You have dropped your horse in price and entered it in a claiming race with a claiming price less than the insured value of the horse. If the horse dies as a result of the race, you will be reimbursed for no more than the price for which you were willing to let the horse be claimed, although you can receive a pro-rated return of the premium that you paid to insure it at the higher amount. Clearly, then, if you are dropping one of your horses in class (for whatever reason), you should immediately request from your insurance broker a commensurate drop in your "sum insured" and thus your premium.

Now take the opposite case. If you have a horse that is skyrocketing in class but you are paying a premium commensurate with a lower class, the insurance company will not "adjust up" automatically to the horse's value at the time of death. Worst case: You have insured your two-year-old for $32,500, then gone on to race him and discovered he was a stakes winner worth possibly millions in combined racing and breeding potential — but if you have not readjusted your premium on the horse since first insuring him, you would only recover $32,500 upon the event of his death.

In other words, it behooves the astute owner and trainer to re-evaluate periodically the mortality premiums being paid on all horses in their stable.

A cautionary note: The wording of most mortality policies clearly indicates that the owner or trainer must notify the insurance company or its agent of any dramatic change in the horse's health or condition. The existence of an abnormality or malaise that is unreported can adversely affect — or even nullify — a mortality insurance claim.

An interesting note: The higher priced the horse, the lower the premium for his mortality insurance may be. In fact, this is quite logical: If you own a stakes-caliber runner, the horse probably will be watched more closely and handled more cautiously…meaning that the risk for the insurance company should be reduced and the premium lowered accordingly.

Claiming insurance: Whoever claims or wins the draw for a horse in a claiming race is completely liable for the horse he or she is claiming the instant the race officially starts. If the horse has to be destroyed as a result of injuries sustained in the race, the claiming owner is still responsible for payment for the pre-agreed claiming price. Thankfully, there is claiming insurance that can cover your losses in the unlikely event that a horse you claim suffers a life-ending injury during the race (or within 24 hours, depending upon the terms of your policy). If you already have a horse (or horses) at the track that is covered by an annual policy, ask your broker whether your policy extends to other horses you may suddenly acquire (i.e., claim). If not, you may want to take out claiming insurance before you enter a claim on a new horse. One problem: You may not be able to get it. Claiming insurance is the loss leader in equine insurance. It is extended only as an accommodation to owners with large stables already insured or to trainers with good histories and good relationships with the insurance carriers. If you can land claiming insurance, it will cost you only 0.75% to 1% of the claiming price listed for the horse, but the policy usually only covers the race and up to 24 hours afterward.

Or if you already have an equine insurance policy, you may purchase an annual insurance policy for horses that you claim, with coverage being bound once the starting gate opens. Contact your insurance agent before you drop the claim slip, however, and inform him or her of your intentions. If your claim is successful, your new horse will be added to your policy and an annual premium will be charged.

Specified (or "limited") perils insurance: Coverage of this type is less expensive but is typically limited to death from perils such as "fire, windstorm, lightning, and transportation." Not covered is any loss due to death from disease or injury (i.e., colic, broken bones, cancer) — anything "medical."

Owners' legal liability insurance: This type of policy is becoming popular in a culture that is increasingly litigious. It protects you, the owner, from claims against your person or estate by third parties suing for property damage or bodily injury inflicted by your horse and provides your legal defense. For example, if a person is standing too close to your horse in the saddling ring and gets kicked, he or she could sue you for damages. Your homeowner's insurance will not cover such a claim nor will there be any appreciable help from the insurance policy of the facility (i.e. the racetrack or training barn) where the incident occurred.

Legal liability insurance is bought in increments (up to $2 million or $3 million), with premiums based on the number of horses being insured at one time:

• $1 million worth of liability coverage for one to five horses costs about $750 per year. The amount of coverage for six to 10 horses would cost approximately $1,000 per year.

• $300,000 worth of liability for one to five horses would run about $350 per year; figure about $500 per year for six to 10 horses.

If you have vulnerable personal assets of any considerable amount, this type of insurance is clearly worth investigating.

Worker's compensation insurance: Worker's compensation insurance for all employees of the stable (including the trainer and any jockeys you use) is usually the responsibility of the trainer rather than the owner. However, in the case of an owner employing his or her own private trainer, then it's up to the owner to provide worker's compensation coverage for the employees of his stable.

Most racing commissions keep close tabs on the upkeep of every trainer's worker's compensation insurance — but there are two things that you, as an owner, should know. First, every trainer, depending on his or her history of claims (whether the claims were ultimately cleared or not), is charged a different percentage per $100 of payroll for worker's compensation insurance. The percentage can be as little as 10% or as much as 30% — and since these charges will be passed on to you via your monthly day-rate bill, it's worth finding out what your trainer pays for worker's comp. Second, if your trainer falls behind on his or her worker's comp premium payments, you may be exposed to liabilities caused by injury to one of his or her employees. Horror stories exist of owners being assessed medical damages when a trainer's exercise rider was injured and the worker's compensation policy had lapsed due to lack of premium payment. So ask your trainer if the worker's compensation is current. Or investigate taking out your own worker's comp policy — owners can and do obtain them. In fact, some racing states, including New York and New Jersey, require that owners carry worker's compensation. If you ship to race, it's best to obtain coverage from a national carrier that can provide coverage in all states, or an "all states endorsement." This will save you from having to obtain coverage in different states. Although your trainer usually handles arrangements for worker's comp, make sure he is aware that in most states he must show proof of such insurance.

While debate surrounds the issue of whether jockeys are considered employees or independent contractors, in California they are covered by a separate insurance fund that is usually paid for by assessing owners a sum per mount ridden. This jockey's insurance costs between $20 and $60 per mount — a figure that usually appears on California owners' monthly statements. In other racing states, the Jockeys' Guild provides insurance, which is usually funded from a portion of the purses or through a surcharge that is attached to the licensing process.

Breeding Stock Insurance

Insurance for breeding stock is not as cut and dried as is coverage for racehorses. In addition to standard mortality insurance, owners of breeding stock may also purchase coverage to protect their interest in a breeding stallion's fertility or to guarantee that a mare will conceive and that she will produce a live foal. Medical insurance is also offered on mares, stallions, and young horses not yet in training to help defray the costs of illness or injury.

Barrenness insurance/conception insurance: This policy guarantees that a mare will conceive and produce a single live foal and that the foal will survive its first 30 days. The premiums charged vary, depending upon the mare's current foaling date (will she foal late, leaving less time to be bred back?) and produce record. Before 2001's mysterious Mare Reproductive Loss Syndrome (MRLS), rates for barrenness insurance ranged between 22% and 25% of the stud fee. Due to the large number of claims caused by MRLS, it's uncertain if this type of coverage, in the short-term, will still be available or at what cost.

Guaranteed live foal/prospective foal insurance: This insurance coverage takes effect once a mare is confirmed in foal and insures that she will produce a single live foal. Its 10% to 11% of the stud fee cost reflects the reduced risk of only guaranteeing a live foal from a mare that has conceived. This type of insurance is commonly used to cover mares purchased at auction. However, MRLS has also made its short-term availability uncertain.

Stallion infertility insurance: Purchased by those with an "insurable interest" in a stallion prospect, this coverage insures that in his first year at stud, a stallion will get at least 60% of his mares in foal. Parameters are set with regards to a minimum and maximum number of mares bred. The cost is approximately 3.75% to 4% of the insured value.

Accident, Sickness, or Disease (ADS): ADS insurance covers owners of stallions or prospective stallions against infertility caused by, you guessed it, an accident, sickness, or disease. It costs between 0.25% and 0.50% of the horse's value and is usually purchased on an annual basis throughout the stallion's breeding career.

For those fortunate enough to own that once in a lifetime fabulously bred and extremely fast colt, an insurance package combining mortality, infertility, and ADS insurance can be purchased for 7% to 7.5% of the horse's appraised value.

Medical insurance: Coverage for surgical or medical expense is not available for racehorses. Medical insurance is available for breeding stock, though, and for young horses not yet in training. For $7,500 worth of coverage, $200 is a usual premium charged, with a deductible of $250 per claim.

Licensing Procedures

In order to race a Thoroughbred, you, the owner, must be licensed. The power to grant a license or revoke it rests with the state racing commission, which regulates racing under laws promulgated by the state.

If you buy a horse at a public sale or auction, you don't need a license. It is only when your horse is entered in a race or you have put a claim on a horse about to race that the licensing process must be underway.

You must have an owner's license before you can enter your horse in a race (and in some cases even before you can bring your horse to a racetrack for training). But once you own a registered racehorse — i.e., through buying at auction or by private purchase rather than by claiming — you will find it a fairly simple process to become licensed. Though it can be more time consuming, many states will license you by mail, although the racing commission may deny you access to the backstretch until you have your picture taken for your photo identification badge.

Most state racing commissions have offices at the racetracks where the current race meet is being held. You must request an application for owner's license by mail or online in order to have it returned to them in sufficient time (about 15 days) before your horse is to race. Further, some states may require you to supply financial background information, be photographed (preferably at the racing commission's office at the track), and, finally, supply a set of fingerprints (which can be done at the commission's office or at a police station). The fingerprints will be used in a background check designed to keep the undesirables out of the horse racing industry.

Finally, you must pay a fee (see Appendix) for the license. When it expires, you may renew it by mail. If you have changed your address since receiving your license, contact your state racing commission as you might not receive the reminder in the mail.

An owner's license will generally provide you with free parking and grandstand or clubhouse admission at most racetracks, but some stipulate that you must have a horse racing at that track to receive privileges.

An important note: If you plan to ship your horse to another state to race, you will have to be licensed in that state unless you have applied for and received a national racing license (see below) and are racing in a state that accepts it.

Some states have reciprocal arrangements to share your fingerprint information, considerably reducing the administrative burden of being fingerprinted in different states. You still must complete the license application, though, and pay the required fees. Many states do offer a temporary license for owners shipping horses in for stakes races. These licenses are usually good for one start or a specified number of days. Check with the racing commission in the state in which you intend to race to see if it is available.

National Racing License

Understanding an owner's need for a simple, multi-state licensing process, a group of forward-thinking commissioners recently developed the National Racing Compact to provide for a single national owner's license. Operating as a central licensing clearinghouse, this compact is an independent, interstate government entity that sets standards for licensure, accepts applications and fingerprints, performs background checks, and issues licenses that are recognized by the compact's participating states.

A tremendous convenience for owners and a time-saver for administrators, this national racing license is accepted in Arkansas, California, Colorado, Delaware, Florida, Illinois, Iowa, Kentucky, Louisiana,

Maryland, Michigan, Nebraska, New Jersey, New York, Ohio, Ontario, Pennsylvania, Texas, Virginia, Washington, and West Virginia. Hopefully, the compact will soon be able to add other states to its list so that a greater number of owners will benefit. The compact's goal is to have the national license accepted in 30 jurisdictions. This should eliminate owners' frustrations with being re-fingerprinted, rephotographed, and relicensed when shipping to race.

The national license costs $150 and is valid for three years on a calendar-year basis. In addition, individual states may charge their owner's license fee. To apply, you must be at least 18 years of age, complete the national racing license application, and select the states in which you intend to race. Additional states can be added later by a simple telephone call. Visit your local racetrack, police, or sheriff's station to be fingerprinted (using the RCI fingerprint card) and then submit the application, fingerprints, a photo (digital or passport), and payment to the National Racing Compact. Contact the National Racing Compact at website www.racinglicense.com, which accepts payment by check or credit card. The compact can also be reached at P. O. Box 184, New Kent, Virginia 23124, or toll free at (877) 457-2538.

RCI Multi-Jurisdiction Licensing Program

The Association of Racing Commissioners International (RCI), a group that promotes uniform regulation in racing, has also worked to streamline the licensing procedure through its multi-jurisdiction licensing program. This program allows owners to obtain licenses in different states through the use of a single application, although individuals still must submit a signed application and license fee to commissions of states in which they intend to race. Currently more than 30 racing states accept the RCI application.

Owners are advised to obtain prints using the RCI's fingerprint card, which will allow those states requiring fingerprints to receive background reports from the FBI. This service, too, greatly reduces the burden of becoming re-fingerprinted in different states.

To obtain a multi-jurisdiction application and fingerprint card, visit the RCI's website at www.arci.com, or contact them at 2343 Alexandria Drive, Suite 200, Lexington, Kentucky 40504, telephone 859-224-7070.

NAPRA's Multi-Jurisdiction License Application

The North American Pari-Mutuel Regulator's Association (NAPRA), has also developed a multi-jurisdiction license application that can be completed and sent to various jurisdictions on-line. While you must still appear at the selected state's racing commission's office to sign the application, filing it electronically beforehand will save you time and headache.

Fifteen racing states are currently accepting NAPRA applications, which can be obtained at www.napraonline.com.

5

Acquiring a Thoroughbred

L et's take the plunge. Let's buy a horse. It's about as easy as buying that one-of-a kind, exotic sports car. Those who go about it in a sensible way can get a thrilling and serviceable vehicle at an appropriate price. Those who close their eyes, hold their noses, and leap might as just as well buy lottery tickets.

Like those shiny cars on a sunny lot, horses can have beautiful bodies. In both cases, however, it's what's underneath that counts.

In buying a horse, there is no consumer guide or so-called "blue book" that sets price ranges. The market determines the cost. Past bull markets have seen untested horses sell for $13 million, based on their conformation and bloodlines. Some of these horses proved to be dismal failures on the racetrack. On the other hand, there have been horses acquired for less than $5,000 that have provided millions of thrills and hundreds of thousands of dollars in purse money.

Keep a simple rule in mind: There isn't a soul in racing who wouldn't sell his house and mortgage his assets to own a horse able to compete in the Triple Crown or Breeders' Cup World Thoroughbred Championship. Everyone who has ever sold a horse has a small voice inside that wonders "have I sent away the big one?"

But breeding, buying, and selling comprise the economic engine that drives Thoroughbred racing. Ask major breeders if they willingly give up the best of each lot they breed, and they will tell you, in deadly earnest, "that's what we are in the business to do." There are broad basic values to consider at the outset of a buying venture. Each contains risk. Each can produce rich rewards. Each demands that you bet both your wallet and your heart on the outcome.

The three most common ways to acquire a Thoroughbred are:

1) Claiming a pre-selected horse at the races.

2) Bidding at an auction.

3) Private purchase from a breeder or owner.

In all cases, you should enlist a professional to help you make your choice. Now is not the time to be leaning on the hunches of Uncle Harry or go it alone. In the case of auctions or private sales, take (or send on your behalf) a bloodstock agent, at least, and, ideally, a trainer and a vet as well. In the case of claiming, you must have a trainer in place before you can make your move.

Claiming

Claiming is the means by which the majority of new owners enters the racing world. It's not only one of the least expensive ways to get into the game, it's the quickest; in as little as two weeks, a new owner can have the chance to see his or her own horse compete — and perhaps win.

Claiming is the ingenious American method for ensuring a sense of parity among horses in any given race. The price at which a horse can be claimed is established as part of the entry qualifications for that race. Knowing that any other owner or trainer can purchase the horse generally discourages owners from putting horses in races where their quality is sure to make them winners. If they do, it will likely mean that their valuable, promising horse will be claimed, and — before the day is out — be the boast of someone else's stable.

The claiming game, popular as it is, is both complicated and fraught with interesting pitfalls — for new owners and experienced ones alike. There are many owners who have been enthusiastic claimers for years and have yet to turn a profit — but there is so much to be gained, so much steady action, and so much still to be learned that they remain as game for the challenge as they were when they began, whether that was two years ago or twenty.

The claiming procedure is carefully regulated and involves a number of precise, prescribed steps. First, you will have spotted a horse you like or have a hunch about one that runs in claiming races within your price range. Before you act on your desire, however, you should find a trainer who either specializes in claiming or, at the very least, is willing to work with you on the claiming process. It is not only practical to go in with a trainer at your side, but necessary: You cannot, by rule, receive your claimed horse without having a licensed trainer (or his or her designated handler) on hand to lead the horse away after the race.

The practical reason to engage a trainer prior to claiming is that trainers see virtually every horse on the grounds during morning gallops and workouts. If your intended claim is not a horse they know, they can generally seek out from the myriad of backstretch workers someone who knows something about the horse you fancy. The trainer will report back to you about what has been learned and knowledgeably turn you on to — or away from — a given claiming candidate. (Thus it's easy to see why trainers of claiming stock can be rather secretive when asked about their horses. But once you've invested time and money in a horse, only to see him claimed when you dropped him in for a "tag" in hopes of winning some sorely needed purse money, you'll quickly understand why trainers give guarded answers when asked about their stock. They are protecting their owners, and their livelihoods, and would rather not give out details that can quickly spread about the backstretch and increase, or decrease, a horse's chance of being claimed.)

If you are new to Thoroughbred ownership and don't already own a horse racing at the meet from which you intend to claim, you must first receive an "authorization to claim" from the state racing commission. This authorization (also known as "eligibility to claim" or an "open-claim certificate") will allow you to claim without having an owner's license. To obtain authorization to claim, stop by the racing commission's office at the track to complete the application for an owner's license and application for authorization to claim. At this time you will be fingerprinted and will pay the required fees. Once the commission is satisfied that you meet the requirements for obtaining an owner's license and have engaged a licensed trainer to receive the horse, you will be authorized to claim. In some states you can complete these steps the day before you intend to claim, while others require more advance notice to complete background checks (see state-by-state claiming rule Appendix). You will not receive your owner's license unless or until you successfully exercise a claim, since one of the qualifications for license is the actual ownership of a racehorse.

Your next stop is the office of the horsemen's bookkeeper or paymaster of purses at the track where you intend to make your claim. You, or your trainer, bearing a letter of authorization from you, must establish an account with funds sufficient to cover the cost of the horse you're after - its' claiming price will be listed in the track program. Since you are not already an owner with an account, the paymaster will prefer that you present a cashier's check sufficient to cover your claim, and don't forget to add in sales tax, which varies from venue to venue (see Appendix). Call the paymaster's office before you have your check cut to make sure it's written for the correct amount. Technically, you could pay by personal check, with a letter of guarantee from your bank, but there's a risk that the check and letter won't be accepted. A wire transfer from your bank is equally shaky, since the banks — in trading your money back and forth — may drop the ball and cost you the chance of executing your claim.

Once you've established your account with the paymaster, who will hand you a blank claim slip, you and your trainer will head to the paddock to study your horse in the saddling paddock. This is the trainer's last chance to pick up suspicious signs from a horse's action or behavior — a limp, tired, or stiff look, unusual sweating — anything that might suggest that the horse is not being "risked" in this claiming race, but dumped. Though it's not unusual, your trainer may advise dropping the claim slip in the trash instead of the box. Your money in the paymaster's office can be reclaimed or left on account for your next try.

But if all systems are go, have your trainer take you to the track's claim-card box to execute the claim. The claim box's location varies from track to track and can be obscure, so have your trainer accompany you on your first trip. Keep an eye on your watch, as you must have your claim card time-stamped and deposited in the claim box a prescribed amount of time before the race, usually either 10 or 15 minutes before post.

When your time-stamped claim card has been deposited in the box, you still won't know your chances of acquiring the horse in question. There is no way of finding out before the finish of the race, how many others are also bidding for the claim.

When the race is over, you will go to the corner of the winner's circle (usually), where the official known as the stewards' aide holds the claiming cards. If there is more than one card, they will be turned face down and numbered on the back. Then, a bottle of "peas," or numbered dice, is shaken, and one pea is drawn. The cardholder coinciding with the number receives a "delivery slip" to present to the horse's handlers and now owns the horse. Again, you can reclaim your money from the paymaster if you don't get the horse, or you can leave it on account.

But wait — the claiming experience is far from over. Several possible surprises and questions are still to come. First, if you made the winning claim, you owned the horse the instant if left the gate (or in some states, stepped foot on the track). If it broke down after leaving the gate, came up lame, or didn't finish, you still own it. You may have drawn the pea and spent up to $100,000, plus tax, for an animal whose racing career is clearly finished — or worse, who has to be destroyed because of mortal injury suffered in the race. You can protect yourself financially from the latter occurrence by obtaining claiming insurance.

The only sense in which you don't yet own the horse is if it finished in the money: the "former" owner, the one who entered the horse, gets any and all purse money "your" new horse earned in the race.

Finally, if your horse was sent to the test barn for blood and urine samples for drug testing, you will have to wait to take possession of the horse until these samples are collected. This may take an hour or all afternoon.

If either the track vet (who follows the horses from the saddling paddock through the race to the finish line) or the state vet has spotted your horse as looking unsound, injured, or bleeding from the nose, it will be placed on the vet's list, and you may not be permitted to enter it into a race anywhere from a few days to six months. You — the new owner — will be responsible for the time and cost of getting the horse legally up to speed before you can race it.

The ultimate test result when claiming will occur privately the morning after the race, when your trainer tells you whether the horse woke up fit and healthy. If it didn't, you may have been tricked into paying too much for too little. Actually, "bluffed" might be a more accurate term: As in poker, this is a fair part of the claiming game. Ninety percent of all racehorses will eventually turn up in a claiming race. The most likely result from a claim will be a raceable horse.

You will now be able to race your new horse as soon as it is rested — provided (in most states) that you raise it in "class," that is, enter it in a race with a claiming price at least 25% more than the one for which you claimed it. To race the horse at a lower level or to sell it for the purpose of racing, you will normally have to wait 30 days. Likewise, racing's rules prohibit you from running your new horse at another race meet or in another state until the meet from which you claimed the horse ends or a prescribed amount of time elapses.

Otherwise, in a couple of weeks or so, you, as the new owner of your claimed horse — much like the owner of any sports franchise — will have your first racing experience as an owner and get to experience firsthand the thrill of victory or the agony of defeat.

General Claiming Rules

The claiming of horses is serious business, as it involves not only an owner's assets but also a trainer's livelihood. The state racing commissions outline specific claiming rules, which are strictly enforced by the racetrack's stewards. While some discrepancies in different state's rules exist, there are some basic general rules that you, as an owner, should be aware of before you ever decide to drop a claim in or drop your horse in a claiming race.

To begin, only owners who are in good standing (meaning that no complaints have been filed against them for unpaid bills, etc.) and individuals who have been issued a claiming certificate or are otherwise authorized to claim by the state racing commission are allowed to claim. These certificates are usually valid for a specific length of time or until their holder successfully claims a horse, at which time the individual is issued an owner's license.

Other general claiming rules include:

No person can claim or cause his or her horse to be claimed for his or her own account.

Owners or trainers cannot collude or make agreements to protect one another's horses and prevent them from being claimed.

Owners cannot claim horses trained by their trainer; likewise, trainers cannot claim horses from their owners.

A horse against which a claim is held (such as a lien, mortgage, or bill of sale) may not be entered in a claiming race unless written consent is on file with the horsemen's bookkeeper.

An authorized agent may make claims, but only for the account of those for whom he or she is licensed as agent.

All claims for horses shall be for the amount so designated in the official program.

Claims are to be made on the official forms supplied by the racetrack or racing commission. All information regarding the horse to be claimed must be correct, including the spelling of its name. No marks are to appear on the claim envelope, other than the number of the race.

No money or equivalent is to be placed in the claim box.

Claim amounts are to be deposited with the horseman's bookkeeper prior to the race.

Claims are irrevocable.

The stewards oversee the administration of claims, making sure that owners have the correct claim amount on deposit and issuing authority for the horse to be delivered after the race to its new owner (this usually occurs in the paddock after the race or in the test or detention barn, with possession being taken by representatives of the horse's new trainer).

If more than one claim is filed for the same horse, the successful claimant shall be determined by lot under the stewards' supervision.

Each title to a horse that is claimed shall be vested in the successful claimant when the stall door of the starting gate opens (or in some states leaves the paddock or steps onto the track), regardless of any subsequent injury to the horse during or after the race.

If the stewards excuse a horse before it is a starter, each claim for the horse shall be invalid.

The stewards, at their discretion, may require a person to provide a written affidavit that he or she is claiming the horse for his or her own account and not for another person.

The claimant of the horse is solely responsible for determining the sex of the horse.

A claimed horse cannot remain in the same stable from which it was claimed.

The engagements of a claimed horse pass automatically with the horse to the claimant, although the new owner is responsible for future payments.

Buying at Auction

Thoroughbred auctions offer the widest selection and often assure fair market values for horses. They are organized and scheduled according to horses' age and intended use. To determine where and when the auctions of horses matching your dreams take place, check with your chosen blood-stock agent and/or look through publications such as *The Blood-Horse* and

Thoroughbred Times. One caution here: If you notify two or three prominent auction companies of your general interest, rest assured that your mailbox will be crammed with auction catalogs as well as announcements from individual sellers calling attention to their sale candidates.

To familiarize yourself with the sales process, attend several as an observer. Consider it a dry run. This exercise should include selecting horses to inspect, evaluating them based upon their pedigree and conformation, and estimating their selling price. As you compare your figures to the actual selling price, you will develop a sense of the market while gaining an understanding of the auction environment.

Buying at auction can be just as exciting as winning a race. You are dueling with other bidders for the horse of your choice, and you can imagine the thrill when it's your bid that the auctioneer's gavel finally confirms. But this is not a simple or relaxed occasion. Anyone can attend an auction and buy a horse. However, there are too many options to consider in too short of time to safely go in without an experienced adviser, such as a trainer or bloodstock agent. Such agents are not only knowledgeable about bloodlines and value of horses, but can also handle the intricacies of bidding, obtain and complete the appropriate applications for credit and transfer of title, procure the official bill of sale, arrange for post-purchase veterinary examinations, and organize the transport of your horse to your chosen barn. For the cost of a flat 5% of the horse's purchase price, the enlistment of a reputable bloodstock agent is a good investment by any standard.

Your agent or trainer will analyze the catalog for you, assess the stock being offered, and give you a short list from a field of perhaps thousands of horses that conform to your goals and fall within your price range.

When you're ready to buy, follow the guidelines below to make sure your experience as a buyer goes smoothly.

Before — The Preliminary Work

Time is precious at the sales. It is essential that you arrive as prepared as possible. The pre-sale work can often be more important than that done at the sale.

First, review the catalog(s). A catalog can be obtained from the auction company. It is generally available three to four weeks prior to the sale and is always complimentary. In addition to a horse's pedigree and hip number, the catalog contains explanations of the conditions of sale — the terms that control the sales proceedings.

1) Complete the paperwork

Review the conditions of sale. Read and make sure you understand each condition. Pay special attention to the warranties and types of defects that enable buyers to rescind the purchase of a horse, as they differ from company to company and between different ages of horses.

Establish credit. The first section of the catalog contains information regarding payment, including sales tax requirements. To secure credit with the sales company, you must complete a credit application prior to the sale. If another party, such as your agent or trainer, will bid on your behalf, the authorized agent form must also be completed. Copies of both forms are contained in the catalog.

2) Select horses.

Study the catalog and select, based upon pedigree, the horses in which you are interested. Nomination information is typically listed at the bottom of each catalog page. Note those nominated to state-bred programs and to the Breeders' Cup. You should confirm with the seller all nominations and state registration.

3) Meet with your agent and/or trainer.

Assign responsibilities. Bidding arrangements, pre-purchase veterinary procedures, pedigree research, and post-sale accommodations should be discussed for each horse identified.

Devise a first-look list. Your agent and/or trainer should revise the preliminary list, adding or eliminating horses in a manner consistent with your plan and budget. Keep in mind that the list is likely to be narrowed as each horse is physically inspected.

Secure the services of a veterinarian. If a veterinarian is not already part of your team, consider consulting one to assist in the selection process. Fees should be discussed and agreed upon in advance.

During — Duties at the Sale

For maximum efficiency, be well organized and stay focused on your objectives.

1) Inspect the horses.

Physically inspect all the horses on your first-look list. To avoid confusion, take notes and assign a grade on the corresponding catalog page. Based upon the inspections, it is quite probable that you will further cull the list of potential purchases to a short list. Inspect your final candidates several times. Don't be afraid to go back for a second or third look.

2) Consider performing pre-purchase veterinary examinations.

Depending upon the degree of interest in a horse on the short list, your budget, and the estimated sales price, you may wish to have a veterinarian perform a pre-purchase exam. Such an examination may include X-rays, an endoscopic exam (involves placing a flexible fiber optic tube into the throat to view the larynx to look for any abnormalities of the larynx/pharynx), and a physical exam.

Most sales companies have a repository where X-rays and other health records on the sales horses are stored. These X-rays are usually taken within a few weeks of the sale. You should have your veterinarian review X-rays in the repository on all the horses that you are interested in bidding on. Participation in the repository is voluntary and some sellers may not place X-rays in it. If there are no X-rays in the repository on a horse in which you are interested, then you should have the horse X-rayed prior to the sale.

If a consignor offers X-rays and/or other test results, such as endoscopic exams, for your review, be certain to find out the age of the information, as the information only has value if it is truly recent. Remember, horses are not machines; their physical conditions can change overnight.

Familiarize yourself with the sales catalog.

3) Be aware of announcements.

Listen to all announcements made from the auction stand prior to the sale of the horse. There are some conditions and warranties that must be announced at time of sale. Updates and corrections to the catalog page are also made at this time.

4) Bid.

It's easy to get caught up in the excitement and atmosphere at a sale. Don't permit yourself to get carried away when bidding. It is imperative that you follow your initial plan and stay within the identified budget. Bid only on horses on your short list, exercise control, and stay within your predetermined price for that horse.

Remember, too, that both title and risk pass to you at the fall of the auctioneer's hammer. You become responsible for the horse and its actions at that moment.

After — Post-Sale Procedures

Successful bidders must make the necessary arrangements for the

Inspect all the horses whose attributes might fit your plan.

board and care of their purchases. This includes purchasing insurance (if desired), making payment, and securing transportation and boarding accommodations.

1) Make payment.

Payment should be consistent with the arrangements made with the sales company. If credit was not established prior to the sale, payment is generally due within 30 minutes of the fall of the hammer. It is not uncommon for consignors to continue to care for the horse while the buyer settles with the sales company and secures transportation services. Ask the consignor first. Upon settlement or confirmed credit, buyers will be given a stable release and, later, The Jockey Club registration certificate will be transferred to the buyer through the sales company.

2) Remove the horse from the sales grounds.

Van companies have representatives at almost every sale. Select a carrier and provide them with a copy of the stable release. The carrier will need that form to remove the horse from the grounds. Horses must be removed from the sales grounds within 24 to 48 hours, depending upon the sale.

Note: Taking possession of the horse constitutes delivery and acceptance. Consequently, it's imperative that before moving the horse, a veteri-

When it comes to bidding, don't get carried away.

narian determines that your horse does not have any conditions that would allow the sale to be rescinded under the conditions of sale. Persons purchasing mares reported to be pregnant should confirm the pregnancy status of those mares. Under most conditions of sale, the purchaser's right to rescind a sale is prefaced upon a veterinary examination occurring on the grounds.

Warranties

Major Thoroughbred auction companies recognize extenuating circumstances that allow buyers to return a horse if the horse has a condition or conditions of which the buyer was unaware at the time of purchase. If the condition was not announced at time of sale or a veterinary certificate was not on file in the repository, then you may have rights to return the horse. These limited warranties are stated in the front of each catalog, under "Conditions of Sale." You must make yourself aware of all the conditions of sale prior to bidding on a horse, as you will be bound by the conditions of sale whether you have read them or not. The warranties listed under these conditions have a very strict time limit, which expire at different times (either 24 or 48 hours) after the sale or upon removal from the grounds (whichever comes first). Clearly, it's wise to have a vet examine the animal on the sales grounds immediately after purchase.

Some Examples of Limited Warranties:

An examination of the horse's larynx and pharynx using a veterinary endoscope (a lighted, metal magnifying tube inserted via the nostril) may reveal problems with the horse's breathing.

Your veterinarian may detect a problem with the horse's eyes.

If you are buying breeding stock and you find a desirable mare in foal, you need to make certain that your "mare in foal" actually is in foal.

Be sure that your horse does not have the habit of cribbing — a stable vice some think can lead to colic, a blockage of the digestive tract that can be fatal.

If it is a yearling or weanling, find out if the auction company has guaranteed against it being afflicted with spinal ataxia (sometimes called wobbler syndrome), which is a spinal condition affecting coordination.

Again, you and your bloodstock agent must review and understand the catalog's conditions of sale and have interpreted anything that is unclear or possibly disadvantageous.

A cautionary note: Literally anyone who wants to call him or herself a bloodstock agent can do so. No license is required for agents to conduct business. However, any auction company issuing a catalog will be willing to offer names of trusted agents in the area. Screening through an advocate organization, such as your state's Thoroughbred breeders and/or owner's association and requesting references are essential steps to take before enlisting your bloodstock agent.

Types of Auctions

The main kinds of Thoroughbred auctions are yearling, two-year-old-in-training, breeding stock, and the mixed sales, which include horses of all ages, including racing age.

The yearling auctions are mainly held between July and October, with the principal arenas being Kentucky, New York, Florida, Maryland, and California. Purchasing a yearling at auction can be one of the least expensive methods of acquiring a racehorse and also one of the riskiest. You will

How to Read a Catalog Page

The first time you open an auction catalog, don't be intimidated by the manner in which the information is presented. Just as you learned to read a horse's past performance in the *Daily Racing Form*, you will quickly learn how to glean information from a horse' page in a catalog. Here are some pointers to get you started.

1 The number identifying the horse, appearing on its hip.

2 The horse's pedigree, traced three generations. At each generation, the sire appears on the top and the dam on the bottom.

3 A synopsis of the sire's racing record and notable progeny.

4 A synopsis of the first dam's racing record and progeny.

5 A synopsis of the racing record of the first dam's most prominent offspring. Each indentation represents one generation.

6 The maternal grandmother.

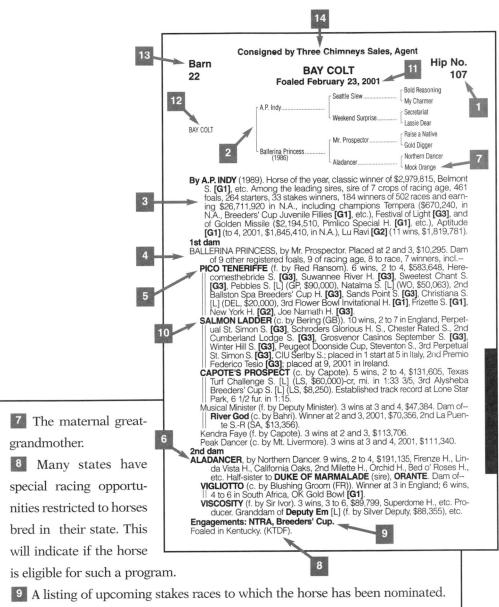

Consigned by Three Chimneys Sales, Agent

Barn
22

BAY COLT
Foaled February 23, 2001

Hip No.
107

BAY COLT

A.P. Indy ....
- Seattle Slew .... Bold Reasoning / My Charmer
- Weekend Surprise .... Secretariat / Lassie Dear

Ballerina Princess ....
(1986)
- Mr. Prospector .... Raise a Native / Gold Digger
- Aladancer .... Northern Dancer / Mock Orange

By A.P. INDY (1989). Horse of the year, classic winner of $2,979,815, Belmont S. **[G1]**, etc. Among the leading sires, sire of 7 crops of racing age, 461 foals, 264 starters, 33 stakes winners, 184 winners of 502 races and earning $26,711,920 in N.A., including champions Tempera ($670,240, in N.A., Breeders' Cup Juvenile Fillies **[G1]**, etc.), Festival of Light **[G3]**, and of Golden Missile ($2,194,510, Pimlico Special H. **[G1]**, etc.), Aptitude **[G1]** (to 4, 2001, $1,845,410, in N.A.), Lu Ravi **[G2]** (11 wins, $1,819,781).

1st dam
BALLERINA PRINCESS, by Mr. Prospector. Placed at 2 and 3, $10,295. Dam of 9 other registered foals, 9 of racing age, 8 to race, 7 winners, incl.--
  PICO TENERIFFE (f. by Red Ransom). 6 wins, 2 to 4, $583,045, Herecomesthebride S. **[G3]**, Suwannee River H. **[G3]**, Sweetest Chant S. **[G3]**, Pebbles S. **[L]** (GP, $90,000), Natalma S. **[L]** (WO, $50,063), 2nd Ballston Spa Breeders' Cup H. **[G3]**, Sands Point S. **[G3]**, Christiana S. **[L]** (DEL, $20,000), 3rd Flower Bowl Invitational H. **[G1]**, Frizette S. **[G1]**, New York H. **[G2]**, Joe Namath H. **[G3]**.
  SALMON LADDER (c. by Bering (GB)). 10 wins, 2 to 7 in England, Perpetual St. Simon S. **[G3]**, Schroders Glorious H. S., Chester Rated S., 2nd Cumberland Lodge S. **[G3]**, Grosvenor Casinos September S. **[G3]**, Winter Hill S. **[G3]**, Peugeot Doonside Cup, Steventon S., 3rd Perpetual St. Simon S. **[G3]**, CIU Serlby S.; placed in 1 start at 5 in Italy, 2nd Premio Federico Tesio **[G3]**; placed at 9, 2001 in Ireland.
  CAPOTE'S PROSPECT (c. by Capote). 5 wins, 2 to 4, $131,605, Texas Turf Challenge S. **[L]** (LS, $60,000)-cr, mi. in 1:33 3/5, 3rd Alysheba Breeders' Cup S. **[L]** (LS, $8,250). Established track record at Lone Star Park, 6 1/2 fur. in 1:15.
  Musical Minister (f. by Deputy Minister). 3 wins at 3 and 4, $47,384. Dam of--
    River God (c. by Bahri). Winner at 2 and 3, 2001, $70,356, 2nd La Puente S.-R (SA, $13,356).
  Kendra Faye (f. by Capote). 3 wins at 2 and 3, $113,706.
  Peak Dancer (c. by Mt. Livermore). 3 wins at 3 and 4, 2001, $111,340.
2nd dam
ALADANCER, by Northern Dancer. 9 wins, 2 to 4, $191,135, Firenze H., Linda Vista H., California Oaks, 2nd Milette H., Orchid H., Bed o' Roses H., etc. Half-sister to **DUKE OF MARMALADE** (sire), **ORANTE**. Dam of--
  VIGLIOTTO (c. by Blushing Groom (FR)). Winner at 3 in England; 6 wins, 4 to 6 in South Africa, OK Gold Bowl **[G1]**.
  VISCOSITY (f. by Sir Ivor). 3 wins, 3 to 6, $89,799, Superdome H., etc. Producer. Granddam of **Deputy Em [L]** (f. by Silver Deputy, $88,355), etc.
Engagements: NTRA, Breeders' Cup.
Foaled in Kentucky. (KTDF).

7 The maternal great-grandmother.

8 Many states have special racing opportunities restricted to horses bred in their state. This will indicate if the horse is eligible for such a program.

9 A listing of upcoming stakes races to which the horse has been nominated.

10 A horse whose name appears in bold capital letters means it is a stakes winner. If its name appears in bold lower-case letters, it is stakes-placed.

11 The horse's birth date.

12 The horse's name. If unnamed, it is described by sex and color.

13 The number of the barn where the horse is located.

14 The name of the consignor (the farm or individual selling the horse).

be buying purely on the basis of pedigree and conformation (i.e., the ideal physical structure of a Thoroughbred). The buyer of a yearling must have both patience and optimism — in spades. Though all Thoroughbreds are born to run, not all are guaranteed to become competitive athletes. Because they are completely untried, any of these yearlings, once they mature, may turn out to have bad knees, weak tendons, or simply be slow runners with no heart for competition. On the other hand, your baby may grow up to be the next Secretariat or Personal Ensign.

The select yearling auctions, held in July and September in Lexington, Kentucky, and in August in Saratoga Springs, New York, involve only a few hundred handpicked colts and fillies, which go for an average price of several hundred thousand dollars. Most buyers may be better served at the non-select sales in late summer, where yearlings of every kind and in every price range are available. The September sale in Lexington is the largest auction of its kind in the world, offering up to 4,000 yearlings. Here is where the trainer or bloodstock agent with a good eye can find you a top-flight athlete, whether a colt or filly, for less than $50,000.

Average prices for yearlings in Florida, Maryland, California, and other regional sales are considerably less. Many horses can be purchased out of these sales for less than $10,000. Is a $10,000 horse worth the investment? For the new owner intent on finding an ownership path that can be comfortably trod, there is no difference in the learning experience, regardless of the horse's cost.

Since all horses' birthdays are officially January 1 of the horse's birth year, the yearling is anywhere from 10 to 18 months old. Therefore, the new owner and trainer may have up to a year of boarding, breaking, training, feeding, repairing childhood injuries, medicating, and schooling the horse before it can actually demonstrate its fettle. But this horse probably will be like a child to you by then — and its first race can definitely be a day worth waiting for.

In case you don't understand the age calculation, here is the calendar of Thoroughbred breeding: The gestation period for horses is 11 months. Mating usually begins in the middle of February to ensure that the foal is born after January 1. If by some accident, it were born prior to January 1, in racing terms it would be one year old, while in actuality it is one month old.

Like children, horses mature at different rates. They are ready for racing when they are ready. You can't force it and expect wondrous results. Mating ends sometime in late June or early July. Thus a "late" foal would be born in June and therefore take more time to grow before being ready to race. Is it better to have an "early" (March or April) foal or a late (May or June) arrival? Opinions vary. The one uncontestable fact is that a majority of Kentucky Derby winners are May foals.

The "two-year-olds-in-training" auctions are held beginning in February in a wide variety of locales (although they tend to be concentrated in Florida, Kentucky, and California).

The very logical rule of thumb at auctions in general is that the more a horse has been proven, the more you will pay for it (in the case of yearlings, a proven sire and/or dam with proven bloodlines is what you're paying for). Horses for sale at two-year-old auctions have already been broken and schooled. The top sales will offer only horses that have had a minimum of 90 days worth of training — i.e., breaking and galloping. At these auctions, the fillies and colts will often be "previewed" — which means they are galloped, worked, or breezed to clockers' stopwatches. The standouts will be obvious, and everyone will be bidding for them.

These fillies and colts are very close to being able to race. (Some horses sold at Keeneland's April sale race during that meet.) Since their soundness and fitness has, to some extent, been demonstrated, and since their owners have invested another year in keeping and breaking them, the two-year-olds-in-training are about twice as expensive as yearlings. In fact, you may discover that the two-year-old you're about to buy was a yearling you looked at in one of last year's auctions. Likely, he was bought by a specialist known in the racing world as a pinhooker. The pinhooker is an investor who, you might say, likes to gamble before the racetrack — that is, he or she spots a yearling, invests six months or so breaking and training it, and if the filly or colt pans out, sells it for a great deal more that its yearling purchase price at one of the two-year-old auctions. Although you will be paying more for a two-year-old-in-training than for a yearling, you will still be paying less than for a two-year-old already racing.

At the breeding stock auctions (usually held November through January), you can buy not only weanlings, but also some of the most valuable Thoroughbreds available at auction, anywhere: top-quality broodmares. Buying such a mare is one of the few affordable chances to get a foal that, at exactly three years old, might be one of the 20 or so Thoroughbreds — out of approximately 33,000 others turning three that year — great enough to race in the Triple Crown series.

Though there is always the hope of acquiring a top national winner through claiming, any horse showing that kind of promise is rarely risked on the claiming ladder. The same tends to hold true of hugely talented two-year-olds; they simply don't come onto the open market. If you, like most of us, lack the purse to spend a quarter of a million dollars on a single, top-

Advantages/Disadvantages Associated with Different Age Purchase

Age	Advantages	Disadvantages	When Sale Held
Yearling	Large selection; owner can oversee all breaking and training; pinhooking options.	8-12 months until ready to race — expenses incurred during this time.	July-Dec.
Two-year-old	Ready to race; further along in development; better able to assess ability	Smaller selection; horses may be rushed through training for sale.	Feb.–June
Weanling	Reasonably priced; pinhooking options; can oversee development.	Hard to evaluate at this early an age; 18 months until ready to race.	Oct.-Feb.
Broodmare	Can choose matings; can sell foals or enjoy success of homebreds.	Pregnancy can be complicated; lots of risk, time, and cost involved.	Oct.-Feb.

bred yearling, then the road to your personal racing nirvana may be to buy good mares and breed your own history-making champions (See Chapter 15, Breeding Your Own). It's a dream that has come true before.

The mixed sales (usually from October through February) tend to be catch-all sales where horses are being auctioned as the result of a legal dissolution of partnership, a stable surplus, the settlement of an estate, or because they simply are no longer desirable to their owners. The auctions can include fillies, mares, weanlings, colts, horses, geldings, and broodmares. In other words, the mixed sales provide the opportunity for you to buy (at a single event) one or two of almost anything you have in mind for your stable and within almost any budget range. Most of the horses offered have at least some form on record and are not likely to be the worst of surprises. Neither, by the same token, are they likely to be history-making diamonds in the rough. Here, above all other arenas, is where a thorough veterinary exam is an absolute essential.

Thoroughbred Auction Calendar

Month	Auction Type/Location
January	Barretts Mixed Sale/Los Angeles
	Heritage Place Sales Co. Mixed Sale/Oklahoma City
	Keeneland Breeding Stock Sale/Lexington
	Ocala Breeders' Sales Co. Mixed Sale/Ocala
February	Arkansas Thoroughbred Sales Co. Mixed Sale/ Little Rock
	Fasig-Tipton Florida, Inc. Select Two-Year-Old in Training Sale/Miami
	Fasig-Tipton Kentucky, Inc. Mixed Sale/Lexington
	Fasig-Tipton Midlantic, Inc. Mixed Sale/Timonium, Md.
	Ocala Breeders' Sales Co. Select Two-Year-Olds in Training Sale/Miami
March	Barretts Selected Two-Year-Old in Training Sale/Los Angeles
	Fair Grounds Sales Co. Two-Year-Old in Training Sale/ New Orleans
	Fasig-Tipton Two-Year-Old in Training Sale/Dallas
	Ocala Breeders' Sales Co. Select Two-Year-Olds

	in Training Sale/Ocala
April	Keeneland Two-Year-Old in Training Sale/Lexington
	Louisiana Thoroughbred Breeders Sales Co. Mixed Sale / Lafayette
	Ocala Breeders' Sales Co. Two-Year-Old in Training Sale/ Ocala
May	Barretts Two-Year-Old in Training Sale/Los Angeles
	Fasig-Tipton Midlantic, Inc. Two-Year-Old in Training Sale/ Timonium, Md.
June	Ocala Breeders' Sales Co. Two-Year-Old in Training Sale / Ocala
	Dan Arrigo Sales Co. Horses of Racing Age Sale/Chicago
	Illinois Thoroughbred Breeders & Owners Two-Year-Old Sale/Chicago
	San Antonio Horse Sale Co. Mixed Sale/San Antonio
July	Keeneland Select Yearling Sale/Lexington
	Fasig-Tipton Kentucky, Inc. Select Yearling Sale / Lexington
	Fasig-Tipton Midlantic, Inc. Two-Year-Old and Horses of Racing Age Sale/Timonium, Md.
August	California Thoroughbred Breeders Assoc. Yearling Sale/ Del Mar
	Fasig-Tipton New York, Inc. Select Yearling Sale/ Saratoga
	Fasig-Tipton New York, Inc. Preferred Yearling Sale/ Saratoga
	Fasig-Tipton Summer Yearling Sale/Dallas
	Louisiana Thoroughbred Breeders Sales Mixed Co. Sale/ Lafayette
	Ocala Breeders' Sales Co. Select Yearling Sale/Ocala
	Ocala Breeders' Sales Co. Yearling Sale/Ocala
September	Keeneland September Yearling Sale/Lexington
	Oregon Thoroughbred Breeders Assoc. Annual Mixed Sale/Portland
	Washington Thoroughbred Breeders Assoc. Yearling Sale/ Seattle

October	Arizona Thoroughbred Breeders Assoc. Mixed Sale/ Phoenix
	Barretts Yearling Sale/Los Angeles
	Barretts Mixed Sale/Los Angeles
	Breeders Sales Co. of Louisiana Yearling Sale/New Orleans
	Fasig-Tipton Kentucky, Inc. Fall Yearling Sale/Lexington
	Fasig-Tipton Midlantic Inc., Eastern Fall Yearling Sale/ Timonium, Md.
	Fasig-Tipton New York, Inc. Horses of Racing Age Sale/ New York
	Heritage Place Sales Co. Mixed Sale/Oklahoma City
	Illinois Thoroughbred Breeders & Owners Yearling Sale / Chicago (sometimes held in September)
	Ocala Breeders' Sales Co. Mixed Sale/Ocala
	San Antonio Horse Sale Co. Mixed Sale/San Antonio
November	Fasig-Tipton Kentucky, Inc. Selected Fall Mixed Sale/ Lexington
	Keeneland Breeding Stock Sale/Lexington
December	Arkansas Thoroughbred Sales Co. Mixed Sale/Little Rock (may be held in October)
	Dan Arrigo Sales Co. Horses of Racing Age Sale/Chicago
	Fasig-Tipton Kentucky, Inc. Mixed Sale/Lexington
	Fasig-Tipton Midlantic, Inc. Mixed Sale/Timonium, Md.
	Fasig-Tipton Texas, Inc. Mixed Sale/Dallas
	Washington Thoroughbred Breeders Assoc. Mixed Sale/ Seattle

Private Purchase From Breeder or Owner

Private purchase is the only avenue by which sure-fire, stakes-quality horses can be bought, and they may go for prices you'd have to expect for the rarity of a horse racing near-guarantee.

Private transactions offer the buyer an opportunity as well as the option of a pre-purchase exam. Furthermore, the purchaser is not restricted to only those horses offered for sale, but may make an offer on any horse considered desirable, including those not necessarily advertised for sale. Again, consultants play a vital role in finding, selecting, and inspecting prospects.

You may live in an area where you have access to breeding farms, owners' farms, or training barns. If so, some combination of word-of-mouth, your own eyes and instincts, and a relationship with a local horseman may have led you to take an interest in the stock of a particular farm, or in a particular Thoroughbred. You may also get a lead from your trainer or bloodstock agent who knows of a promising but little-known farm and possibly has entry there.

Purchasing one of these horses privately has its upsides and downsides. You and your trainer and vet can take all the time you want to consider and examine the horse and to research its lineage without the pressure and emotional frenzy of an auction. On the other hand, you will be dealing with a set price from the owner. A wild lucky buy is not likely. Remember that. As with the mixed auctions, there is a reason the owner is willing to sell the horse you're looking at. Part of what you must try to do as a prudent buyer is find out why.

There are many reasons for selling a horse, ranging from pure economics to personal taste to veiled chicanery. There is no reason for the owner to reveal all his reasons, so it's up to you to do the research. Is the owner really overwhelmed by current expenses? Is the owner really considering moving to a smaller property? Why isn't the owner planning to race the horse? Remember, you're buying the end of someone else's dream — even if the animal is a yearling. That doesn't mean it isn't good. It simply means that you should be sure it fits your dream.

As with other purchase options, proper arrangements must be made and various factors should be considered, as follows:

1) Make an inquiry regarding purchase opportunities.

If you are interested in purchasing a particular horse, contact the horse's owner, trainer, or owner's agent and inquire if the horse is for sale.

2) Inspect the horse.

After ascertaining that the horse is for sale, a thorough physical examination should be conducted. Follow the same guidelines as those associated with inspecting horses at public auction. If you are serious about the purchase, employ a veterinarian to perform a physical examination evaluating the soundness, general health, wind capacity, and reproductive ability of the animal.

3) Negotiate price.

The sales price should reflect the quality of the horse's pedigree, conformation, and race record. To determine an offering price, also evaluate the following factors:

The level at which the horse has been competing. If the horse competed in claiming races, what was the claiming price?

The future earning potential. How much longer will the horse be able to race and at what level?

The residual value. Will the horse have value as breeding stock?

When a purchase price has been determined, make a formal offer.

4) Present a written agreement of sale or purchase and a bill of sale.

A written agreement of sale or purchase should be prepared and should include the names of the parties, identification of the horse, terms of sale, warranties of sale, contingencies and deadlines, and site of the transaction, as sales tax may be a factor. It may be prudent also to include a procedure for resolving disputes, as well as a provision acknowledging the right for a complete veterinary exam. In most cases, insurance providers require a veterinarian exam before a policy will be issued. Where questions or suspicions exist, good business practice suggests that a title search should be made to ascertain that the seller's title is free of liens.

Upon acceptance of the offer, the purchaser should request a bill of sale. A security agreement may be imposed by the seller to secure payment if the seller is financing any portion of the purchase price. At the closing, the purchaser should receive the horse's Jockey Club certificate, as well as copies of its health records.

Leasing

While this form of ownership is not widely used, leasing a horse can have several advantages and can be just as much fun.

Compared to other ways of acquiring a horse, leasing requires very little capital. Ordinarily, the lessee simply assumes responsibility for all costs associated with the board and care of the animal during the term of the lease. In exchange, the lessee enjoys the benefits of ownership, with the obligation to share some of the benefits with the lessor per the terms of the lease. Depending upon the purpose of the lease and/or the type of horse leased, i.e., racing prospect or broodmare, the parties may share in revenues derived through racing or sale or in the ownership or management of progeny.

It is recommended that a professional be consulted before entering into a lease. There are several issues that deserve special attention and may be overlooked without professional consultation.

Partnerships

Few will argue that the thrill of owning part of a racehorse matches that of sole ownership. Because of this and other practical considerations, many first-time owners elect the partnership route. The proportional initial capital expenditure combined with reduced recurring expenses affords most an economical entry into the business.

There are generally two paths to becoming involved in Thoroughbred partnerships:

1) Purchasing shares in an existing partnership.

2) Forming a partnership with a group of friends or associates.

Opportunities to become involved in partnerships in Thoroughbred racing abound. Before plunging into one, though, it's important to look into the individuals involved, as some partnerships are more reputable than others. When considering partners and partnerships, make sure to find a match for your goals, philosophies, and financial budget. And, ask questions!

Before Plunging into a Partnership — Ask Questions!

To find partnership opportunities, contact local horsemen's associations, trainers, and other industry professionals. Or, refer to either the *TOBA Membership Directory* or *The Source*, a directory for the Thoroughbred industry published by *The Blood-Horse*. Then, compile a list to contact and request a copy of their written plan or prospectus.

When reviewing this material, determine if the partnership is 1) a racing, breeding, or pinhooking partnership; 2) involved at the level at which you desire (claiming, allowance, or stakes horses?), and 3) a general or limited partnership, as this distinction will affect your expense liability and your right to participate in the decision making.

After identifying partnerships that pique your interest, ask to meet with their managing partners. Ask him or her the following questions, along with any others you may come up with.

1) What are the partnership's goals, and how will they be achieved?

The managing partner should be able to clarify objectives and how he or she intends to achieve them. Is there a developed plan? Does it appear realistic? What are the partnership's goals and are they consistent with yours? How will success be determined — by profit alone, caliber of races won, social activities, etc.?

2) Who are the players?

What are the managing partner's credentials? Experience in the industry? Does he or she have a financial interest in the partnership? Who are the other professionals involved, i.e., the trainer, pedigree adviser, veterinarian, farm manager, and bloodstock agent? You may want to meet them and verify their resources. Also, who are the other partners, how many will there be, and what percentage will they own? Are any related to the managing partner? Remember, these are your business partners. You should be confident in your compatibility and find them trustworthy. Don't forget the horses — determine how they are acquired and how closely their purchase price reflects the price of the partnership.

3) What type of business entity is used?

Tax and liability implications of the partnership's form of business should be analyzed.

4) How are the finances handled?

Frequently, the managing partner is compensated for his or her experience, time, and related expenses; compensation may be a management fee, equity in the horse, or a commission for finding or selling the horse. You should be informed of this arrangement.

Before making your initial investment, ascertain what is included in the offering price and the number of horses in which you are purchasing an interest. Some partnerships offer packages while others offer individual horses.

In addition to the cost of a share in a horse, there are other expenses such as training, veterinary and blacksmith bills, accounting fees, vanning, etc. Know who authorizes these expenditures and how investors will be notified and billed.

When income occurs from purse money or sales, does it flow directly to investors or is it maintained in an account to cover future expenses? When does the partnership settle up — monthly, quarterly, annually? Does each partner receive a statement reflecting cash receipts and disbursements? If so, how often?

5) How are decisions made and by whom?

Depending on the expertise of the managing partner, it may be desirable for him or her to have the final say in decisions. Likewise, other partners having significant expertise might ought to have a say. To keep everyone happy, or at least try to, it is imperative that a clear understanding exists about how decisions will be made, whether they are made democratically or by an individual.

6) What services are provided to investors?

When will reports on the condition, progress, and location of your horse(s) be sent? Who is responsible for them, and how will they be sent? Will you be provided with perks, such as race day seating and passes? Will you have access to the stable area? Will you be supplied with a financial statement for tax purposes?

7) How are shares transferred, and how will the partnership be dissolved?

Many partnerships require that investors first offer their shares to the existing partners; however, determining a transfer or sale value can be difficult. While occasionally a partnership will employ an expert to determine a share's value, it is far more common to disburse partnership interests at public auction.

You need to know how long you are committed to participate in the investment and what happens to the partnership when a horse is retired from racing.

8) Consider forming one yourself.

Why not form your own partnership? Ask a trainer, bloodstock agent, or other consultant to match you with other interested partners. While this approach may be more time consuming, it enables you to create the partnership that will allow you and your partners to reach common goals. Be sure to use this list, though, when outlining the partnership's criteria.

6

Pedigree – The Family Tree

A s a racehorse owner, you may not be a devotee of pedigree study — you may prefer your action on the track and not the breeding farm. But in order to round out your knowledge of Thoroughbred racing, it's important that you have a basic understanding of pedigree terminology and breeding theories.

A horse's pedigree refers to its family tree — its sire (father), its dam (mother), and all of the forebears who make up its ancestors. In order to determine a horse's value, much weight is given to its lineage, as many believe that the performances of a horse's ancestors are strong predictors of the animal's potential.

There are many students of Thoroughbred pedigrees, and analyzing familial ties in the equine world is for some a fascinating hobby and for others a lucrative career. It's somewhat surprising that none of the colleges in the Bluegrass region offer a "Thoroughbred breeding" diploma. With as many theories existing about pedigrees as theories about how to make money in the stock market, pedigree analysis can be an enjoyable endeavor for the analytical mind. But no matter what time you devote to learning about Thoroughbreds, you should be familiar with basic breeding premises. Some pedigree consultants pay great attention to "inbreeding"and/or "nicking," while others focus on the physical or aptitudinal characteristics certain families tend to have, such as speed or classic performance. Having a basic understanding of different theories will allow you to focus on those you find most appealing.

Before buying or breeding, remember, though, that the two greatest genetic influences on a horse are its immediate sire and dam. A horse's sire and paternal ancestors appear on the top of its pedigree, while its dam and maternal kin appear on the bottom. Both a horse's sire and dam should be analyzed most carefully before taking breeding theories into consideration.

Sire Information & Considerations:

How many foal crops has the sire had, and what is the number of foals in each crop?

What percentage of his progeny are starters, winners, and stakes winners?

What type of horses does he tend to produce: Do his horses race better on turf or dirt? Does he produce better colts or fillies? Do they tend to make many starts or are they finished racing after only a few starts? Are they sprinters or stayers, better two-year-old runners, or do his foals develop more slowly?

How old is the stallion? Has he had a chance to prove himself? The first couple of years can be a roller-coaster ride for a young stallion trying to attract a quality book of mares.

Mare Information & Considerations:

What are the mare's race and produce records of her female side going back at least two generations?

How many of her foals have started? What was their race record, including number of starts, wins, and purse money earned? How long did they withstand training? At what level did they perform?

How many full or half siblings have been stakes performers?

Once armed with this information, you might want to take into consideration some of the more complex breeding theories. But remember, they are called theories for a reason…

Female Family Influence: Professional breeding analysts cite the importance of a horse's female family as paramount, and they place far greater emphasis on it than on other factors in a horse's pedigree. While theoretically the sire's and dam's family should carry equal weight, many believe the dam's genetic influence plays a greater role.

Inbreeding: Inbreeding is the term used to describe breeding in which the same ancestor appears in both the sire and dam sides of the horse's first four generations. For example, if the same ancestor appears in the third generation on its sire's side and then again in the fourth on its dam side, the horse is referred to as being inbred 3 x 4. The theory of inbreeding is based on the postulate that the ancestor to which the particular horse is inbred will have greater influence and thus emphasize its certain characteristics. Most believe it radical for a horse to be inbred closer than 3 x 3.

Outcrossing: Outcrossing is the opposite of inbreeding, meaning that none of the horse's ancestors are repeated within five or more generations. As you may remember from your high school biology class, outcrossing is thought to foster hybrid vigor.

Nicking: Nicking refers to the compatibility of certain bloodlines or how well they "nick." Although there are rarely enough examples of offspring created by two bloodlines to be statistically significant, it's hard to dispute that some nicks work very well and in some instances have changed the course of the breed. The Nasrullah—Princequillo nick produced some outstanding specimens, including the great Secretariat, while the Storm Bird—Secretariat nick has generated leading sire Storm Cat and grade I winner and top stallion Summer Squall. Remember, breeding is more of an art form than a science, and although a theory, nicking has some basis in fact. Why do nicks work? Possibly it's due to two bloodlines merging their genotype and phenotype (how genes manifest themselves in conformation, temperament, and physical aptitude) in a superior way.

It's important to place nicking in its proper perspective, though, and not let its use overshadow the immediate attributes and performance of the sire and dam before you.

Dosage: Although not a simple concept, dosage is used by both breeders and handicappers alike to determine a horse's propensity for speed versus stamina based upon his pedigree. It was first popularized when used as an indicator of which horses would be ready to race a mile and a quarter on the first Saturday in May. However, its value to breeders is somewhat dubious as it only analyzes half the horse's pedigree, the sire side, and ignores the dam's influence. Thus, one can as easily be misled as be informed by dosage numbers.

Modern dosage theory analyzes a horse's first four generations to determine which *chef-de-race* stallions appear. The term *chef-de-race* refers to certain stallions whose speed or stamina abilities are determined to influence the breed. These stallions' aptitude for speed or stamina is categorized as brilliant, intermediate, classic, solid, or professional, with "brilliant" representing a horse with extreme speed, and "professional" representing one with extreme stamina. The "intermediate," "classic," and "solid" represent varying degrees in between, with the middle marker classic representing a horse that can carry speed over the "classic" distance of a mile and a quarter (or a mile and a half in Europe).

A horse's dosage index (DI) is calculated by a rather complex formula that assigns points to the *chefs-de-race* that appear in a horse's pedigree and thus reflects a horse's tendency to be fast versus its ability to stay a distance. The higher the DI, the more speed a horse has in its pedigree. The average DI for North America is 2.4, so a horse having a dosage of 3.0 would have considerable speed in its pedigree. A horse with a dosage above 4.0 is not considered to be able to stay the classic American distance of a mile and a quarter.

While an interesting tool, dosage should only be used to measure a horse's distance capacity and not its relative worth. It does not give significant information as to the quality of a horse's pedigree, as it is possible for a horse by a moderate regional sire to have the same dosage index as one by a world-class one.

Performance Indexes: Just as the financial markets have indices that help investors gauge stock and bond performance, indices also exist for those who invest in Thoroughbreds to help determine bloodstock value. These performance indices are also used as tools when planning matings.

Average Earnings Index (AEI): The average earnings index compares how much purse money the offspring of one sire has earned, on average, in relation to the average earnings of all runners in the same years. The average earnings of all runners in a given year is set at 1.00, so a stallion with an AEI of 2.00 would have runners that earned twice as much as the average. The AEI is used in conjunction with the "comparable index" to show if a stallion improves a mare's produce compared to when another stallion is bred to her.

However, a stallion with one superior runner can skew his AEI, resulting in a distorted number that doesn't truly represent the rest of his progeny's earnings. For example, millionaire John Henry was the only significant runner by Old Bob Bowers, giving his sire a skewed and misleading AEI number.

Comparable Index (CI): The comparable index indicates the average earnings of offspring produced by mares bred to one stallion, compared to the earnings of the offspring produced when the mare was bred to other stallions. If a stallion has an AEI greater than his CI, he is considered to "move up" the mares bred to him and thus is considered an above-average stallion. For example, if a stallion's AEI were 2.5 and his CI 2.0, then he is considered to improve the mares bred to him.

Racing Index (RI): The Racing Index is based on the average earnings per start for North American runners. It is calculated by taking all foals born in a given year and determining that crop's average earnings per start for each year that the crop raced, and then comparing it with the AEI. The average earnings per start for a crop for a given year is set at 1.00. A horse with a RI of 2.00 would have earned twice as much per start during a given year than a horse of the same sex, from the same crop, and having a RI of 1.00. Colts and fillies are separated for the calculation. After five years of running, an individual runner's RI doesn't change, even if it continues to race.

Sire Index (SI): An average of the RI's for all of the stallion's foals that have started three or more times in North America. This index is designed to show the racing ability of a sire's foals.

Comparable Sire Index (ComSI): The average of the RIs of progeny produced from mares bred to the subject stallion, excluding foals by that stallion. When compared to a stallion's SI, it indicates whether a stallion improves the mares to which he is bred. If a stallion's SI is 1.3 and his ComSI is 1.7 he is not considered to "improve" his mares.

Broodmare Sire Index (BSI): An average of the RI of all foals out of the sire's daughters that started at least three times. For BSI to be calculated, a broodmare sire must be represented by a minimum of 75 starters. This index is designed to show the racing ability of a mare's foals. Many times a mare may not produce black-type stakes-level foals but may be producing quality foals that win upper-level claiming and allowance races on the major racing circuits. If so, this will be reflected in her BSI.

What is "Black Type"?

Listen to horse people discuss the relative merits of a horse's family, and you will invariably hear them discuss how much "black type" is in its pedigree. But just what exactly is this black type?

Black type refers to a horse that has won or placed in a stakes race. A horse whose name appears in bold letters (a.k.a. "black type") is one that has placed in a stakes race, while a horse whose name appears in bold and is capitalized is a stakes winner. While it's true that the more black type a

---

Catalog Style Pedigree vs. 6-Cross Family Tree Pedigree

For considering the merits of a horse's pedigree to determine its value, the acceptable pedigree used by industry professionals is a catalog style pedigree, and not a six-cross family tree pedigree that is offered by various pedigree software companies. While the six-cross pedigrees are useful when analyzing hypothetical matings, studying nicks or inbreeding, or dosage, they need not be used when determining a horse's value. The commonly accepted pedigree for appraising purposes is a catalog style one, which shows a horse's female family, race record, and produce record, if applicable.

---

horse has in its pedigree the more desirable it is, you need to be aware that not all black-type horses are equally desirable due to the simple reason that a stakes winner running at Yavapai Downs in Arizona is not of the same caliber as a stakes winner at Belmont Park.

By definition, for a race to be given black-type status, its entries must close 72 hours before it is run. Fees must also be paid toward the purse by owners and/or additional (added) money contributed by or through the host racetrack. Most importantly, a stakes race must have a total purse value distributed on race day of $35,000 or more. While the size of the purse does not factor into whether a race is called a stakes race, it must meet the purse criteria to qualify for black type under the International Cataloging Standards Committee.

To help differentiate the quality of various stakes races, other symbols are used with which you should become familiar.

Graded races, the most lucrative of competitions, are designated with a (G) in a sales catalog, although in some countries they are known as "group" races. These are considered the highest quality of all stakes races; they must have a purse of at least $100,000 and have no restrictions other than age or sex. Graded stakes are further classified into three categories: grade I, grade II, and grade III. Grade I races are the cream of the crop. The Breeders' Cup World Thoroughbred Championship races all carry grade I status, as do the Triple Crown races (the Kentucky Derby, Preakness, and Belmont Stakes), and approximately 90 other races in the United States. Approximately 150 grade II races are run throughout the country each year, while about 220 grade III races occur.

The grading given a race by the American Graded Stakes Committee is not static in nature. Each year the committee members meet to discuss American stakes grading and decide which stakes will keep their grading status and which will be upgraded, downgraded, or removed from the list. Many a racetrack executive has nervously held his or her breath awaiting the outcome of the committee's meeting, as a track's ability to hold graded stakes directly affects its ability to attract top horses.

A notch below the quality of graded stakes come listed races. Listed races are those that, for various reasons, have not qualified for graded status but have a total purse value of $75,000 or more and have no restrictions for entry other than sex and age. In a pedigree, a listed race is identified by the name of the race, followed by the designation (L). The name of the track will then appear, along with the purse earned by the horse.

Next are restricted races, which, as the name implies, are restricted to certain types of horses such as state-breds, non-winners of a stakes race,

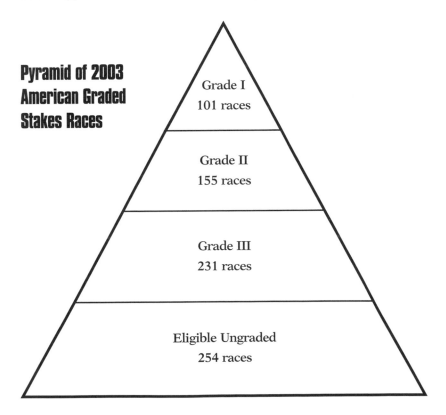

Pyramid of 2003 American Graded Stakes Races

Grade I
101 races

Grade II
155 races

Grade III
231 races

Eligible Ungraded
254 races

etc. Examples of restricted stake races are those run on California Cup Day and Maryland Million Day. In a pedigree, a restricted race is identified by the designation (R), along with the name of the track where the race was held and the purse earned.

Finally, there are simple black-type races, which are stakes races having a purse between $35,000 and $74,999. In a pedigree, they are identified by name only, followed by the name of the track and the purse earned. Be careful when weighing the merits of a horse with plain black-type races, for in some cases allowance races carrying no black-type offer higher purses and stiffer competition. A horse winning a high-class allowance race will not receive black type, although he may be superior in class to a horse that gains black type by winning a small stake. That's where your analytical skills, and knowledge of the racing game, come into play.

It's Easy to Obtain a Pedigree On-line

Studying pedigrees can provide a fascinating glimpse into your horse's family tree and offer up useful information on its worth and potential. And with the advent of modern technologies, it's easy to obtain a myriad of pedigrees, race records, and statistical information from your computer in the comfort of your own home.

Simply contact the following companies that will, for a small fee, download and transfer the requested information. A wealth of information awaits at your fingertips.

www.equineline.com — maintained by The Jockey Club Information Systems, Inc.

www.brisnet.com — Bloodstock Research Information Services, Inc.

7

Conformation

Developing an "Eye" for a Horse

No horse is perfectly conformed. Remember this when assessing horses, for if your goal is to find a horse with correct conformation, you will pass up many runners in the process. Good conformation is important, though, when searching for durable horses that can withstand years of training and racing in pursuit of purse money. Keep in mind that when you are examining a horse's conformation, your purpose is to exclude those with physical faults that you and your advisers deem unacceptable.

When a horse is first presented to you, consider the overall picture. Does the horse appear balanced? Is its frame well proportioned? Does it suit its musculature? What about its "bone"? Does it appear substantial and not too light? Horsemen generally prefer to see a horse with good bone mass, although mass is not necessarily an indication of density. For

Conformation is a key part of the equation in choosing a racing prospect.

example, look at the horse's cannon bone. Does its size fit with the horse's overall body type? A large, muscular horse supported by pencil-thin cannon bones is not desirable. How about intelligence? Does the horse seem in control, aware of its surroundings, and alert? Finally, is the horse athletic in appearance? Does it look physically capable?

Once you have gained an impression of how a horse looks overall, you can then start to focus on its individual parts.

Side View

Feet: A horse's hooves must be able to withstand a great deal of pressure. Consider the proportion, substance, and size of the hoof. Large or small feet are not disadvantageous as long as they are proportionate to the size of the horse. Hooves should have about a 45-degree slope to them. Avoid those that are vertical or dish-shaped (meaning they have a concave appearance). The heels should appear healthy and not be tight or constricted. The hoof's surface should be smooth and devoid of cracks. The underside of the hoof should have a slightly oval shape with some depth. Some believe that a horse with large feet might have an aptitude for turf racing.

Pasterns: The region in the foreleg or hind leg between the hoof and the ankle, the pasterns provide a horse with leverage when moving forward and act as shock absorbers when the hoof lands. A horse's pastern should be at an angle that matches its hoof angle. Its length should be proportionate to the horse's overall body type; too long a pastern could indicate weakness and tendon strain while too short a pastern may absorb too much concussion, thus stressing the bone structure.

Ankle: As with pasterns, the ankle (or fetlock) joint size should be proportionate to the rest of the leg. Beware of spread or prominent sesamoids, the small bones at the rear of the ankle where the pastern and cannon bone meet. These small bones serve as pulleys for the flexor tendons. A prominent appearance could signal sesamoiditis, an inflammation of the sesamoids that causes lameness.

Cannon bones: Ideally, the cannon bone, the bone that connects the knee to the ankle in the front leg, and the hock to the ankle in the hind leg, should be short, strong, and have good mass. The front cannon bone should exit the lower knee cleanly and be well centered and not offset, while the hind cannon bone should connect the hock and the rear pastern in a straight line.

Knee: Bones in and leading to the knee should line up and not tilt forward ("over at the knee") or back ("behind" or "back at the knee"). A horse that is over at the knee will be constantly out of balance due to the knee's position over the lower leg, which can strain joints, ligaments, and tendons. When viewed from the side, a horse with this conformational defect will have a knee with a convex shape. A horse that is back at the knee has a more serious condition, as its knee is bent backward in a concave shape. This defect commonly results in bone chips, causes tremendous strain on

Look at a horse from all angles. A front view can reveal certain leg defects.

tendons and ligaments of the lower leg, and can cause lameness in the pasterns and ankles.

Shoulder: The shoulder of a horse begins at its withers and extends down and forward to its chest. A long shoulder with a slope in the neighborhood of 45 degrees is desirable, as this structure allows a horse to maximize its forward extension. However, the exact slope of good shoulders will vary from horse to horse – it's more important that a horse's shoulders be set back and angled out to an appropriate degree. A horse that has a short shoulder with a relatively steep slope will have a short, choppy stride. Such steep shoulders do not absorb the concussive forces caused by the short stride, allowing concussion to work its way upward into the body.

Neck: A horse's neck is important to its balance and maneuverability; thus, it should not be too short or too long but fit in proportion to the horse's body. For example, a long-backed horse with a short neck is out of proportion and, ultimately, out of balance. The neck should flow smoothly into the withers, or the point where the neck, shoulders, and back meet. Horses that carry their heads high from their neck may have restricted airflow and an inefficient stride. Likewise, horses with "ewe" necks, necks having a concave shape, are not desirable.

Head: Beauty is in the eye of the beholder, and the particulars of a

Many buyers manually inspect a horse's legs and feet.

horse's head can be a matter of personal preference. Plain-headed horses can have just as much ability as those with more refined heads. You often will see experienced horse people placing a fist under the horse's jaw, the thinking being the wider the space, the roomier the air passage. Nostrils should be wide, about twice the size of a silver dollar, with elastic sides that can expand to take in great quantities of air.

Eye: The eyes should be big and bright. Look for an intelligent, keen eye. Horses with "pig-eyes," or small eyes set back in the head, should be avoided as their vision is reduced.

Back: The distance from the withers (where the neck, shoulders, and back meet) to the top of the croup (where the back and pelvis bones meet), should match the length of the horse's neck from the poll (the top of the head) to the withers. This matching length gives a horse good balance and allows for a well-sloped shoulder that will produce a good stride. Horses with long backs tend to have straighter shoulders, and thus shorter strides, while short-backed horses tend to turn over their feet more often, giving them a quicker stride. Such short-backed horses may have a tendency to show early speed but have difficulty sustaining it over a distance. Sway-backed horses, or those whose backs have a severe dip, have weak backs and should be avoided.

Hip/buttocks: The hip, croup, and buttocks of a horse are the most variable area of the horse, meaning that a variety of shapes can be desirable. The croup, the top of the horse's hindquarters above its tail, should have a gentle slope, not too steep or flat. Too steep a croup will impede a horse's extension to the rear and shorten its stride, while too flat a croup will impede a horse's forward extension of its hind legs. The gaskin, the area above the hock, should depict some strength and should complement the muscles of the quarters. A horse with a good length of croup and round, fully developed quarters has the good mechanics that will produce good power.

Hocks: A horse's hock is the joint of the rear leg that connects the cannon bone to the tibia bone in the gaskin area. Hocks play an important role in movement as they transmit energy, via tendons stretched over them, from the hooves to the hindquarters. They should not be straight as a post, nor curved so deeply as to be "sickle-hocked," but somewhere in between. "Post-legged" horses whose hocks have little angle pass concus-

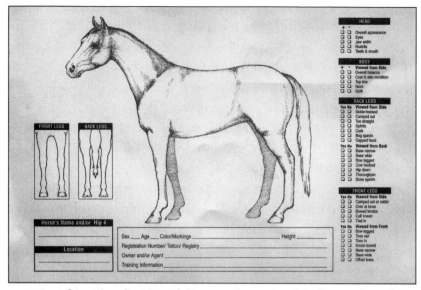

A conformation chart is useful in assessing a potential sales purchase.

sion farther up the leg, making the horse predisposed to lameness. Sickle-hocked horses have too great an angle in their hocks that can, depending upon the severity, put too much stress on the hock and also cause lameness. When looking at the hock area, see whether the horse stands with his hocks tucked up underneath the body, being sickle-hocked, or behind the body like a German shepherd. Both are considered defects. The horse should be standing balanced and straight.

Frontal View

Feet: Look for balanced, symmetrical feet. Avoid misshapen, dished, or cracked feet. Notice if a horse has a clubfoot, a condition in which one has a steeper slope. Such hooves absorb concussion less effectively, which can lead to lameness.

Cannon bones: From the front, the cannon bones should appear straight and be of the same length. Keep an eye out for splints (bony growths) under the knees or on the sides of the foreleg's cannon bones.

Knees: The knees should sit squarely on top of the cannon bones. A horse's knees should not be severely offset, meaning that both the cannon bone below the knee and the foreleg above should align with the center of the knee and not to one side or the other ("offset knees").

Chest: A horse's chest should be broad and appear powerful. Differences in the chest may show which horses are likely sprinters and which are stayers. A large chest will provide ample space for a horse's lungs to expand, although too much width may interfere with the horse's action. Broad chests may give the horse ample oxygen for quick bursts of speed, although such large mass may prevent the horse from sustaining his speed over a distance. Horses with narrower chests may not be as quick, but they are more likely to sustain their speed over longer distances. Narrow-chested horses are said to lack power.

Shoulders: Look for balance, symmetry, and good muscling.

Rear View

Hocks: When you are looking at the horse from the rear, the hocks should appear to point straight at you and not turn in ("cow hocked") or turn out ("open at the hocks"). Horses with severe cow hocks may interfere with themselves (the hocks strike each other during movement) and stress the hocks. However, some cow hocks may improve when the horse is training and its hindquarters develop more muscle that improves the action of its rear legs. Look for a horse that moves his rear legs in a reasonably correct manner, for as long as the hock action doesn't cause the horse to forge or interfere with himself, they may be fine.

Hip/buttocks: The hind end is the horse's engine. Definition and development are key attributes. Large, well-muscled hindquarters may predispose a horse to sprinting, while those horses that are lighter behind may be inclined to run a distance of ground. Take the horse's pedigree into consideration as well, for certain sires produce specific body types that can explain why a horse is shaped they way he is.

Walking Stride

Front/Rear view: The horse should move straight as it walks toward and away from you. Observe whether the horse toes in or out as it walks. Horses whose toes angle inward as they step ("toeing in") will tend to paddle when they walk. This condition is not as serious as "toeing out," which stresses the inside of a horse's knee and can contribute to splints. A horse that toes out significantly is also in danger of striking its lower legs as it moves.

Side view: Check for an overstep, meaning do the hind feet reach beyond the front hoof prints? This is considered a sign of athleticism. Observe the horse's head. Be certain it does not bob unusually when walking, as this may indicate soreness or lameness.

Walk: Look for a smooth, athletic stride. A horse should have some swing in its hips, and his rear legs should reach well up under himself. An overstep, where the horse's hind leg steps over the hoofprint left by his front leg, is highly desirable. Finally, observe the horse's overall presence – does he appear confident? Is he interested in his surroundings? Is he balanced as he moves, or does he stumble and trip? Look for a horse with a good walk – it's one of the signs of a potential athlete.

Final Impressions

Remember, every horse has some physical faults. The art or science of evaluating a horse involves deciding which faults are less likely to affect the horse's performance. It is helpful to be familiar with the horse's pedigree when viewing the animal, as some sires pass similar conformational faults to their offspring, some of which have little or no consequence with respect to a horse's racing success. Be reminded that a horse's greatest attribute can't be seen, and that is the size of his heart.

Everyone has different thresholds with regards to what constitutes acceptable faults. Establish your own thresholds, but be realistic considering your budget.

8

Operating Costs

S o you've dug deep into your pockets, taken the plunge, and purchased a racehorse. Congratulations…that was a down payment.

As with any piece of valuable real property, your horse will require ongoing upkeep such as daily training, physical maintenance and repair, extra expenses for special occasions (such as race day), insurance, and, of course, the inevitable dues to Caesar in the form of taxes. Part of assuring yourself a non-traumatic experience as a Thoroughbred racehorse owner is knowing what expenses to expect — and making sure you have the money to meet them.

Most of the big-ticket expenses are noted and explained elsewhere in this manual, but for easy reference (and arithmetic), everything you're likely to be paying for is listed below.

These figures are laid out so that you can, if you wish, prepare an operating budget for each horse in your stable. Cost management is recognized, even by experienced owners, as one of the great enigmas in racing — and, unless you have bottomless pockets or don't care much for the business — it is a crucial exercise, one to be undertaken thoughtfully and monitored regularly. Cost management seems to derive from an axiom in Murphy's Law that says, "work expands to meet available budget." So, to some extent, figure all the costs of keeping a racehorse.

No fixed rate actually exists for anything mentioned below (with the exception of taxes, some jockey fees, and your particular trainer's worker's compensation premiums). Apparently, costs are set by what the market will bear — a fact illustrated by the differences in costs to train a horse throughout the country.

Costs of Racehorse Ownership

Trainer's day rate: The day rate is the daily rate your trainer charges to keep a horse in his or her barn. It covers feed, labor, worker's compensation, and miscellaneous items such as bandages, vitamins, etc. Day rates range from $35 to upward of a $100 a day, depending upon the trainer's locale and success. Most trainers operating at the same racetrack will usually be within 5% of one another. (See Appendix for further details.)

A cautionary note: As you shop for a trainer, keep in mind that reputable people generally won't work for terrific cut rates. If a trainer in your locale is offering a discounted day rate, beware. Such individuals may be able to offer discounts by cutting corners on your horse's care or by not keeping their worker's compensation insurance up to date. If the latter is true, you, as the owner, have an increased risk of being held liable for an injury that may occur to a stablehand.

Veterinary fees: Most owners run a vet bill of $200-$300 per horse per month, which includes pre-race Lasix injections, routine vaccines, and endoscopic examinations to check the horse for signs of nasal capillary bleeding after a race or strenuous workout. Other possible costs include X-rays, drugs, surgeries, and serious injuries or illnesses – these can significantly affect your monthly statement. (See Chapter 9, Veterinary and Farrier Care, for further information.)

Farrier: Your horse must be shod about every four weeks. Regular shoeing includes hoof trimming and attaching new shoes and costs about

A trainer's day rate includes stabling and feeding of the horse and labor.

$85-$120 per horse. Again, the price of shoeing varies depending upon your horse's locale and your farrier's expertise. When it comes to special or remedial shoeing and procedures, farriers – like dentists – will charge according to their reputation, experience, and what the local market will bear. (Chapter 9 gives greater detail on shoeing costs.)

Equine Dentistry: This will be a rather small fee that will only be charged a couple of times a year. The rates to "float" a horse's teeth, or file their rough, worn edges, range between $35 and $75.

Farm Day Rate: Occasionally your horse may need time off from the rigors of race training to rest, relax, and, possibly, recuperate at a farm. Farm day rates range anywhere from $8 to $25 a day.

Transportation: Figure in transportation costs if you are shipping to race. These costs vary widely depending upon your horse's travel plans. (See Chapter 11, Shipping to Win, for further information.)

Race Day: Race day brings some additional costs. Hopefully, they will be more than offset by purse earnings.

Trainer's Commission: Trainers earn commissions when a purse is earned. They generally charge 10% of any purses earned, although some may only charge for first- through fourth-place finishes. A small barn stake of 1% to 3%, to be split among the barn crew, may also be charged on wins.

Jockey's Fee: A minimum of $35-$100 is paid for a jockey to ride in a race. If your horse comes in first, the jockey receives 10% of your share of the purse. He or she is paid 5% of the earned share of the purse for second- and third-place finishes.

Other Race Day Costs
Pony-to-post: $10-$25
Lasix shot: $10-$25
Fluid & Vitamin "jugs": $25-$35
Endoscopic exam (if necessary): $50-$75
State taxes: Purse earnings are taxed as income.

Income Generation

A common cycle of conditioning will put each horse into a race about seven times a year. While it is nearly impossible to predict where your horse will finish or what it will earn in these races, you can project some income if you place your horse where it will be competitive and finish in the money.

Let's assume that your horse will win at least one race during the year and finish in the money in three other races. Check the condition book to determine the average purse for which your horse will be racing and then refer to Chapter 13 to see the percentage of purse paid to specific placings. While such income projection will never be on the nose, it is possible to roughly estimate income your horse may earn.

If you go through this exercise, one observation will probably jump out at you: It costs just as much to keep a horse that wins huge purses as it does to keep one that wins small ones.

9

Veterinary and Farrier Care

Veterinary Care

Veterinary expenses are probably one of the least understood and most frustrating aspects of Thoroughbred ownership. The monthly vet bill is anticipated with as much relish as the monthly credit card statement, only with more maddening symbols and hieroglyphics (ESE, ATCH, Eastern/Western, EIA) detailing what treatments and medications a horse received.

To lessen the surprise, it's important to have a clear understanding with your trainer about how approval for treatments and administering of medication will be handled. If you are a hands-off owner who feels

Veterinarians at a sale reading X-rays.

comfortable with your trainer's decisions in this area, you might need just a heads-up if a large bill is on the horizon.

For other owners, though, it's worthwhile to discuss with your trainer how veterinary care will be approved. Many trainers are more than happy to keep owners in the loop about veterinary work because, by doing so, the owner shares the responsibility for a course of treatment that, in hindsight, wasn't a success or that generated large bills.

Whatever level of communication you choose or your time permits, be sure to ask your trainer if the veterinary care is itemized in his or her monthly training statement or if the veterinarian will bill you directly. In the latter event, you will be better served if the trainer reviews the veterinarian's statement for accuracy before forwarding it to you. Training barns are busy places, and inadvertent billing mistakes do occur, so ask that your trainer review and initial the veterinary bill as a courtesy to you. Finally, don't be shy about asking the veterinarian or his or her office personnel about the charges you will be expected to pay.

The authors urge all owners to ask questions regarding what medications your horse is receiving and if any of it has the ability to result in a

Performing an endoscopic exam to determine a horse's soundness of wind.

positive post-race test (see Chapter10, Medication Implications). With racing laboratories' testing procedures becoming increasingly sensitive and with purse money on the line, the wise owner knows what medications his or her horse is receiving.

Managing Your Monthly Vet Bill

Like all professional athletes, your horse will have its share of aches, pains, minor injuries, and, sometimes, major injuries as a result of training and competition. Some horses require fewer treatments than others, and some trainers rely less heavily on medications and veterinarians than others. Nevertheless, at one time or another you will probably own a horse that will suffer a serious illness or injury that will cost a lot of money to treat.

The only defenses against being surprised by a large vet bill are 1) to understand, as much as possible, the purpose of each treatment, 2) to have some realistic sense of its cost, and 3) to keep in contact with your trainer so you are prepared for any unusual medical outlays.

To create an effective budget, ask your trainer how extensively he or she uses the veterinarian. You might also set a dollar ceiling beyond which your trainer must consult you before authorizing treatment.

Keep in mind, too, that trainers, by law, are not allowed to be in possession of a syringe in the barn. Therefore, the trainer cannot administer injectable medications or substances to any horse — and that includes such common necessities as vitamin supplements, emergency colic remedies, Salix® (commonly known as Lasix), hyaluronic acid for joints, and even deworming medications. Thus any of these items your horse might need will appear on your veterinarian 's statement — although decoding them can be somewhat daunting.

Decoding Your Vet Bill

Keep in mind when considering the overall trainer/vet symbiosis that good veterinarians take pride in their work and want their client's horses performing at the top of their game. Most veterinarians will visit each of their trainers' barns every day and take the time to examine any horse with a questionable condition. The trainer's veterinarian assumes responsibility for watching all of his or her patients for medical developments and is motivated to catch them as early as possible to prevent illnesses or injuries. Although veterinarians do not charge for their daily visits, their work will be reflected in their monthly statement, which is usually categorized by each horse they treat.

To make conversations with your trainer about veterinary work easier and to increase your understanding about veterinary care, here's a list of common medications and therapies, diagnostic tests and examinations, and injuries.

MEDICATIONS

Routine Items	When Performed	Approx. Cost
Flu/rhino vaccination	Every 2-3 months	$45
West Nile Virus vaccination	Annually	$35
Tetanus vaccination	Once or twice/year	$13-$18
Standard deworming	Every 2-3 months	$20-$30
Teeth floating (dentistry)	Every 3-4 months	$50-$75

Antibiotics .... $8-$40/day, $180/day for Amikacin
Penicillin, Tetracycline, Gentamicin, Baytril, Naxcel, Amikacin, Tribrissen, Trimethylsulfate, Trimethoprim Sulfate
Treatment of bacterial infection. Amikacin is used primarily for respiratory tract infections

Anti-inflammatories............... $15-$25/day (injection), $2-$4/day (orally)
Phenalbutazone, Banamine®, Naproxen, Motrin®, Ketofen® (all are non-steroidal, but their use can be restricted on race-day – check with your local jurisdiction). Azium®, Naquasone®, Vetalog®, Prednisone, Dexamethasone (these are steroidal and need to be used with caution when racing).
Reduction of inflammation in muscles and joints.
Banamine is also used in the treatment colic.

Bronchodilators $10/day
Clenbuterol, Albuterol
Work to open constricted airways. Also have expectorant properties that work to clear mucous and debris from airways and reduce inflammation.

Ulcer therapy

Tagamet, Carafate .... $60-$150/month

Gastrogard .... $48/day, or $1200/month

Treat stomach ulcers

Bleeder Medication

Lasix/Salix® .... $15-$25/per treatment

Reduces severity of exercise-induced pulmonary hemorrhaging

(EIPH)

Premarin.. $65-$95/per treatment

Used with Salix® for problem bleeders.

Robinul®, Amicar®, Methergin, Adaenosena ..... $15-$25/per treatment

Used with Salix® as a breathing aid for workouts only. Most cannot
be used pre-race.

Muscle relaxants

Robaxin® ....$5-$15/per treatment

Musculoskeletal soreness

Hormones

Winstrol, Equipoise, Deca Durabolin, Testosterone ..... $30-$60 per shot

Regumate®.. $200/month

Suppresses ovulatory cycle

Corticosteroids

Depomedrol®, Vetalog®, Celestone® .... $50-$75/joint

Intra-articular injection that provides short-term relief from joint inflammation.

*Anabolic steroids used to stimulate muscle development and appetite, repair tissue, and accelerate recovery from disease or injury. Anabolic steroids may cause aggressive behavior in mares or geldings and may have adverse effects on the reproductive function of mares and stallions.

VITAMINS AND FLUIDS

ESE (vitamin E & selenium) .... $25/per treatment

Used to treat muscle soreness

Fluids & vitamins (Jugs).. $25-$35/per treatment

Electrolyte solutions administered intravenously to replace essential
elements depleted by workouts, races, or Salix® use.

THERAPIES

Hyaluronic acid.. $125-$150/joint

Hyaluronate, Hyvisc®, Hylartin®

Intramuscular/intravenous injections that promote joint health and prevent degenerative joint disease.

Adequan/Legend...$75-$90/week

Treatments last from three to five weeks, or indefinitely

Intramuscular/intravenous injections that promote joint health and prevent degenerative joint disease

Neutriceuticals

Cosequin®, shark cartilage, Synoflex®,

Flexfree®, Cortiflex® .... $60-$120/month

Natural products that may be effective in maintaining joint health.

TESTS, EXAMINATIONS, & COMMON PROCEDURES

X-rays or radiographs .... $60-$85 for knees or ankles, $80-$100 for stifles.

Images injuries in bone

Ultrasound .... $100-$125 per scan

Images injuries in soft tissue

Endoscopy .... $50-$75

Diagnoses breathing problems such as malfunctions, infections, or bleeding.

Tracheal wash (swabbing) .... $75-$100 to obtain sample, $100 for lab work.

Used to check for respiratory infection

Routine soundness exam.. No charge

Palpation, gait analysis, hoof-testing, etc.

Basic pre-purchase soundness exam ....$50-$75

Additional X-rays and endoscopic exam......................................$500-$700

CBC (complete blood count)..$30-$45

Additional blood chemistries..$40

Routine castration............................$125-$200, plus cost of tranquilizers, tetanus shots, and antibiotics.

Coggins test (to check for equine infectious anemia)..................... $20-$35
Needed in order to transport horse

Blistering .... $35 blistering agent
Procedure used to increase blood circulation to a localized area
such as a horse's shins or front ankles. A caustic agent is applied directly
to a horse's skin to produce a reaction in the soft tissue. This reaction
causes more blood to circulate throughout the affected area, which
increases healing.

Internal blister.. $50- $75
Procedure in which mild caustic agents are injected beneath the
skin of an affected area to increase blood supply to it and thus increase
healing. Internal blisters are used on such areas as a horse's back or stifle.

Pin-firing... $200
A severe form of "counter-irritation" whereby multiple holes are
burned in the skin by a hot pin-sized iron. This firing produces
acute inflammation that increases circulation and speeds healing of the
affected area.
Local anesthetics are applied before the process, and a horse is
tranquilized during the procedure. A horse receives 30 days of rest after
being pin-fired. Pin-firing is primarily used to heal bucked shins, although
it is not as commonly used as it once was.

Freeze firing.. $75-$150
A procedure that is similar to pin-firing, except liquid nitrogen is used
to freeze the affected area instead of burning it. An advantage of freeze
firing is that a horse can return to training after 15 days.

COMMON INJURIES

Exercise-induced pulmonary hemorrhage (EIPH), also known as
bleeding, is characterized by bleeding from the lungs after strenuous exercise. Research has shown that 70% to 100% of racehorses experience
EIPH to some degree. It is believed that horses experience EIPH during
exercise due to the unusually high blood pressure in the blood vessels that
lead from their heart to the lungs. This pressure causes the walls of the

vessels to break and release blood into the airways. Many times an endoscopic examination is needed to determine if a horse has bled after a race or workout, as bleeding may occur without external symptoms. The diuretic Salix® (Lasix) works to lower blood pressure slightly in the lungs, which is thought to reduce bleeding.

Bone chips: Pieces of bone broken off at a joint, usually caused by racing stress. If they remain attached, they may not interfere with the horse's action but can be extremely painful and sometimes require removal by arthroscopic surgery. Such surgery costs between $1,500 and $2,000 and is followed by six to 12 weeks rest and an additional three to four months of retraining.

Bowed tendon: An inflamed or ruptured superficial flexor tendon, which is the tendon running from the back of the knee to the fetlock or

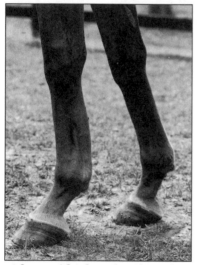

A horse with a bowed tendon in his left foreleg.

ankle area. Bows are usually caused by severe strain, although horses that are back at the knee, have long and weak pasterns, or are trimmed to have a long toe and low heel may be predisposed to them. The bowed appearance is due to the formation of fibrinous tissue. Many bows are undetectable to the eye but can be seen on an ultrasound if caught early. Bows are classified as low, medium, or high, depending on their location. Treatment usually requires long periods of rest – six months to a year on the farm is normal. While enzyme injections and laser and surgical procedures are being used to treat this injury, less than 50 percent of horses suffering a bowed tendon return to racing.

Bucked shins: A bucked shin is an enlargement on the front cannon bone between the knee and fetlock joints. Bucked shins are caused by microfractures to the periosteum (the thin sheath covering the bone) and occurs most often in young horses in heavy training. Treatment options include giving a horse a two- to-three-month rest, pin firing, periosteal scraping, or continuing with light training with a gradual increase in intensity.

Colic: Colic is a general term used to describe gastrointestinal pain. The number one killer of horses, colic can happen at any time and for many reasons. Treatments vary depending upon type and severity, with a simple colic treatment costing about $100. More severe or prolonged cases can cost several hundred dollars, while cases requiring surgery can cost several thousand or more.

Condylar fracture: A fracture occurring in the cannon bone. The condyle is a protuberance at the bottom of the cannon bone where it fits into the fetlock joint. Condylar fractures can be repaired surgically for about $1,500-$2,500. The prognosis for survival and return to racing soundness depends on the severity of injury. In uncomplicated cases, after surgery the horse usually is given stall rest for one month after surgery, followed by another month of stall rest combined with some hand-walking. After this 60-day period, X-rays are taken to determine the rate of healing. If all is going well, another two to four weeks of light exercise are likely before the horse resumes training. In cases of more severe fractures, the recovery period could span many months before the horse is ready to return to training.

Curb: An inflammation or strain of the plantar ligament, which is located immediately below the point of the hock. Treatment options include rest, firing, or blistering. Costs range from $100-$200, while time off is usually 30-60 days.

Fractured bone in leg: Surgery to repair a fractured bone in the leg requiring the placement of screws in the cannon bone or pastern will cost $2,000-$3,000 or more, depending upon the fracture's complexity. After surgery, the horse will require four to eight months of rest and another three to four months of retraining.

Grabbed quarter: Tearing of skin and tissue caused by a horse "grabbing" a front hoof with a hind hoof. Cost and amount of training time lost depend on the extent of injury. This can be a major or minor injury. Special shoes, such as Z-bar shoes, can help.

Hoof abscess: A localized collection of pus underneath the hoof wall. They usually occur in the hoof sole as the result of a bruise to the foot, although they can also appear at the coronet band. They can be major or minor depending upon the amount of hoof affected and if they undermine the hoof wall.

Quarter cracks: Cracks occurring in the hoof that are caused by stress or improper shoeing. They can become a source of great pain and sometimes include development of infection in the exposed soft tissue underneath. This injury can be corrected with a fiberglass or epoxy patch and proper shoeing. The cost and amount of training time lost, if any, depend on the extent of the injury.

Respiratory illness: Acute respiratory illness, such as pleural pneumonia, is often related to stressful events, such as transport. It requires extensive treatments that can last for months. It is diagnosed through the use of ultrasound or thoracic radiographs and is treated with antibiotics. Depending upon the extent, this type of illness can be major or minor. Treating pneumonia can cost thousands of dollars.

Sesamoid fracture: The sesamoids are two small, delicate bones at the back of the fetlock that are held in place by ligaments. They serve as pulleys over which the deep digital flexor tendons pass. A fracture to the sesamoids usually involves an injury to the suspensory apparatus. Depending upon the severity of the injury, surgery can be performed to

A splint can be seen on the inside of this foreleg.

treat the fracture, and horses may return to racing after six to eight months of rest. Surgery costs about $1,500-$2,500.

Slab fracture: A fracture at the knee whereby a "slab" of a carpal bone splits and the front part becomes detached. This can often be repaired surgically for about $2,000-$2,500, after which a horse is given six to seven months of rest. While not necessarily career ending, a slab fracture is a serious injury.

"Popping" a splint: Inflammation leading to bony growth that occurs on the splint bone. Splints are most commonly caused by concussion with a hard surface. Blistering, surgery, and rest are all treatments. Time off is anywhere between two weeks and two months, depending upon severity of the splint.

Torn suspensory ligaments: The suspensory ligaments run from the top end of the back side of the cannon bone, knee, and hock down to sesamoids and the pastern bone. These are among the most stressed of all tissues in the racehorse's body and are, therefore, one of the most common sites for injury. Treatment is usually six to nine months of rest followed by three to four months of retraining. Little can be done medically to treat these injuries.

FARRIER WORK — KEEPING FEET FLEET

It's all truly riding on the hoof.

Your success as a Thoroughbred owner could conceivably boil down to the four inches of hoof that keep your horse connected to the ground. More than one owner has realized this after having his or her dreams put on hold due to a misplaced nail, poor shoeing work, or a stubborn hoof abscess that just won't heal. So don't overlook the importance of a good

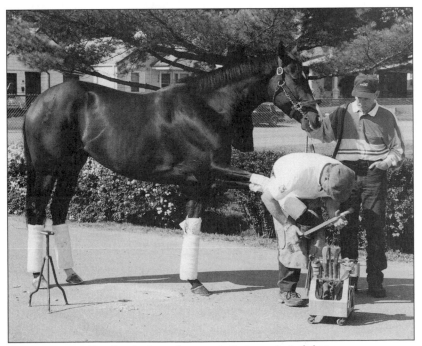

Routine footcare is a must of a horse in training.

farrier in your quest for the winner's circle.

On average, horses are shod every three to five weeks, although this can slightly vary depending upon the time of year and climate. Hooves, which are similar in composition to your fingernail, tend to grow faster during the summer. Horses living in cold climates can be more prone to dry, hard hooves, while horses living in hot, wet climates can be susceptible to soft hooves.

Farriers, who are paid per horse shod, can easily shoe a horse in 20-30 minutes. And for about $125 a horse, horseshoers enjoy a good living. But their jobs are truly backbreaking.

A farrier first untacks and pulls off a horse's old shoes, trims and balances the hoof, and then nails on new shoes. Most racehorses are used to the process and stand patiently. Watching a good farrier shoe a horse is worth observing, as his quick-yet-precise moves carefully craft a hoof into racing shape.

Shoeing horses involves more than simply tacking racing plates onto a hoof, though. Good farriers know the importance of properly balancing and shaping a horse's hoof before attaching a shoe. They closely observe a horse's foot movement, wear patterns on old shoes, and type of racing it will be doing before selecting a shoe that will allow the horse to give his best performance. They even take the weather into consideration, as rainy weather may require different shoes, while extremely wet or dry conditions require them to be on the lookout for quarter cracks.

A Balanced Hoof and Proper Fit Essential

A properly balanced hoof will evenly distribute the impact of a horse's weight without causing undue stress. To achieve this balance, the farrier should observe the horse in motion. The feet should hit the ground flat, with the angle of the hoof and pastern in alignment. Like the footwear of their human athlete counterparts, horses' old shoes should be checked for wear patterns – a useful tool in determining proper balance.

Serious problems can develop when out-of-balance conditions occur. If a horse's toe is not properly trimmed and left too long, increased strain occurs on the flexor tendons and knees. Proper trimming can reduce this stress.

It's important that a horse's shoes fit properly. Proper fit means the shoe must be formed to the shape of the foot, be level, and not cause pressure on the sole. If the shoe has a "toe grab," which is similar to a cleat, it should be exactly centered with the apex of the frog. Toe grabs that are not properly aligned can cause ligament injuries as the foot is forced to break over unnaturally.

A small amount of excess shoe should also be left around the heel to allow for its natural expansion when contacting the ground at racing speeds. If not left, the hoof may grow out over the shoe and result in corns or under-slung heels. Under-slung heels, or heels that are extremely sloped, can create stress on ankles and tendons.

It's also important to maintain ample sole on a horse's foot for protection and strength. The bars of the heel should remain intact so as to keep the heels strong and to prevent the heel from rolling under the foot.

Running Shoes for Horses

Not all horses' shoes are alike, nor do they serve the same purpose. Turf courses require different shoes than dirt tracks, as most grass courses ban toe grabs, which tend to damage their running surface. Likewise, wet weather can call for different shoes than dry, as some trainers believe adding mud or jar calks, nails, or stickers will increase their chance of winning races.

Below is a list of shoes commonly used on racehorses in training. While the decision of which shoe is best left to your trainer and farrier, it's always good to be familiar with the shoe your horse is wearing and its cost.

Aluminum shoes .... average $100
   Lightweight shoe most commonly used for racing.

Flat steel training plates .... average $100
   For horses in light training.

Queens plates .... average $100
   Light-weight aluminum training plates without a toe grab.
   Used primarily on turf horses.

Egg-bar shoes .... additional $25/shoe
                              (if worn in front, a pair is used for balance)
   Special shoe used for horses with quarter cracks, broken coffin bones,
   or sore or under-slung heels. They are oval (or egg-shaped) and work
   to distribute weight over a larger circumference.

D-bar shoes .... additional $25/shoe

Similar to egg-bar shoes, they distribute weight over a larger area and help to relieve the soreness of navicular disease and hoof cracks. A bar at the rear of the shoe connects the heels, giving the shoe a "D" shape.

Z-bar shoes .... additional $100 per shoe
Oddly-shaped shoes (they look like a "Z") that are a form of a D-bar shoe. They are used on horses with grabbed quarters as their shape supports the foot while relieving pressure from the affected heel.

Half aluminum bar pads (frog plates) .... additional $25 per shoe
Shoes used to relieve pressure from the heel portion of the foot. They aid horses with sore heels, as well as those with navicular disease, broken coffin bones, and bruised frogs.

Glue-on shoes... $350 per pair, plus $50 to apply.
Unlike most shoes, which are nailed to the hoof's outside wall, glue-on shoes are adhered to the hoof using a strong bonding agent. They are useful for horses with thin hoof walls or those with chronically sore feet. Glue-on shoes are normally applied to the front feet and stay on surprisingly well.

Bonded shoes .... additional $15
Shoes having an additional rim pad to absorb shock. The rim pad also acts as a "spacer," keeping the soles of the feet up and off the ground.

Outer-rim shoes .... averages $100
Mainly used for turf horses. Their outer perimeter is slightly raised, creating a small ridge that aids traction.

Toe grab .... no additional charge
A toe grab acts as a cleat on the toe of the shoe, providing additional traction. Like most cleats, they are available in both a small and large grab. Aluminum shoes with toe grabs are the most common shoes used on racehorses.

Quarter Horse grabs .... may be slight additional charge
Large toe grabs that are primarily used on the hind feet for traction.

Jar calks .... may be slight additional charge
Cleats placed in the heel portion of the shoe to provide additional traction in the mud.

Stickers .... may be slight additional charge
Cleats on the outside rim of the shoe. They are commonly used for additional traction in the mud, as well as on horses that hit (interfere

*with) themselves while running. This shoe may take the foot out of
balance and thus create additional problems.*

Mud nails or pyramid nails .... no additional charge
Traction devices used on wet or muddy tracks.

Blocked heels .... no additional charge
*Two cleats placed at the farthest portion of the heel on the inside and
outside rim of the shoe for added traction especially in the mud. Blocked
heel shoes are placed only on the hind feet, and they may also be used
on horses that run down (burn their pasterns) or overextend themselves
behind as the cleats raise the heel and reduce sliding.*

Patches .... $200-$300 plus shoeing
*Epoxy patches are used to help horses recover from quarter cracks,
abscesses, and grabbed quarters. A tough fiberglass cloth is used with
the epoxy to form a patch that supports the foot as it grows out its
affected area. Patches last about 30 days, usually a second one is needed
to complete the recovery.*

Do Toe Grabs Increase Breakdowns?

Are toe grabs bad? Can that little piece of metal centered on the toe of
your horse's shoe increase the chance he will go lame, or worse yet, suffer
a breakdown?

Industry leaders in California think so and are backing up their belief
with a two-year study of shoes worn by Thoroughbreds racing at California
racetracks. Information gleaned from this study will help the University of
California Davis researchers determine if and how toe grabs, rim shoes,
and other traction devices increase the chances of lameness and fatal
injuries in racehorses. This study was sparked by preliminary research that
showed horses wearing front toe grabs were 3.5 times more likely to suffer
a fatal musculoskeletal injury than those without front toe grabs. The study
also showed that horses wearing front "low" toe grabs were six times more
likely to suffer a fatal suspensory apparatus injury, while horses wearing a
"regular" height toe grab were 16 times more likely.

Alarmed by these somber statistics, California's racing industry decided further study on the effects of toe grabs was needed, as UC Davis' preliminary research was conducted on only 200 horses. When completed,
UC Davis' two-year study will analyze horses on a much larger scale.

How do toe grabs affect soundness? By providing extra traction and acting as cleats, their added height changes the hoof angle, creating additional strain on the soft tissue of the lower limb when the horse pushes off when running.

The results of this two-year study will soon be available. Until then, be aware that the use of toe grabs could play a role in your horse's soundness.

10

Medication Implications

The use of medication in racehorses is subject to endless debate. Purists who think that horses should race on only hay, oats, and water decry the use of anti-inflammatories, anabolic steroids, and breathing aids in racehorses, claiming their use allows horses with problems to continue to compete, ultimately weakening the breed. Others believe that racehorses should not be denied the benefits of modern medicine, the judicious use of which allows horses to overcome ailments more quickly and reduce the amount of training time lost to illness or injury. While both sides argue valid points, it is hard to fathom the industry outlawing the use of therapeutic medication, as many owners and trainers depend on its use to keep their horses competing for checks.

Whichever side you take, the use of medication in American racing is bound to continue. That is why you, as an owner, need to understand some of the basic issues that surround medication and how its use could ultimately affect your bottom line.

Medication rules differ from state to state.

Different Rules for Different Jurisdictions

Different racing states have different rules regarding medication, and although the industry is working toward and desperately needs some standardization in medication rules, such uniformity has yet to be attained. What may be legal in one state can be illegal in another. For example, in Kentucky it is legal to give two non-steroidal anti-inflammatory drugs, one corticosteroid, and anabolic steroids in any combination and in any dosage, up to four hours prior to a race. In other states, such as New York, it is illegal to administer those same medications within 48 hours of a race. As an owner, it is not imperative that you memorize the medication rules in every state. You do, however, need to be aware that each state is different so that if you ship to another state to race you can ask your trainer and veterinarian if your horse's medication regimen will cause any problems.

Drug Testing

To keep the playing field level and to assure the betting public's confidence in fairly run races, each state's racing commission oversees the testing of racehorses immediately after they compete. The testing procedure begins when blood and/or urine samples are collected from, at the minimum, the winner of each race, and usually from beaten favorites and a handful of randomly chosen horses. These samples are divided into two separate samples, one of which is shipped to an approved laboratory to undergo analysis for prohibited substances or too great of an amount of an authorized medication. The second sample is retained by the commission and is commonly referred to as the "split" or "referee" sample.

Currently, most states classify drugs according to their potential to alter performance, with a Class I drug violation incurring the stiffest penalty and a Class V drug carrying a warning or small suspension. (See "Drug Classifications" later in this chapter.) If a positive for one (or more) of these substances is detected, the trainer can request the second sample (the split or referee) be tested by a different lab to confirm the drug's presence (note: Massachusetts and New Hampshire do not allow split samples). If the second test confirms the first, the trainer is provided a hearing before the board of stewards, which either fines or suspends the trainer (or both), depending upon the severity of the infraction. The horse is normally disqualified, and any purse is forfeited and redistributed to the other horses in that race. The race will not appear as part of the horse's record.

Current detection methods allow labs to measure the presence of a substance in picograms — or a billionth of a gram. That is like finding one speck of salt in an Olympic-sized swimming pool. While it is difficult to determine whether substances found in such small quantities have a performance-enhancing effect on a horse, it is equally as difficult to monitor what a horse ingests on a 24-hour basis. Many naturally occurring substances, such as chocolate and coffee, can cause a positive for caffeine, while poppy seeds can cause a positive for morphine. Positives are further complicated by the fact that, just like humans, horses metabolize substances at different rates, and different medications take varying times to leave a horse's system. A therapeutic drug legally used to help a horse overcome an illness could, weeks later, cause a positive from a residual amount left in its system.

Understanding the negative light in which racing is portrayed when such "positives" are found, some racing jurisdictions have instituted threshold levels below which a positive finding is not reported. These levels are set only after scientific research shows that substances found in amounts beneath the set limit do not affect a horse's performance. If a substance is found in amounts below a threshold level, a positive will not be reported. But not all states have adopted threshold levels, leaving owners and trainers to wrestle with officials when a positive is declared.

While these stringent regulations may at times seem draconian, rememb that changes in speed of less than 1% are extremely difficult to demonstrate statistically, yet an improvement of only 1% represents about six lengths in a race over one mile. In short, the regulations are there to maintain racing's integrity and protect your interest as a horse owner.

Technicalities aside, ownership should be an enjoyable experience, not one that involves the legal system and strips you of a purse. So make sure that your trainer is on top of medication rules, pays attention to how medication is administered in the barn, and is working to insure that one of your horses does not incur a "positive." In other words, be a proactive owner. Read your vet bills, look at the medications being used on your horse, and understand what they are. If you have questions, ask your trainer.

And don't slip your favorite horse chocolate kisses or candy bars.

Drug Classifications

The Association of Racing Commissioners International (RCI) has developed a process to classify drugs for regulatory purposes. The Drug Testing Standards and Practices Committee, a panel of scientists chosen by RCI, meets annually, sometimes more often if necessary, and classifies drugs based on pharmacology, drug use patterns, and the appropriateness of a drug for use in the racing horse. Most states' regulatory bodies refer to this classification scheme when ruling on a drug positive in their state. The scheme classifies drugs into five categories:

Class I: Stimulant and depressant drugs that have the highest potential to affect performance and that have no generally accepted medical use in the racing horse. Substances include opiates, opium derivatives, synthetic opioids, psychoactive drugs, amphetamines, and drugs that are potent stimulants of the central nervous system.

Class II: Drugs that have a high potential to affect performance, but less of a potential than drugs in Class I. These drugs are 1) not generally accepted as therapeutic agents in racing horses, or 2) they are therapeutic agents that have a high potential for abuse. Drugs in this class include psychotropic drugs, such as diazapam (Valium™), central nervous system and cardiovascular system stimulants, depressants, neuromuscular blocking agents, and local anesthetics.

Class III: Drugs that may or may not have generally accepted medical use in the racing horse but the pharmacology of which suggests less potential to affect performance than Class II drugs. They include bronchodilators and other drugs with primary effects on the autonomic nervous system, procaine, antihistamines with sedative properties, and certain diuretics.

Class IV: This class includes therapeutic medications that would be expected to have less potential to affect performance than those in Class III. They include less potent diuretics, anabolic steroids, corticosteroids, antihistamines and skeletal muscle relaxants without prominent central nervous system effects, expectorants and mucolytics, hemostatics, cardiac glycosides and anti-arrhythmics, topical anesthetics, antidiarrheals, and mild analgesics. This class also includes the non-steroidal anti-inflammatory drugs (NSAIDs) at concentrations greater than established limits (i.e., phenylbutazone at 5.0 µg/ml).

Class V: This class includes therapeutic medications for which concentration limits have been established by the racing jurisdictions as well as certain miscellaneous agents such as dimethylsulfoxide (DMSO) and other medications as determined by regulators. Included specifically are agents that have very localized actions only, such as anti-ulcer drugs, and certain anti-allergic drugs. Anticoagulant drugs are also included.

11

Shipping to Win

S hipping your horse, either by van or by air, is an inevitable part of owning a potentially winning stable. Not only do race meets move from track to track throughout the year, but as your horse rises or drops in class and ability, you may have good reason to ship to another track or state, even if only for a single race.

Though your trainer will have his or her own preference with regard to transport companies and will make the actual arrangements, it's useful for the owner to have an overview of the process.

There are a couple of things to remember when shipping. One is that every time a horse is shipped to race, its Jockey Club certification papers must be on file in the racing office of where it is to compete. If the horse has not been described on its papers since it was a yearling, its identifying markings may have changed radically — so radically that the official known as the horse identifier may not accept it as the horse it is represented to be. This is a disaster that can take weeks to rectify — and will certainly keep you out of the race you went to the trouble to ship for! Item number two to remember is your silks — make sure a set ships with your horse or your trainer.

Interstate transport

Vanning rates vary widely depending on where a horse is being shipped, how many other horses are on the van, if single stall, stall and a half, or box stall is used, and the price of fuel. A price variable also involves whether the company has horses to bring back from the destination; again, there will be a differential based on the number of horses being shipped.

It's important to know that whenever a horse is shipped into another state to race, the horse racing commission in that state will require that the owner be specifically licensed to race there. The racing commission will also require a health certificate (including a negative Coggins test for equine infectious anemia). The health certificate must include the name of the testing laboratory, the laboratory identification number of the sample, test results, and the date of the test, which must have been conducted within one year of shipping (except for California, which requires one no more than six months old). Again, these formalities are customarily coordinated by your trainer, but as always, you, as the owner, will be the one ultimately liable – and very disappointed – if all is not in order.

Local Ground Shipping

Most of the ground transport companies work a given route or area, i.e., Lexington, Southern California, Florida.

In Los Angeles, Miami, New York, and San Francisco, the vanning costs for an owner who ships a horse that is training at one local track to race at another local track is picked up by the racing associations. In Los Angeles and San Francisco, any vanning company can be used, while in Miami and New York the horse must ship on a designated shuttle. For example, a horse stabled at Santa Anita is entered in a race at Hollywood Park during one of its meets. The cost to ship the horse back and forth to Hollywood Park to race is paid for through the track from a fund generated from a fraction of the handle.

In case you are curious, some trainers ship their horses to across town meets on the morning of race day: the mesmerizing ride in the van, some believe, tends to relax and quiet the horse. Every trainer has his or her own philosophy, however, and some will ship particularly nervous or immature horses a day or two in advance of the race to settle the horses and accustom them to the new environment. Other trainers will have their raced horses rest overnight at the host track before returning them to their home barn.

Air Transport

There are two ways for your horse to go when flying. One is via a charter airline company specific to the large-animal business, while the other is on commercial airlines, using air cargo rates and terms. Equine charter companies use long ramps that horses walk up from a van into a stall in the plane, while horses being shipped on commercial airlines are usually loaded onto a pallet of three stalls that is then lifted into the cargo hold.

The cost to fly your horse depends upon both the destination and whether you send your horse first class (a box stall), business class (a stall and a half), or coach (a single stall). Stalls on a plane are narrow and can be compared to those on a horse van, so often times a horse will be given more legroom with a stall and a half or box stall.

Rates for equine airfare also vary depending upon the cost of fuel and the number of horses being flown. A ballpark cost to fly a horse from coast to coast in the United Stakes in the commonly used stall and a half is about $4,500, one-way. Flying a horse to or from Kentucky from either coast is a bit cheaper – about $4,000 (again, one-way). Shipping overseas is significantly more expensive, although many times the overseas racing association hosting big events will pick up the cost of transport (including Dubai, Hong Kong, and Singapore racing associations). To fly a horse from New York to England costs between $12,000 and $15,000; flying from Los Angeles to either Australia, Japan, or Hong Kong will cost between $22,000 and $25,000 (again, these are one-way costs).

When flying a horse within the United States, also figure in the vanning costs from the airport to the track. Not all airports accept equine cargo, the ones that do include Chicago, Dallas, Indianapolis, Lexington, Los Angeles, Louisville, Miami, Newark, Oakland, Ontario, San Jose, and Seattle.

When shipping internationally, these fees encompass a great deal of detail work, including the acquisition of passports for the grooms or handlers accompanying the horses; arrangements for necessary health certificates; USDA inspection, pre-export quarantine facilities and paperwork; ground transportation to and from the carrier, export certificate, and registration of the horse in the host country. Usually, the shipper must leave the horse's official Jockey Club registration at the border, and in return, an export certificate will be issued. If the horse is not going for sale but only to race, the export certificate will be handed in and the Jockey Club registration form returned to stay with the horse in perpetuity.

Insurance for air transport outside continental North America (United States and Canada) is available — as most equine mortality policies will not cover horses outside the United States and Canada. Shipping insurance, which covers transport and 30 days afterward, can be endorsed onto a policy for a fraction of a percent of the insured value. Some policies may be purchased that include worldwide transit — check with your agent to determine availability.

Safeguards: Though accidents, injuries, and fatalities are not common during vanning, they do, of course, happen. These are high-strung animals, and everyone knows the perils of highway travel. It is entirely possible that you, as an owner, could have the unhappy experience of being called out of the blue and told that the van carrying your horse was in a bad accident. That news would be shattering on an emotional level, but when the recovery of costs for treating — or actually losing — your horse come to the fore, the news is financially crushing as well.

If your horse was killed during vanning or so badly injured that it had to be put down and if you had mortality insurance covering that horse, you would be able to recover some or even all of your financial loss.

What if the injuries caused in the vanning incident are not life threatening, but are serious enough to require surgery, long-term care, or lay-up? What if, even after all that, it is clear that the horse's racing career is over? Such losses can easily amount to hundreds, if not thousands, of dollars. You would logically turn to the transport company for recovery of your losses (particularly if there is indication that the company or its driver was negligent or at fault). You would be in for a rude shock, on top of the one you're already enduring, when learning that the transport company's limit of liability is only a few thousand dollars, regardless of what the horse was worth.

The rueful fact is you have agreed to that limit of liability whenever your trainer or his employee affixes a signature to the bill of lading handed him by the transport driver — a signature that must be in place before the driver can allow your horse to be loaded. The relatively small limit of liability is there, unarguable – and so far legally irrefutable — in the fine print of every bill of lading. Your only option for more coverage, at this point, is to ask the transport company for its higher limit of liability on a per-horse, per-trip basis.

At the fairly low rates transport companies are currently charging the Thoroughbred industry, and with the kind of insurance they carry, it would be impossible for them to offer anything even approaching full loss-of-use compensation on their expensive cargoes.

12

The Races

If there's a psychological break point in racing — a wisdom fulcrum upon which your success as an owner will consistently balance — it is judging the race that's right for your horse.

Few owners say it aloud as they watch the connections of a winning horse make their way, smiling, fists raised in victory, to the winner's circle of an important race: "I should be winning big races with my horse." It's just plain human nature. The best advice is to ignore that magnetic dream. Reality is the road to success, and placing your horses in races that might lack the luster you'd like but can well pay the freight is the first step toward someday making your own run at a great stakes winner. If you insist on running your horse in a race in which its morning line is 30-1, keep in mind that horses with those odds win only 4% of all races.

Sometimes, it's hard to get real, not only for the owner, but for the trainer as well. Months of work and hundreds, and even thousands, of dollars have gone into the training of your horse. None of that was committed with anything but the most optimistic plans. Inherent in the for-

Choose reality over optimism when picking the right race for your horse.

mula, therefore, is the possibility of overreaching, of placing the horse where it is unlikely to win.

The owner's most important task is to balance expectations against reality, enthusiasm against opportunity. Sure, there are times when goals become blurred. After months of intensive and costly work, it is hard to accept that, for reasons known only to some higher power, your horse is much closer to the bottom of the competitive ladder than the top.

It may be necessary to risk the horse at a claiming price that will leave red ink on your investment ledger, but, for all involved, the risk is well worth taking. If the alternative is placing the horse beyond its ability to win, then holding on brings headaches and heartburn. You may even find it is necessary to send your horse to less competitive racing circuits in or out of the state.

Buying the horse is the most important decision you make; choosing the trainer right for you comes next — but you also must answer the toughest question: What and when is the next race that is right for my horse?

Understanding the Condition Book

The condition book is usually published every two weeks. It is available to everyone and can be obtained in the racing office. The condition book is the basic bible of the backstretch, as it lists the races offered in the two weeks ahead at that track. If one of your horses is race-ready, your trainer will eagerly try to find a race suited to your horse. When a new book is out, jockeys' agents are also quick to obtain one and then filter through the backside, negotiating mounts for their riders in the listed races.

The racing secretary writes the roster of races, keeping in mind the type of horses residing at the track. If there are a preponderance of maidens and claiming horses, a host of races will be written to accommodate them. The racing secretary must also write races for state-breds if required by law. An appropriate number of high-purse and stakes races must also be written so that owners of top-class horses have a chance to make good on their investments.

Though a glance at race descriptions atop each page of the program could easily convince you that racing secretaries are pathological obfuscators, if not downright sadists, the secretary's main role is to painstakingly design a level field — races, both for the sake of bettors and owners, in which all the horses will be closely competitive.

Not only is theirs an extremely detailed and difficult job, but the secretaries will be the first to admit that the listed qualifications often seem a tangled web. No one — least of all you or your trainer — should hesitate to contact the secretary for an explanation of any condition that is even slightly unclear. The secretary must fill eight to ten races a day. If an owner or trainer hangs back from entering because of a confusing condition and that race then fails to fill, the secretary's job just got several hours harder.

There are trainers who consider an owner with a condition book as dangerous as an alien with a Tommy gun. But your understanding of the book and the process of entering can save you and your trainer frustration, friction, and even needless mistrust.

Before looking through the condition book, you might want to be certain you are familiar with the terms and titles you'll be seeing.

Kinds of Races

Claiming race: A race with conditions in which every horse entered is available for the price stated in the condition book, as well as the program. The claiming price is what keeps a level field in these races.

Allowance race: A race with conditions but without a claiming price. The elaborate conditions specified in these races (particularly concerning the horse's racing record) keep the field even. In these races, all prior earnings from claiming races — regardless of how much — are disregarded.

Classified allowance: Designed for a horse that has run through his allowance conditions but isn't a stakes-quality horse. Restrictions are placed on horses that have won a certain number of races or amount of money within a given time period.

Optional claiming/allowance: Horses may be entered two ways: either they are eligible for the allowance conditions or they may run for a "tag" or claiming price (and can be claimed out of the race).

Maiden race: Restricted to horses that have yet to win a race ("break their maiden").

Maiden claiming: Horses that have yet to break their maiden and are running in a race from which they may be purchased.

Starter race: An allowance race in which the basic condition is that the horse has raced within a given time in a claiming race with a stated price of "x" dollars or less.

Stakes race: Races in which the owners of the entered horses contribute to the purse, usually through a nominating fee and an entry fee.

Added: If the word "added" appears after the purse amount, as in "$100,000 added," it means that the racing association will add the owners' nominating, entry, and starting fees to the advertised purse, increasing the value of the race.

Guaranteed: If a stake race has a guaranteed purse, the track adds an amount to the sum of the owners' nominating, entry, and starting fees to bring the amount up to the advertised purse.

Handicap: A race in which the racing secretary sets conditions and, with a staff committee, assigns weights to each horse individually based on the horse's earnings and past performance, with the better horses carrying more weight. The racing secretary is using weight to try to have each horse reach the finish line at the same time, which makes for a competitive event that bettors will wager on.

Graded stake: Premier racing events that are internationally recognized. Grade I (or Group I in Europe) races carry the most prestige, then Grade IIs, and then Grade IIIs.

Invitational stake races: The racing association of the current live meet invites individual horses to compete in a given race without requiring owners to contribute to the purse.

Overnight stakes race: Stakes that are not part of the track's official printed (listed) stakes schedule but are developed during the course of the meet. They are usually of a lesser caliber than a stakes race.

Match race: A rare event in modern times, a match race is a special duel race between two "star" horses and is usually hosted by the track.

Substitute race: A race, described in the condition book for a particular day, that will be used should any of the races in the book fail to fill.

Extra race: Extra races are written the day before entries are taken and are posted on the overnight sheet and announced over the public address system during morning workouts. They are used in the event a race listed in the condition book fails to fill.

Conditions

Conditions concern a horse's racing record, sex, and age (and sometimes even color; races have been written strictly for grays and roans by creative racing secretaries), and play a large role in which race your horse is eligible for and competitive in.

While conditions mostly apply to allowance races, there are tracks around the country that write conditional claiming races. Like claiming prices, conditions are used to level the playing field and keep races filled with horses of similar ability to make for competitive events that bettors will wager on.

But learning to read and understand a race's conditions isn't easy. It's somewhat akin to algebra; while it may seem challenging at first, eventually the light will come on, and you will be able to quickly determine whether a race fits your horse.

The accompanying condition book excerpt shows a day of races at Hollywood Park. The following discussion explains the conditions for substitute race No. 1 and other terms in the book.

"For Fillies and Mares Three Years Old and Upward which have not won either $3,000 three times other than Maiden, Claiming, or Starter or which have never won two races (first condition).

This condition has two subparts, the first being "...which have not won either $3,000 other than Maiden, Claiming, or Starter..." and the second being "or which have never won four races." A horse need only fit one of these conditions to be eligible for this race, not both.

For your horse to be eligible for this race under the first subpart, it cannot have won three races in which the winner's share of the purse was more than $3,000, unless the race was a maiden, claiming, or starter race. Purse money won from a first-place finish in these races doesn't count when determining eligibility for this particular race. However, your horse can have earned more than $3,000 when finishing second through fifth and still be eligible. It's only the winner's share of the purse that counts when determining eligibility.

Or, your horse can be eligible for this race under the second subpart if it has not won four races, of any type, during its lifetime.

If your horse does not fit the conditions of this race it can still be entered if entered for a claiming price of $100,000.

Once again, a horse can be eligible for this race if it fits one of the parts — it doesn't have to fit all three.

This condition book excerpt contains various other terms, some of which are self-explanatory and some that aren't.

The first, third, sixth, ninth, and substitute race No. 2 are claiming races. The price indicated is the amount for which a horse can be claimed from that race. In each race, a two-pound weight reduction is given if the horse can be claimed for a lower price.

The second and fourth races are restricted to state-bred horses, California-breds in this case.

The fifth, six, seventh ninth, and substitute races offer a purse bonus or supplement for a state-bred earning a purse in open company.

The seventh and substitute race No. 1 are optional allowance/claiming races, meaning that a horse may or may not be claimed from this race, depending upon whether it was entered under the allowance conditions or for a claiming price.

The eighth race is an added stake, meaning that the track will add the advertised amount to the nominating, entry, and starting fees. The text provides a description of nomination, entry, and starting fees and other conditions for the stake.

In general, the distance of each race is prominently displayed. A furlong equals one-eighth of a mile.

If gender is not mentioned, either colts or fillies may be entered.

The racing secretary may elect to use a substitute race if one of the other races listed fails to fill.

Fiftieth Day -- Sunday, June 30, 2002
(Entries Close on Friday, June 28, 2002)
(Scratch Time 10:00AM Thursday, June 27, 2002)

1 FIRST RACE	CLAIMING
PURSE $26,000. FOR FILLIES THREE YEARS OLD.	
Weight	122 lbs.
Non-winners of two races at a mile or over since April 29 allowed	2 lbs.
One such race since then	4 lbs.
CLAIMING PRICE $20,000, if for $18,000, allowed	2 lbs.
(Maiden and claiming races for $16,000 or less not considered).	
	ONE MILE AND ONE-SIXTEENTH

2 SECOND RACE	MAIDEN
PURSE $43,000. FOR MAIDENS, TWO YEAR OLDS, BRED IN CALIFORNIA.	
Weight	119 lbs.
(Horses which have started for $40,000 or less in their last 3 starts least preferred).	
	FIVE AND ONE-HALF FURLONGS

3 THIRD RACE — MAIDEN/CLAIMING

PURSE $19,000. FOR MAIDENS, FILLIES AND MARES THREE YEARS OLD AND UPWARD.

Three Year Olds	118 lbs.
Older	123 lbs.
CLAIMING PRICE $32,000, if for $28,000, allowed	2 lbs.

SIX FURLONGS

4 FOURTH RACE — MAIDEN

PURSE $43,000. FOR MAIDENS, FILLIES AND MARES THREE YEARS OLD AND UPWARD, BRED IN CALIFORNIA.

Three Year Olds	118 lbs.
Older	123 lbs.
(Horses which have started for $40,000 or less in their last 3 starts least preferred).	

SIX FURLONGS

5 FIFTH RACE — CLAIMING

PURSE $38,000. (PLUS UP TO $4,560 TO CAL-BRED WINNERS FROM THE CBOIF) FOR FOUR YEAR OLDS AND UPWARD.

Weight	122 lbs.
Non-winners of two races since April 29 allowed	2 lbs.
A race since then	4 lbs.
CLAIMING PRICE $50,000, for each $2,500 to $45,000	2 lbs.
(Maiden and claiming races for $40,000 or less not considered).	

FIVE AND ONE-HALF FURLONGS (On the Turf)

6 SIXTH RACE — CLAIMING

PURSE $46,000. (PLUS UP TO $5,520 TO CAL-BRED WINNERS FROM THE CBOIF) FOR FILLIES THREE YEARS OLD.

Weight	122 lbs.
Non-winners of two races since April 29 allowed	2 lbs.
A race since then	4 lbs.
CLAIMING PRICE $80,000, for each $5,000 to $70,000	2 lbs.
(Maiden and claiming races for $62,500 or less not considered).	

SIX FURLONGS

7 SEVENTH RACE — ALLOWANCE/CLAIMING

PURSE $62,000. (PLUS UP TO $18,600 TO CAL-BREDS) FOR FOUR YEAR OLDS AND UPWARD WHICH HAVE NOT WON $24,500 TWICE OTHER THAN CLOSED, CLAIMING, OR STARTER AT A MILE OR OVER IN 2002 CLAIMING PRICE OF $100,000.

Weight	122 lbs.
Non-winners of $60,000 at a mile or over in 2002 allowed	2 lbs.
$60,000 at a mile or over in 2001	4 lbs.
Such a race other than claiming or starter since April 13	6 lbs.
(Allowance horses preferred).	

ONE MILE AND ONE-QUARTER (On the Turf)

The Races

8 EIGHTH RACE   HANDICAP

The 56th Running of
Cinema Breeders' Cup Handicap
$200,000 Added - GRADE III

A HANDICAP FOR THREE YEAR OLDS. By subscription of $150 each on or before Wednesday, June 19 or by supplementary nomination of $7,500 each by 3:00 pm Saturday, June 22. $1,500 additional to start, with $150,000 added and an additional $50,000 from the Breeders' Cup Fund for Cup nominees only. The host associations added money and all fees to be divided 60% to the winner, 20% to second, 12% to third, 6% to fourth and 2% to fifth. Breeders' Cup monies also correspondingly divided provided a Breeders' Cup nominee has finished in an awarded position. Any Breeders' Cup monies not awarded will revert to the fund. Weights Sunday, June 23. Starters to be named through the entry box by closing time of entries. Preference will be given in the following order: Highweights will be preferred under the following conditions-Breeders' Cup nominees will be preferred over Non-Breeders' Cup nominees assigned equal weights on the scale. Total earnings in 2002 will be used in determining the preference of horses with equal nomination status and equal weight assigned on the scale. All fees for entrants that fail to draw into this race will be canceled. A trophy will be presented to the winning owner. Breeders' Cup Limited shall also present a trophy to the winning owner.

ONE MILE AND ONE-EIGHTH (On the Turf)

9 NINTH RACE   CLAIMING

PURSE $37,000. (PLUS UP TO $4,440 TO CAL-BRED WINNERS FROM THE CBOIF)
FOR FILLIES AND MARES FOUR YEARS OLD AND UPWARD.

Weight	122 lbs.
Non-winners of two races at a mile or over since April 29 allowed	2 lbs.
One such race since then	4 lbs.
CLAIMING PRICE $40,000, if for $35,000, allowed	2 lbs.
(Maiden and claiming races for $32,000 or less not considered).	
(Horses which have started for $25,000 or less in their last 3 starts least preferred).	

ONE MILE AND ONE-SIXTEENTH (On the Turf)

S1 SUBSTITUTE RACE NO 1   ALLOWANCE/CLAIMING

PURSE $55,000. (PLUS UP TO $16,500 TO CAL-BREDS) FOR FILLIES AND MARES THREE YEARS OLD AND UPWARD WHICH HAVE NOT WON EITHER $3,000 THREE TIMES OTHER THAN MAIDEN, CLAIMING, OR STARTER OR WHICH HAVE NEVER WON FOUR RACES OR CLAIMING PRICE OF $100,000.

Three Year Olds	118 lbs.
Older	123 lbs.
Non-winners of two races other than maiden, claiming, or starter since April 29 allowed	2 lbs.
Two such races since March 1	4 lbs.
Such a race since April 29	6 lbs.
Claimers which have won for $80,000 or more in one of their last two starts allowed only	2 lbs.
(Allowance horses preferred).	

SIX AND ONE-HALF FURLONGS

S2 SUBSTITUTE RACE NO 2	CLAIMING
PURSE $35,000. (PLUS UP TO $4,200 TO CAL-BRED WINNERS FROM THE CBOIF) FOR FILLIES AND MARES FOUR YEARS OLD AND UPWARD.	
Weight	122 lbs.
Non-winners of two races since April 29 allowed	2 lbs.
A race since then	4 lbs.
CLAIMING PRICE $40,000, if for $35,000, allowed	2 lbs.
(Maiden and claiming races for $32,000 or less not considered).	
	SEVEN FURLONGS

Common Condition Book Terms

Nominator: The person who nominates the horse in a stakes race. The owner at time of entry pays the nominating fee. If ownership has changed since nomination, the current owner collects the purse.

By subscription: Designates that an entry fee is required.

Maiden: A horse of any age or sex that has never won a race in any recognized jurisdiction.

Fillies: Female horses two, three, or four years old.

Mares: Female horses that are five years (as of January 1 from their year of birth) or older.

Colts: Male horses (not gelded) that are two, three, or four years old.

Horses: Male horses that have not been gelded and that are five years old (as of January 1 from their year of birth) or older.

Geldings: Male horses over two years old (as of January 1 from their year of birth) that have been castrated.

Ridglings: Male horses that have one or both testicles undescended or that have (for whatever reason) only one testicle.

Bay: The entire coat of the horse may vary from a yellow-tan to a bright auburn. The mane, tail, and lower portion of the legs are always black, unless white markings are present. Abbreviation indicated by "B."

Black: The entire coat of the horse is black, including the muzzle, the flanks, the mane, tail, and legs, unless white markings are present. Abbreviation indicated by "Blk."

Chestnut: The entire coat of the horse may vary from a red-yellow to a golden-yellow. The mane, tail, and legs are usually variations of coat color, unless white markings are present. Abbreviation indicated by "Ch."

Dark bay/brown: The entire coat of the horse will vary from a brown, with areas of tan on the shoulders, head, and flanks, to a dark brown, with tan areas seen only in the flanks and/or muzzle. The mane, tail, and lower portion of the legs are always black, unless white markings are present. Abbreviation indicated by "Dk b. or br."

Gray: The majority of the coat of the horse is a mixture of black and white hairs. The mane, tail, and legs may be black or gray, unless white markings are present. Abbreviation in programs and on forms is "Gr."

Roan: The majority of the coat of the horse is a mixture of red and white hairs or brown and white hairs. The mane, tail, and legs may be black, chestnut, or roan, unless white markings are present. Abbreviation indicated by "Ro."

Sprint: Short races of 7 1/2 furlongs or less.

Route: Races of a mile or more, and that generally cover two turns or more on the track.

Turf race: A race that is run on the grass course.

Dirt race: A race that is run on the main track's dirt surface.

Entering in Races

Once you've learned to read the condition book, you and your trainer will soon spot a race that's right for your horse. It's best to leave the entering of your horse to your trainer, as he or she has done it many times and

Different Fees for Stakes Races

Most North American stakes races have nominating, entry, and starting fees that an owner must pay in order to run. These fees help reduce the amount from the general purse fund taken for stakes, allowing more for the bread and butter lower-level races that produce the majority of the handle. Stakes fees originated before the advent of pari-mutuel racing, when owners of top horses would "stake" that their horse would win by directly contributing to the purse.

Owners are usually allowed to break the nominating, entry, and starting fees into separate payments, helping their cash flow and preventing them from having to make one large lump sum payment immediately before the stake is run. The payment structure also works to generate a larger pool of fees.

The nominating fee is due first, usually ten to fourteen days before the stake, although some stakes have a supplementary nominating fee that is paid at time is familiar with the process. You'll be pleased to learn, though, that with the exception of stakes races, there is no cost to enter a horse in a race. The track wants you to enter, and enter often, as races with full fields generate more wagering handle than those with only a handful of runners.

You should be familiar with the process and understand that your horse may not always get into a desired race. At most tracks, entries are taken 48 hours before a race is run, although some exceptions are made on "dark" days, where entries may be taken 72 hours before to accommodate the days during the week when the track is closed.

Before any entry can be made, usually the specific horse must be registered with the track's clerk of the course (in the racing office) and its foal registration papers (its registration certificate issued by The Jockey Club) must be on file in the racing office.

Your trainer contacts the racing office in the morning when entries are taken (usually from 7 a.m. until about 10 a.m.) and tells the entry clerk the name of the horse, which race in the book is being entered, the owner, what jockey will be used, and other details, including the use of Salix® (formerly known as Lasix), blinkers, and whether the horse has been gelded since its last start. The clerk notes the information on an entry card, checks the horse's eligibility to run, and makes sure that the horse's foal papers are

---

of entry and is usually higher than the original nominating fee. However, some stakes' nominating fee falls far in advance of the race. These stakes will usually have a second "sustaining" payment and a late nomination fee (which is more than the original fee) to accommodate late-developing horses.

The entry fee is then paid when the horse is entered, which is normally 48 to 72 hours before the race. The final fee is the starting fee, which is billed directly from the owners' purse account after the race has been run and only if the horse officially starts in the race. If for some reason the horse fails to start (i.e., scratched at the gate), this fee is not applied.

These fees are included in the purse of the stake, although they do not always increase its advertised value. If a stake is considered guaranteed, then the track adds to the sum of these fees to bring it up to the advertised purse. If the race is considered "added," these fees are added to the advertised purse, thereby increasing the race's value.

in the office. Horses not having their papers in the office will not be allowed to run, a fact that has made more than one owner and trainer hasten to the FedEx office to overnight papers to a distant track. *Make sure your horse's foal papers are on file at the track where you intend to run.*

During entry hours, the racing secretary constantly monitors which races are filling and which need some help. If a race isn't attracting sufficient entries, the racing secretary may decide to use a substitute race in the book or quickly add an extra race, the conditions of which he or she quickly announces through the backstretch public address system or prints on the overnight entry sheet. Astute trainers keep an eye and ear out for such announcements, for a race may quickly appear that suits one of their horses.

Or the racing secretary may decide to hustle some entries and call upon individual trainers to enter a horse in a race to help it fill. A trainer may decide to help the racing office out and enter, knowing he or she has now done the office a favor and can call upon the racing secretary to write a race with favorable conditions for one of his or her horses in the future. Good racing secretaries understand the need for favorable relations with trainers and understand that reciprocal back scratching is necessary to get the job done.

After the racing secretary decides the races have sufficiently filled or realizes additional horses can't be enticed to run, he or she determines which races will be used to make up the day's program, or "card," and the order in which they will be run. The "final" is announced, usually mid-morning, of all the confirmed entries for the day's written races. For any races that can accommodate more horses, entries will continue to be taken until the draw is held. If a race overfills with entries, the actual starters will be chosen based on preference conditions. Depending upon how the race has been written (refer to the condition book), a given horse may be preferred based upon races previously run or on the class in which the horse most recently competed. Most often, preference will be based on the date system, meaning the horse that has started most recently is the least preferred. This is done to give all horses at the meet an opportunity to run.

When the final is announced, jockeys' agents, trainers, and often owners assemble to witness the drawing of post positions. Usually a steward will monitor the procedure and resolve any dispute that may arise. A member of the racing office staff will coordinate the draw, utilizing one of the horsemen to select the numbered "pills" that represent post positions. Once the draw is completed, the racing office generates the "overnight," a sheet listing the races, horses, and jockeys drawn for the race card 48 hours hence. As soon as the overnight is published (usually by midday), the sheet is available by fax from the racing office. This sheet has other useful tidbits regarding upcoming races and general backstretch announcements.

Don't be upset if your horse doesn't get into your desired race. It happens often, especially if your horse is running in a first condition race, popular claiming level, or is a maiden. He may be placed on the "also eligible" list and may be allowed to race if a horse entered in that race is "declared" (scratched). Upon entering a race, your horse will be given an entry date and will have a better chance of getting into a race the second time around, as horses with the oldest entry date are given preference in future races. In fact, your trainer may enter your horse with no intention of running it just to get a date. Leave these decisions to him or her, as he or she is at the track every morning and is in the best position to know when to enter your horse.

Racing Officials & Their Functions

Racing secretary: Individual in charge of the racing office who supervises the racing officials, writes the condition book, and oversees the draw. He or she also allots stalls and assigns weights in handicap races.

Paymaster of purses or *horseman's bookkeeper*: Official in charge of purse distributions; nominating, entry, and starting fees (for stakes races); and keeping records of owners and trainers on-track accounts and transactions. The paymaster also allocates jockeys' earnings.

State veterinarian: The state vet enforces the rules and regulations of the racing commission regarding medication, supervises or performs all blood and urine tests on specified horses, and participates in the postmortems — and investigations into — injuries or deaths of any horses at the track. The state vet manages the receiving and detention barns.

Racing or track veterinarian: The racing veterinarian's several duties include 1) Examining all horses before they enter their first race to determine their soundness and fitness for racing (the racing vet may prohibit any horse he or she considers unfit from racing until such time as the horse gains good condition). 2) Assisting the state vet in conducting pre-race examinations during his or her morning rounds. 3) Accompanying the horses all the way from the paddock through the post parade to the starting gate, reporting to the stewards any horses in questionable physical condition. 4) Following and observing (from the ambulance following the race) the horses in a race and examines any mounts that appear in distress after a race. The racing veterinarian has the authority to have a horse placed on the vet's list and is expected to recommend to the stewards the placement of horses on the steward's list. 5) Lastly, it is the racing veterinarian 's responsibility to administer emergency treatment to horses in a race in the event of injury or accident. He or she has the authority (acknowledged by owners, trainers, and the racing commission) to destroy humanely — on the spot — any animal that is, in his or her opinion, injured beyond repair.

Stewards: These officials, appointed by the state racing commission, are charged with supervising the actions of all licensees operating at the track and with governing the conduct of the race meeting "in every particular." Their jurisdiction extends to suspending licenses, levying fines, and even barring individuals from the racetrack. They also sit as judges in medication violations (except in California, where such judgment is given by the court of administrative law) and are the final arbiters of objections during a race.

Paddock judge: This individual supervises the assembly of horses in the saddling paddock prior to a race, oversees the saddling of horses, and keeps a record of all equipment used on each horse. They also give the "Riders up!" call and are responsible for getting the field onto the track in sufficient time for the post parade and loading into the gate.

Clerk of scales: This racing official runs the jockeys room, weighing the jockeys before a race and reporting any discrepancies in their weight to the stewards. His or her job is to make certain the jockeys are at the legal weight for that race's (and their mount's) allowance. The clerk of scales also notes and reports any changes of jockeys or riding silks and provides the paymaster of purses with a list of riding fees due each jockey that day. This official is the one that can be seen next to the winner's circle after the race recording the weight of each rider (and his or her gear) after he or she dismounts to make certain that no weight was dropped after the jockey's pre-race weigh-in.

Clerk of the course: This person maintains the record of a horse's Jockey Club registration certificates (foal papers) and certificates of eligibility for all the horses that will be racing during a meet. This clerk also verifies the ownership of horses, is responsible for the proper transfer of certificates on claimed horses, and is usually the one who issues horse owners their admission and parking passes.

Horse identifier: Prior to a racehorse's departure to the post, the horse identifier inspects each horse's lip tattoo (usually in the paddock or receiving barn) and compares its coloring and markings with its Jockey Club registration papers. The identifier also inspects and verifies the identity of any horse new to the track and supervises the tattooing of all horses on the grounds.

Patrol judges: These are the judges stationed at the poles during races, "spotting" for the stewards and relaying reports. They also run the videotape room for the stewards and jockeys who wish to have a race replayed to check for infractions or violations or study photo-finishes and objections.

Placing judges: These officials work in a station above the finish line, placing horses in order of finish and posting information on the tote board. Placing judges determine the results of photo finishes.

Starter: The starter oversees the loading of horses into the starting gate before a race and is responsible for ensuring an equal and fair start for all horses running. At the moment the starter deems all the horses ready, he or she opens the gate simply by pressing a hand-held button. (Generally, this button is connected via electric leads to electromagnets holding the gates shut; pushing the button breaks the magnetic current of all gates simultaneously, and they fly open on spring-loaded hinges.) The official starter also maintains the starter's list and gives the okay when a horse has been sufficiently schooled at the gate to run.

Horseshoe inspector: This official checks the shoes of every horse entered in a race before it leaves the paddock for the post, reporting to the stewards any improper (or illegal) shoeing. The horseshoe inspector is authorized to correct the shoeing of any horse (at the request of the stewards) and can initiate a stewards' scratch from the race.

Clockers: Stationed in a booth above the "gap" (an opening in the track's outer rail where horses enter and leave for morning workouts), the clockers are responsible for taking official timings of the distances worked by specific horses. They not only relay times and distances to the stewards and state vet (for removal from their official lists), but record the figures that will be used by everyone from casual handicappers to the *Daily Racing Form*. Clockers are not to be confused with timers, the officials who record the exact times of actual races.

Stewards and Other Officials

Usually located in the vicinity of the racing office are three people charged by the state with the supervision in every particular of the conduct of the race meeting — its attendants and management, its enclosures, the races themselves, and the behavior of every one of its licensees (owners, trainers, veterinarians, jockeys, exercise riders, and stable hands). The actions they take to police racing become public knowledge, yet they remain isolated in aeries above the track or in obscure offices somewhere. Most fans think of stewards only as invisible ogres who have often wrecked a good pari-mutuel ticket by setting down or disqualifying a winning horse for some infraction. Owners, however, must regard them for what they are. Stewards have, and use, the authority to levy fines, issue penalties, suspend licenses, bar individuals from the track, and temporarily remove horses from racing.

Stewards might also be looked upon as the circuit court of the racetrack. Everyone, from grooms to warring owner-partners, comes to them for settlement of grievances, objections, and financial complaints against one another. They are not the final court, however. Any involved party wanting to appeal a matter decided by the stewards can take its lawyers to the racing commission for ultimate determination. As one veteran steward put it, "It has been said that old-time licensees never dared ask for justice, only mercy. Today, they not only deserve due process, they damn well better get it."

The steward's responsibilities, all of which involve ensuring the absolute integrity of the sport, settle out into fairly predictable (often prescribed) categories. Following is a list of those categories and the issues that most commonly come up under each.

Inquiries: These are incidents with which everyone is familiar — the ones that delay posting the "official" sign on the tote board and thereby the cashing of tickets and the owner's jog down to the winner's circle. The inquiry is one of the three ways in which an owner can lose purse money (for the others, see protests [below] and medication, Chapter 10).

An inquiry can be called for by the stewards, by their patrol judges (see Officials), by an owner or trainer of a horse in the running, or by a jockey.

The jockey may allege to either a patrol judge or the clerk of scales that another jockey caused interference that affected the outcome of the race or committed a whip violation. Although the stewards have closely watched the race on television monitors, are on walkie-talkies with their spotters (the patrol judges), and although they have rerun the videotape of the race during the time the horses are returning to the finish line, they will hold up the "official" declaration if a jockey alleges misconduct.

Likewise, any owner or trainer can use the racetracks "claim foul" phones to request an inquiry and delay the final race result until the stewards are certain.

Objections: These most often concern the eligibility of a certain horse for entry in a race and are usually made by a competing stable.

In fact (other than the rare objections placed by a racing official), only owners or trainers with a horse in the same race can file an objection involving a competing horse. Objections to the entry of a horse in a race must be made no later than one hour before post time and must be confirmed in writing. Grounds for objection include the following:

1) that there has been a misstatement, error, or omission in the entry under which the horse is to run.

2) that the horse entered to run is not the horse it is represented to be at the time of entry or that the age is erroneously given.

3) that the horse is not qualified to enter under the conditions specified for the race, that the allowances are improperly claimed or not entitled to the horse, or that the weight to be carried is incorrect under the conditions of the race.

4) that the horse is owned in whole or in part by a person ineligible to participate in racing or otherwise own a racehorse;

5) that the horse was entered without regard to an existing lien.

Protests: Protests are usually made against a horse that has already run in a race, and they must be submitted in writing and signed by the protester within a set amount of time (usually 72 hours) after the race, excluding non-racing days. Again, a protest can only be made by owners, trainers, and jockeys with a horse entered in the same race or by racing officials. In some states, protests are not allowed after a race has been declared official.

Protests are akin to inquiry requests. They are filed on the following basis:

1) The order of finish as officially determined by the stewards was incorrect due to oversight or errors in the numbers of horses that started the race.

2) A violation of the riding rules was committed during the race, and that such violation affected the order of finish.

3) The jockey, trainer, or owner of a horse that started in the race was ineligible to participate in racing.

4) The weight carried by the horse was improper, by reason of fraud or willful misconduct.

5) An unfair advantage was gained in violation of the racing rules.

Pending the outcome of the investigation of a protest, the stewards can withhold the distribution of a purse. If a purse has already been distributed and the stewards ultimately vote to disqualify a horse, all monies and prizes awarded to the horse must be returned and redistributed. Furthermore, all fines imposed by the stewards must be paid by the guilty party within a set amount of time after being levied, usually 72 hours.

Mediations: Believe it or not, the stewards are most often called on for mediations between co-owners or partners. Where money or fame is concerned, even friends will war over whose silks the horse should race in, how much (or how little) the horse should be allowed to run for, or what percentage of the purse another owner is entitled to. The stewards will have to examine such items as paid (or unpaid) bills, written or alleged agreements among partners, win-loss histories, The Jockey Club registration papers — anything and everything that angry owners may bring to the table to make their cases. (The stewards devoutly wish that co-owners and partners would put every detail of the agreements in writing.)

Complaints: Complaints taken to the stewards fall into two categories: informal, in which anyone from a groom on up can walk in and complain of an unpaid bill, an unfair parking ticket, a dog running loose, or any conceivable infraction by another licensee (these are usually resolved with a phone call) — or formal complaints, which are submitted to the racing commission and referred to the stewards for resolution. Formal complaints are usually made over financial issues and involve the filing of official paperwork, which can, in turn, lead to a hearing. Furthermore, if they remain unresolved, they can land the involved horse on the steward's list.

Race condition interpretations: These involve owners or trainers who are disputing with the racing secretary their horse's eligibility for a race (usually on questions of weights and allowances).

Penalties: These are most often levied against jockeys — for using illegal whips, for cruel or punishing behavior to a mount, for failure to maintain a straight course, for crossing-over without sufficient clearance, for bumping, for being a no-show rider, for failing to make the required weight, or even for arriving late to the jockeys' room. But the really serious penalties for an owner are the ones that involve non-permitted medications.

Steward's list: Your horse (i.e., your investment) can be suspended from racing by being placed on the steward's list for a number of reasons. One, as mentioned above, is an unresolved conflict among owners, a dispute over ownership, or even a financial dispute between owner(s) and trainer. Other grounds for a horse being placed on the steward's list are lapse of a license (of anyone in your stable); the lack of a recent, timed work for a horse entered in any race; erratic or apparently uncontrollable behavior by your horse on the track; or an unduly poor performance (i.e., 30 lengths behind the pack) by your horse in a race.

Placement on the stewards list for poor performance can and must be rectified by a demonstrated work by the horse in a decent time. The lack of a recent timed qualifying work (obviously, this is applicable to horses that have never raced) will prevent your horse from being eligible to enter in a race. This can be rectified by scheduling a work (timed by the official clocker) that shall then be submitted to the stewards. Although stewards in different states require different work patterns to remove a horse from their list, an example of their requirement can go something like this: If a horse has not worked in more than 30 days (up to 60 days), one work will be required; if the horse has not been worked, per the clocker's worksheet, in 60 days (up to 90 days), two timed works will be required. If the horse has not raced in 90 days or more, three timed workouts, recorded by the clocker and reported to the stewards, will be required before the horse can qualify for entry in a race.

Transfer of ownership: Once a horse has been registered with the racing secretary for an active race meet, and/or is residing on the grounds of an active track, that horse's ownership cannot be transferred (except in the case of a claim) without notifying the board of stewards. Usually, a transfer of ownership form must be filled out and accompanied by a formal notarized bill of sale signed by both the registered buyer and registered seller.

Starter's list: The official starter (who checks blinkers at the gate, witnesses the loading of horses and presses the button to start the race) may place on his list any horse that acted up in the gate or refused to load. Removal from the starter's list can be accomplished when the horse's trainer is ready to demonstrate that the horse has been schooled to load and wait in the gate properly. Until that demonstration satisfies the official starter, however, the horse cannot be raced at any track.

Vet's list: Any horse that has failed to finish or is observed by either the state or the track veterinarian to be sore or bleeding from the nose post-race will be placed on the vet's list and barred from entry in a race for anywhere from a few days to six months. Depending upon the reason why a horse was placed on the vet's list, he may automatically be removed after a set amount of time (usually five days) or may be required to work a prescribed distance in a set amount of time before being removed.

Certainly most troublesome of all, for the owner, is the issue of bleeding and the vet's list. Bleeding from the nose and larynx, as we have discussed elsewhere in this handbook, is not uncommon in Thoroughbred racehorses under the stress of hard workouts or racing. Bleeding may develop — and disappear — at any point in a horse's racing career. (Seventy percent or more of racehorses will exhibit signs of bleeding during their career). Nevertheless, this is a legally defined and monitored affliction, for purposes of racing, and must be attended to with prescribed measures. The first time your horse is observed by the state veterinarian, the track veterinarian, or the stewards to bleed from one or both nostrils after a race, the horse will be placed on the bleeder's list. If the horse is then put on prophylactic medication for bleeding, the official veterinarian must be notified. If the horse then runs a race and is observed bleeding from one or both nostrils post-race, it will be put on the vet's list for, in most states, 14 days.

After the prescribed wait, the animal's racing soundness must be proved in a workout witnessed by either the state or track veterinarian — again, an appointment required — in which it must work a pre-set distance in good time and without signs of bleeding or coughing. If, after the work, the horse shows signs of possible bleeding (bloody nose or coughing/wheezing), the state veterinarian will follow the horse back to its barn. Your trainer will page your veterinarian to do an endoscopic examination of the horse's nose and throat; the state veterinarian will look through the endoscope, and only then if all signs are clear will the horse be removed from the vet's list. If there was more blood as a result of the workout — or if the horse is observed bleeding from one or both nostrils in a second race — it shall be placed on the vet's list for 30 days. If the horse bleeds post-race (or post-work) a third time, it will be prohibited from racing for six months (180 days). Removal from the vet's list in these cases will have to be demonstrated exactly as described above: by appointment, with a work in good time, and with no signs of bleeding or coughing.

Post-race blood and urine tests: If the blood test drawn by the state vet after the races comes back from the state-appointed lab showing that the animal was contaminated by illegal drugs — or by an excess of legal drugs — it will be reported to the racing commission, put on the steward's list, and officially investigated. Even if officials find against the horse's condition on the race day in question, the horse may still be raced during and after the inquiry period (for example, if the horse is claimed, the new owner is not affected), but the former trainer will be penalized, and if the horse finished in the money, the former owner will lose every bit of his or her purse earnings.

Here's hoping your horse's name never appears on the stewards', starter's, or vet's list. If it does, its removal can only be authorized by the entity that placed it there.

Jockeys

Your horse was primed, pampered, and ready for a sure win. How in the world did it wind up with an apprentice jockey who is zero for 20 at the current meet? It's an embarrassing question to present the trainer because it might imply your trainer doesn't have sufficient clout to get the rider you both want. Or it may suggest the folks on the backside have determined your horse isn't a likely winner, so the top jockeys have shied away. Maybe, and maybe not.

The top jockeys are going to go with the "livest" horses in any race, no matter when that horse appears on the racing schedule and often no matter who is training it.

The potential race card for this day was first posted as far back as two weeks. Forty-eight hours ago, your trainer entered your horse, after having, in all likelihood, discussed with a jockey agent which jockeys would be acceptable if the race became a go. But the race card has undergone a lot of changes since then (see Entering in Races).

An agent may have committed his rider to a horse and since found out that a more favored horse or, yes, a trainer to whom he owes one needs

The best jockeys are always in demand.

that jockey for the same race. The ensuing trading of favors between your trainer and the jockey's agent may leave your horse to one of the less desirable riders — i.e., the aforementioned zero for 20 apprentice. By the same token, you on another occasion, thanks to your trainer and past dues, may be the one on the favorable side of the trade.

Unless an owner spends an unusual amount of time on the backside, it is hard to break into the comfortable, triangular dialogue that takes place among trainers, jockeys' agents, and jockeys themselves. It's a family thing — sometimes literally. Jockeys and trainers are often the sons or relatives of other jockeys and trainers. Many of them, including the agents, have grown up in the same small world.

Every day jockeys begin to appear in the stable area as workouts begin around dawn. Good professionals, they are concerned about gaining experience on mounts they may have in future races. They are also doing favors as they track horses for various trainers. So jockey participation in morning workouts becomes a part of the weave of trade-offs that can occur.

The jockeys' agents (who earn from 15% to 25% of the jockeys' winnings) are usually the best-informed members of the racing community when it comes to what horse should (or is likely to be) entered in what race. In fact, the agents will often point trainers toward overlooked races that might be ideal for a horse in the trainer's barn and at the same time suggest one of their jockeys for the ride (they may even go as far as to enter a trainer's horse in a given race). For some reason — perhaps because many are former trainers themselves — the jockeys' agents often have the keenest tack on which horses in any race have the best chance of winning. They also know that a trainer can prime his or her horse by placing it in a race that will hone the horse's fitness for the race that follows. All this activity goes on in the absence of the owner. Favors that are hard to explain, trade-offs that occur without any real discussion, agreements that take place without even a handshake are part of the real politick of the backstretch. You have to be there to understand it. And from time to time, it will most surely present you with a hard to understand (and harder to swallow) jockey switch.

Once in a while, a jockey will alter a commitment between the day the condition book comes out and the day of your race. Sometimes it's the trainer who will break the commitment, often at the owner's request. It's just business. Jockeys make their money collecting their 10% on winning mounts. They can't afford to be sentimental (and if they were, their agent, thinking of his own percentage, would nip that tendency, fast).

Even if you don't wind up with the jockey you wanted, take heart. If you have one of your track's top ten jockeys on your horse, you're probably going to get as smart and professional a ride as anyone could ask. Even if you get a bugboy (an apprentice so known because of the bug-like asterisk that follows the apprentice jockey's name in the program), it doesn't mean you are paying a slouch. An apprentice has to ride either three full years, one full year after his or her fifth winning ride, or come in atop 45 winners before becoming a full-fledged journeyman rider. Until then, you will be getting the advantage of a five-pound weight allowance in any race an apprentice rides for you.

It's worth keeping in mind that even the great jockeys will invariably have slumps and will almost always recover from them. Though these are the best-paid individuals in the industry, their lives are hard. Jockeys can't be licensed if they weigh more than 125 pounds. Surviving, for their entire career, on a few hundred calories a day is wracking enough. Being in acute physical danger, danger too frightening for most of us to imagine, as frequently as ten times a day, five or six days a week, for years on end exacts a heavy emotional toll.

A word to the wise owner: Leave direct communication with jockeys to your trainer. As noted, there are languages, balances, and nuances in the strange world of the backside that those of us who don't live there will probably never master. The last-minute instruction the trainer gives as the jockey mounts for the race is usually a mere reminder of the much longer and detailed conversation that took place early in the morning, when the jockey and trainer were chatting on the backside.

In the case of jockeys (and jockeying for them), spare yourself and accept the system for what it is. If you have the time and energy, you can join the backstretch family. Knowledge of their world may not change any of the situations described above, but it will give you a far more accurate picture of how this closed system operates.

A cautionary note: The owner is required to deposit or have on account with the paymaster of purses the minimum jockey's fee (usually $35-$100, depending upon the type of race) before the start of the race. This is the minimum fee (also called the "losing mount fee") the jockey is paid; he or she earns 10% of the horse's earned share of the purse on wins and 5% of the earned share of the purse for second- and third-place finishes. The jockey fee schedule for your track will usually be printed in each condition book.

Silks

The design of your own silks — a unique and personal imprimatur — is, perhaps, even more so than naming great sires and stables, the thread that truly weaves the owner into the rich, romantic tapestry of the Sport of Kings.

Thoroughbred horse racing was first organized as a sport by King Charles II of England, who established a regular race meeting at

Newmarket in 1671 for the pleasure of the nobility. The earliest known meeting in the American colonies was in 1665, on Long Island.

Although the chariot drivers of ancient Rome may have been the first to sport racing colors (they wore identifying capes and headbands of brilliant hues), the concept of using individual silks in horse racing was first introduced in Newmarket, England, in 1762.

The English Jockey Club was, at that time, a completely different proprietary organization peopled by the most prominent racehorse owners of the day. There were, in all, seven dukes, one marquis, four earls, one viscount, three commoners, one lord, and two baronets. To distinguish at a glance which horses in the race were owned by whom, they submitted "colours." One of them, the color "straw," chosen by the duke of Devonshire — is still used by that family's famed stable. But by far the most celebrated of all silks was chosen 25 years later: "black with white cap"... the colors adopted by Lord Derby.

Today, all nations combined, there are more than 20,000 different silk designs registered with The Jockey Club. Given the number of variations permitted in jacket design, combined with sleeve design, individual silks could run into the tens of millions without repeating one another.

There are always purveyors or designers of silks open for business in makeshift offices or trailers in the backside area of tracks with active meets. They are experts in design and color, and they will help you effectively interpret both your self-image and your dreams in your personal silks. Today's silks are made of nylon for lightness of weight, durability, and washability. The silks used in warm climates or in summer are of nylon taffeta; those used in winter (or in stakes races, for high sheen) are satin-weave nylon. But they are still handmade and hand-sewn — every piece — and can range in cost anywhere from $70-$400, although a set averages about $150.

Before deciding on your silk design, you might want to visit the "silks room" at your local major track to go through the silks books for ideas — and to see if your design is already taken. (Even if it is, the rule is that after five years of non-use, or abandonment, by the registered owner, those silks can be adopted by another owner.)

There is no official national registry of silks. More than once two horses from different states racing against each other have registered, in their respective states, with the same silks. In that case, stewards at the racing track determine who runs in the colors and order one jockey's attire be altered accordingly.

In most states, silks may not contain any logos, labels, or designs that may be construed as advertising, although an experiment in California is underway to allow advertising on silks, saddle clothes, and jockey's pants in order to attract corporate sponsors. Silks may not be changed without approval of the stewards and may not be rotated to accommodate a horse's various owners (i.e., if the horse is owned jointly by partners with other business forms in operation at the track). Any owner racing in New York must abide by certain specifications: all designs or emblems must be repeated on both the front and back of the jacket, and the color navy blue is not permitted because it "reads" as black at a distance.

The silks are usually registered with the clerk of the course at the live race meet, although some states require they also be registered with the racing commission. And some western states, including Montana, North Dakota, Oregon, South Dakota, and Wyoming, do not allow private silks except in stakes races. These states use "house" silks whose colors correspond to post position.

Race Day

Not many people, in the course of their lives, get to experience the highs of anticipation, expectation, and sheer glamour that race day provides the Thoroughbred owner. Depending upon the size of your stable, this thrill can recur every few days to few weeks. Whether your horse wins, finishes in the money, or simply runs a good race, the experience of this day, for a horseman, is what life is about.

Your trainer and the barn staff will share your excitement, from the moment they awaken. The horse, if it has raced before, will soon know "what day it is" by the unusual things that happen.

First, the horse's temperature will be taken, just to make sure nothing is amiss. At some early hour, the state veterinarian will be by for a pre-race examination. The veterinarian will examine the horse's forelegs, checking for signs of swelling or heat. He will ask the groom to walk the horse back and forth, to check for soreness or favoring (and in some cases, will ask to see the horse briefly trotted or jogged right there in the barn). Finally, he will check the tattoo on the inside of the Thoroughbred's upper lip and make sure it matches the official Jockey Club registration number appearing on the horse's papers.

At some point in the morning, the horse may be walked or perhaps jogged or even galloped on the track for a few minutes to limber up. After a bath and a small meal, the horse will be muzzled or its hay net, feed tub, and water will be removed to keep it from any further eating. Like all professional athletes, it will compete better on an empty stomach.

If the horse is a known bleeder, the trainer's veterinarian will come by about four hours before post time and give it a Salix (formerly known as Lasix) shot. This is a completely legal drug (in proper doses) that will lower the horse's blood pressure and reduce the risk of bleeding from the small, thin-walled capillaries of its nose, throat, and lungs under the stress of hard running.

Some trainers will have the horse stand in a foreleg ice bath for up to 90 minutes to relieve any nagging discomfort that might distract it from running its best race. Some states require a sign be tacked on the horse's stall noting that it is "In Today," and warning others to stay away. You might heed this sign, too, as now is not the time to distract or annoy your horse by fussing over him — just give him his space and wait until after the race to reward him with pats and peppermints.

An hour or less before the designated race time, your trainer will receive the 20-minute call, summoning your horse to the receiving barn for a final walk-by witnessed by the official veterinarian. The horseshoe inspector will check to see that your horse's shoes are legal and in good condition. An official called the horse identifier will again verify the horse's lip tattoo, as well as its color and markings, against its papers and photograph on file. After that, your horse will proceed to the saddling paddock where it will meet you and your trainer, and where it will come under the watchful jurisdiction of the track vet veterinarian. At this point, the paddock judge will check and note the gear your trainer has brought for your horse. There are a half-dozen or more bits that may be used to curb a horse's tendency to drift in or out. A tongue-tie is used to be sure the horse's tongue won't obstruct its air passage. Blinkers, hood-goggles, and even earmuffs are part of racing equipment for many horses: they may keep a flighty or fractious horse's mind on the race. But the use of —

or decision not to use — these devices must be cleared with the paddock judge prior to the race (and in the case of blinkers, prior to the issuance of the overnight). Finally, the jockeys' valets bring out their saddles and help the trainers saddle your horse.

Once in the walking ring, the trainer will often introduce you to your jockey and then discuss with the jockey what kind of race the horse is like-

Learning The Poles

The placement of poles on the racetrack is crucial to those involved in the training and racing of Thoroughbreds. Jockeys, trainers, and owners use the poles to measure how far a horse has traveled and how far they have to go.

The easiest way to become acquainted with the poles is to start at the finish line, or wire, and count the poles backward, or clockwise. In North America, the distance between the poles is one-sixteenth of a mile. Black poles represent one-sixteenth of a mile, green poles one-eighth of a mile, and red poles indicate quarter mile fractions.

Start at the wire and begin to count the poles backward. The first pole (black) you reach is the one-sixteenth-mile marker, the second pole (green) is the one-eighth-mile marker, the third pole (black) is the three-sixteenths-mile marker, and the fourth pole (red) is the quarter-mile marker. As you continue to work your way backward around the track, add one-sixteenth of a mile to every pole you reach. Doing this, you will pass the five-sixteenths pole (black), three-eighths pole (green), seven-sixteenths pole (black), and the half-mile pole (red). Continue to count your way around, passing the three-quarters pole (red) and finally back to the finish line, which would be the fourth and final quarter-mile marker on a one-mile track.

However, not all tracks in North America are the same size. So before you begin counting poles, determine the size of the racetrack to make sure your pole count comes out correct.

Armed with this knowledge, you'll know when to start and stop your stopwatch when your trainer informs you your horse is going to work seven furlongs from the three-quarters pole. – *Lucinda Mandella*

ly to run. Every eye in the paddock of spectators near the saddling pad-dock will at some point be on your horse, your trainer, and you.

Unless your horse is in the first race of the day, you will already have been seated for the race and can now return to your box or table. Most major racetracks provide owners of horses racing that day with free admission and usually free clubhouse or turf club seating. The perks for such occasions vary in generosity from track to track and from race to race. At least one day in advance of your horse's race (or as soon as the overnight is published), please remember to contact the track's horse-man's liaison (most have them) in the racing office and arrange for the complimentary services for you. Many times your trainer will take care of these details, so be sure to ask him or her before doing so yourself. The horseman's liaison can also help you find suitable accommodations and transportation if you are coming in from out of town for the race.

Once the trumpet and the post parade and the loading into the gate have taken place, the race — from the words "And they're off!" — is like-ly to become a mighty adrenaline blur (not to mention a surrealistic time-warp) for any devoted owner. Your heart will quicken as the horses race down the backstretch, building to a crescendo as you scream and holler for your horse to "Come on!" If your racing luck holds and the racing gods are smiling upon you, you will probably feel faint of heart as your horse crosses under the finish line first!

Don't hesitate! Start down to the winner's circle, bringing along whomever you want to help you celebrate, and savor every step. The track photographer will be there to record the scene of your trainer and jockey on and around your winning horse, and you beaming close by. The track will make available to you (yes, for a price), not only this winning photo, but often a videotape of the race, and even a copy of the photo finish, if there was one.

After the race, the horse (as a winner) will immediately visit the deten-tion barn (no stops along the way) to have blood drawn and urine samples, which are sealed and signed in the presence of the trainer or the trainer's representative. The horse will be bathed, cooled out, and eventually returned to his barn for his evening meal and some well-deserved rest.

Drug-testing notes: Winners are not the only horses tested. Usually the second- and third-place finishers in stakes races are also selected, along with a horse randomly chosen from each race or an odds-on favorite that finished poorly.

Purse payment notes: Though you look forward to your purse check (barring any positive drug tests), you will unfortunately not be able to physically take possession of your win money for a few days. To avoid any further delays in collecting your money, make certain that, if you cannot pick up the check yourself, you have (by original, signed authorization) nominated someone else — either a partner or your trainer — to collect from the paymaster of purses any money your horse may have won. Or, you can leave your winnings on account with the paymaster at the track, making future claims and the depositing of jockey's fees an easier matter. If your horse has been claimed, on the other hand, you can collect your sum the same day (but only if you do it quickly: the paymaster's office usually closes very soon after the end of the last race of the day).

No matter how your horse finished (provided it was not injured), you will have had a great day...a day that few others on the planet, and only a few score in history, can truly appreciate.

Congratulations!

13

Purses & the Paymaster

While many are undoubtedly attracted to Thoroughbred ownership by the pure spectacle of the sport and the chance to own their own sporting franchise, there's no disputing that the quest for purse money is what keeps most owners in the game. While Thoroughbred ownership is a risky undertaking, with no guarantee of profit or breaking even, owners do have the chance of recouping their investment and even making a substantial profit through this country's rich purse structure.

Purses are generated by the betting public. Each time a wager is placed, a portion of that bet is retained (the "takeout") and returned to you (as an owner) in the form of purse money. This takeout, which is an amount determined by the state that will be withheld from the total wagered "handle," is also divvied up among the track, as its commission; the state; and, in some states, the breeders and other recipients.

Takeout rates are complex. Not only do they vary from state to state, they also vary depending upon the type of wager placed. A greater percentage is taken from exotic wagers (exactas, trifectas, etc.) than from straight win, place, and show bets. With the advent of modern simulcasting, figuring the amounts generated for purses from the takeout has become even more complex, with purses receiving different percentages from on-track vs. off-track bets (as only a small portion of the takeout from off-track wagers is paid to the track where the race originates). The growth of account wagering and international simulcasting is sure to make the division of revenue derived from takeout more confusing.

Different racing circuits offer different purse structures, with the biggest purses tending to be offered in major metropolitan areas with a rich tradition of horse racing, such as Los Angeles, Miami, and New York. These locations have large populations that like to wager, and they bet a dizzying amount on a daily basis. Other states, such as Kentucky, have such a strong tradition of racing that their smaller local populations, coupled with their deep fields of quality horses, are able to attract sufficient on-track and simulcast bettors to offer substantial purses.

But no matter where you race, you will probably find your local track offers enough purse money to keep your stable running in the black. Winning a $20,000 maiden claiming race is just as exciting as capturing the big stake, and probably easier, too.

(The track's racing secretary, usually working in conjunction with the local horseman's organization, decides which races receive what purse amount. Balancing the purse program is a delicate act and one that is constantly evolving. In California, the owners' organization (the Thoroughbred Owners of California) has taken over a large part of this process and has a purse committee that works with the local racing secretaries to determine the purse structure, including what percentage of the general purse fund should be allocated to their stakes program. A purse contract is usually signed between racetrack management and the horsemen to ensure that purses are correctly and promptly paid.

While a glance at the chart showing different tracks' average daily purse distribution may entice you to run your horse at a track with rich purses, remember that the quality of the horses running at a meet can almost always be correlated with the quality of purses offered there. So, if you are going to choose your racing circuit specifically because of its purses, make sure that your racing stock is up to the task and will be competitive.

2002 Approximate Average Daily Purse Distributions
& Percentage Paid to Top Finishers

Track	Av. Daily Distribution (Approximate)	Av. Overnight Purse (Approximate)
Aqueduct, NY	$375,000	$40,000
Arlington Park, IL	$300,000	$26,500
Bay Meadows, CA	$173,000	$17,500
Belmont Park, NY	$560,000	$40,000
Calder Race Course, FL	$228,000	$17,800
Canterbury Park, MN	$106,000	$10,800

Track	Av. Daily Distribution (Approximate)	Av. Overnight Purse (Approximate)
Charles Town, WV	$132,000	$12,800
Churchill Downs, KY	$413,000	$31,700
Colonial Downs, VA	$202,000	$16,700
Delaware Park, DE	$291,000	$28,900
Del Mar, CA	$470,000	$39,500
Ellis Park, KY	$195,000	$17,500
Emerald Downs, WA	$94,000	$8,200
Fair Grounds, LA	$263,000	$20,000
Fairplex Park, CA	$246,000	$20,200
Finger Lakes, NY	$78,000	$8,200
Golden Gate Fields, CA	$163,000	$17,000
Great Lakes Downs, MI	$85,000	$7,900
Gulfstream Park, FL	$314,000	$24,300
Hawthorne Park, IL	$225,000	$20,500
Hollywood Park, CA	$394,000	$32,000
Hoosier Park, IN	$170,000	$13,800
Keeneland, KY	$608,000	$44,000
Kentucky Downs, KY	$270,000	$28,000
Laurel Park, MD	$180,000	$18,600
Lone Star Park, TX	$228,000	$18,300
Louisiana Downs, LA	$158,000	$12,200
The Meadowlands, NJ	$216,000	$20,200
Monmouth Park, NJ	$313,000	$27,000
Mountaineer Park, WV	$166,000	$17,100
Oaklawn Park, AR	$205,000	$15,900
Penn National, PA	$68,000	$7,400
Philadelphia Park, PA	$145,000	$13,700
Pimlico, MD	$235,000	$19,500
Prairie Meadows, IA	$123,000	$16,500
Remington Park, OK	$80,000	$8,900
Retama Park, TX	$99,000	$8,300
River Downs, OH	$64,000	$6,900
Rockingham Park, NH	$91,000	$8,800
Sam Houston, TX	$109,000	$9,700

Track	Avg. Daily Distribution (Approximate)	Avg. Overnight Purse (Approximate)
Santa Anita, CA	$440,000	$35,500
Saratoga, NY	$616,000	$42,800
Sportsman's Park, IL	$239,000	$22,000
Suffolk Downs, MA	$86,000	$9,400
Tampa Bay Downs, FL	$104,000	$8,900
Thistledown, OH	$71,000	$8,300
Turf Paradise, AZ	$77,000	$6,800
Turfway Park, KY	$169,000	$13,500

Some tracks have multiple race meets throughout a year. The above figures represent an average of their meets.

Purse Percentage Distributions by Track, and When Available

Surprising differences occur in how purses are paid at individual tracks. Some pay a portion of the purse down to fifth or sixth place, while others pay a portion to all the starters in a race in an attempt to allow all owners a chance to recoup some of their costs. The purse percentages paid for various placings vary from track to track, although the winner's share is usually about 60% of the purse. As second place earns 20% (on average), it literally pays to win.

Here are different track's specific purse payouts, and when purse earnings are released to owners.

Track	Purse Percentages	Released
Aqueduct	1st-5th; 60%, 20%, 11%, 6%, 3%	48 hours after race
Arlington Park	1st-5th; 60%, 20%, 11%, 6%, 3%	48 racing hours
Bay Meadows	1st-5th; 55%, 20%, 15%, 7 %, 2 %	48 hours
Belmont Park	1st-5th; 60%, 20%, 11%, 6%, 3%	48 hours
Calder Race Course	All starters in overnight races; 1st, 60%; 2nd, 18-20%; 3rd, 10-13%; 4th, 4-6%; 5th-12th, 1%; 1st-5th in stakes, 60%, 20%, 11%, 6%, 3%	72 hours for wins, all others 24 hours

Canterbury Park	All starters; 1st, 60%; 2nd, 18-20%; 3rd, 10%; 4th, 4%, 5th - 12th, 1%	48 hours for overnight races; 1st-3rd in stakes races are held until drug test clears
Charles Town	Overnights 1st-6th; 60%, 20%, 10%, 5%, 3%, 2%; Stakes 1st-5th; 60%, 20%, 11%, 6%, 3%	The Friday following the drug test clearing; horses not tested, next race day
Churchill Downs	1st-5th; 62%, 20%, 10%, 5%, 3%	48 racing hours
Colonial Downs	Overnights 1st-6th; 57%, 21%, 11%, 6%, 3%, 2% Stakes 1st-5th; 60%, 20%, 11%, 6%, 3%	When drug test clears, usually 3-4 days
Delaware Park	1st-5th; 60%, 20%, 11%, 6%, 3% 6th-on receive a bonus of $200-$300 each, depending upon purse	1st-place money all others 24 hours
Del Mar	1st-5th; 60%, 20%, 12%, 6%, 2%	48 hours
Ellis Park	1st-8th; 60%, 20%, 10%, 5%, 1% 1%, 1%, 1% (Unused %'s revert to winner)	48 racing hours
Emerald Downs	1-5th; 55%, 20%, 15%, 7.5%, 2.5% Stakes winnings are released only upon the drug test results	24–48 hours;
Fair Grounds	1st-5th; 60%, 20%, 11%, 6%, 3%	For winners and other horses being drug-tested, 7-10 days. All others, 48 hours
Fairplex Park	1st-8th; 55%, 17%, 12%, 7%, 5%, 2%, 1%, 1%	48 hours
Finger Lakes	State-bred races 1st-5th; 60%, 20%, 11%, 6%, 3% Open races 1st-8th; 60%, 20%, 10%, 5%, 2%, 1%, 1%, 1%	First 3 finishers in trifecta races, purse held 3 days; First 2 finishers in exacta races, purse held 3 days; All others, 24 hours

Golden Gate Fields	1st-5th; 55%, 20%, 15%, 7.5%, 2 5%.	48 hours
Great Lakes Downs	All starters in overnight races: 1st, 59-63%; 2nd, 19-20%; 3rd, 10%; 4th, 6%; 5th on 1% Stakes races 1st-5th; 60%, 20%, 11%, 6%, 3%	72 hours
Gulfstream Park	All starters in overnight races: 1st, 60%; 2nd, 18-20%; 3rd, 10-13%; 4th, 4-6%; 5th-12th, 1% Stakes races 1st-5th; 60%, 20%, 11%, 6%, 3%	24 hours
Hawthorne Park	1st-5th; 60%, 20%, 11%, 6%, 3%	48 racing hours
Hollywood Park	1st-5th; 60%, 20%, 12%, 6%, 2%	72 hours
Hoosier Park	All starters in overnight races: 1st, 60%; 2nd, 20%; 3rd, 10%; 4th, 5-6%; 5th, 1-4%; 6th, 1-2%; 7th, 1%, 8th, 1%; 9th, 0.5-1%, 10th, 0.5% Stakes races 1st-5th; 60%, 20%, 11%, 6%, 3%	24 hours
Keeneland	1st-5th; 62%, 20%, 10%, 5%, 3%	48 racing hours
Kentucky Downs	All starters in overnight races: 1st, 60%; 2nd, 20%; 3rd, 10%; 4th, 5%; 5th, 2%, 6th-on, 3% divided equally. (If only 6 starters, 5th gets 3% and 6th 2%) Stakes races 1st-5th; 62%, 20%, 10%, 5%, 3%	48 hours
Laurel Park	1-6th in overnight races; 1st, 57%; 2nd, 21%; 3rd, 11%; 4th, 6%; 5th, 3%; 6th, 2% Stakes races 1st-5th; 1st, 60%; 2nd, 20%; 3rd, 11%; 4th, 6%; 5th, 3%	Minimum of 72 hours; In Maryland, if a race has more than six horses, an owner's mount and "gate" fees are paid by the track
Lone Star Park	1st-5th; 60%, 20%, 11%, 6%, 3%	1st & 2nd place week (to allow for test results); all others, immediately

Louisiana Downs	1st-5th; 60%, 20%, 11%, 6%, 3% Some stakes 1st-6th; 60%, 20%, 10%, 5%, 3%, 2%	8-10 days for horses that were drug tested (or until test clears), all others 24 hours
The Meadowlands	All starters in overnight races; 1st, 60% 2nd, 18-20%; 3rd, 10-12%; 4th, 4-6%; 5th-14th, 1-3%; Listed stakes; 1-5th, 60%, 20%, 11%, 6%, 3%	72 hours
Monmouth Park	All starters in overnight races; 1st, 60% 2nd, 18-20%; 3rd, 10-12%; 4th, 4-6%; 5th-14th, 1-3%; Listed stakes; 1-5th, 60%, 20%, 11%, 6%, 3%	72 hours
Mountaineer Park	Overnights 1st-8th; 58%, 20%, 10%, 5%, 3%, 2%, 1%, 1% Stakes 1st-5th; 60%, 20%, 11%, 6%, 3%	The Friday following the drug test clearing; horses not tested, next race day
Oaklawn Park	1st-5th; 60%, 20%, 10%, 6%, 4%	96 hours
Philadelphia Park	1st-5th; 60%, 20%, 11%, 6%, 3%	Winners & other horses visiting the test barn, 7 days; all others, 24 hours
Pimlico	1-6th in overnight races; 1st, 57%; 2nd, 21%; 3rd, 11%; 4th, 6%; 5th, 3%; 6th, 2% Stakes races 1st-5th; 1st, 60%; 2nd, 20%; 3rd, 11%; 4th, 6%; 5th, 3%	Minimum of 72 hours; in Maryland, if a race has more than six horses, an owner's mount and "gate" fees are paid by the track
Prairie Meadows	Overnights 1st-5th; 60%, 20%, 12%, 5%, 3% Stakes 1st-6th; 60%, 20%, 10%, 5%, 3%, 2%	Usually 5 business days

Remington Park	All starters in overnight races; 1st, 60%; 2nd, 18-20%; 3rd, 10-13%; 4th, 4-6%; 5th on, 1% Stakes races 1-6th; 60%, 20%, 10%, 5%, 3%, 2%	1st & 2nd place (and others visiting the test barn) 7–10 days, all others 24 hours
Retama Park	1st-5th; 60%, 20%, 11%, 6%, 3%	1st & 2nd place week (to all for test results); all others, immediately
River Downs	All starters in overnight races; 1st, 60%; 2nd, 20%; 3rd, 10%; 4th, 5%; 5th on, 5% divided equally Stakes races 1st-6th; 60%, 20%, 10%, 5%, 3%, 2%	72 hours
Rockingham	Overnights 1st-5th; 60%, 20%, 10%, 5%, 3%, with remaining 2% going to jockeys' insurance fund Stakes 1st-6th; 60%, 20%, 10%, 5%, 3%, 2%	48 hours
Sam Houston	1st-5th; 60%, 20%, 11%, 6%, 3%	1st & 2nd place week (to all for test results); all others, immediately
Santa Anita	1st-5th; 60%, 20%, 12%, 6%, 2%	72 hours
Saratoga	1st-5th; 60%, 20%, 11%, 6%, 3%	48 hours
Sportsman's Park	1st-5th; 60%, 20%, 11%, 6%, 3%	48 racing hours
Suffolk Downs	Overnight races 1-5th; 1st, 60%; 2nd, 20%; 3rd, 10%; 4th, 5%; 5th, 3% (remaining 2% is paid to an injured jockeys' fund) Stakes races 1st-6th;60%; 20%; 10%; 5%; 3%; 2%	48 hours, excluding weekends and holidays
Tampa Bay Downs	All starters in overnight races: 1st, 60%; 2nd, 18-20%; 3rd, 9-13%; 4th, 3-6%; 5th on, 1% (Percentages vary depending upon number of starters. Stakes races 1st-6th; 60%, 20%, 10%, 5%, 3%, 2%	48 hours

Thistledown	All starters in overnight races;	48 hours
	1st, 60-65%; 2nd, 18-20%;	
	3rd, 9-10%; 4th, 3-5%; 5th on, 1%	
	Stakes races 1st-6th; 60%, 20%, 10%,	
	5%, 3%, 2%	
Turf Paradise	All overnights & most stakes	If horse is drug-
	1st-5th; 60%, 20%, 10%, 6%, 4%	tested, 7-10 days;
		all others, 24 hours
Turfway Park	1st-8th in overnight races:	48 hours
	1st, 60%; 2nd, 20%; 3rd, 10%;	
	4th, 5%; 5th, 3%, 6th-on, 2% divided equally	
	Stakes races 1st-5th; 62%, 20%, 10%, 5%, 3%	

The Paymaster

The paymaster, otherwise known as the horseman's bookkeeper, is the individual charged with overseeing that the daily purses earned are correctly deposited into winning owners' accounts from the general purse fund. This person also oversees the collection and redistribution of amounts used to claim horses, making sure that an owner wishing to claim has the necessary amount on deposit and ensuring that the owner whose horse was claimed receives this amount in his or her account. The paymaster also withholds the jockey's earnings or mount fees, placing them in a separate account for each individual rider. At the end of the year, the paymaster also issues IRS Form 1099 to those owners earning purse funds.

If you are new to a track and are running a horse that is likely to earn a portion of the purse, find the paymaster's office, introduce yourself, and give the paymaster your address, telephone, and social security or federal tax identification number. By establishing your purse account in person, you have ensured that the office has your correct information, and you will be familiar with the person from whom you will later collect your purse earnings.

If you don't take the time to visit the paymaster or if you are shipping a horse to race and won't be attending, take a minute to call the paymaster's office and make sure the horseman's bookkeeper has your correct information. This simple step will ensure that your account statements will always reflect the correct reporting information.

At most tracks you will need to have on account the jockey's mount fee before being allowed to race. Other tracks allow you to race without it and then bill you for the fee. As the jockey's mount fee is usually less than $150, we encourage you to have it on account before you enter – it's just a good business practice.

Purse money is not immediately available after the race. Purses can be collected anywhere from two to seven days after your horse has run, depending upon the track. You can either visit the paymaster in person to collect your check, call and ask that a check be sent, or leave your purse earnings on account for future claims or riding fees. If you still have purse funds on account at the end of the meet, the track will send them to you in the form of a check, or you can ask the paymaster to transfer those funds to another track. Purse funds left on account will not automatically transfer to the next live meet; they will be mailed to you unless the paymaster is notified otherwise.

If you are shipping out of state to race, a simple call to the paymaster's office by you or your trainer to make sure the office has the information necessary to set up your account is appreciated. To collect your funds from out of state, simply call the paymaster and ask that they be sent to you.

Partnerships are treated differently by different paymasters, depending upon the volume of owners and partnerships. Some will accommodate partners' requests to divvy up earnings into separate accounts, while others, overwhelmed by the paperwork presented by multiple ownership, will only issue a check that matches the ownership of the horse, as in "pay to the order of Smith, Smith, and West." Checks issued this way can present a cashing problem, unless all three of these partners are able and willing to go to their local bank simultaneously. It might be better for you if the check is written as payable to "Smith, or Smith, or West," which will allow any of the three partners to deposit the check and split the earnings. In order to do so, you will need to contact the track's clerk of the course and request that the ownership on the horse's papers be changed to "Smith, or Smith, or West." In some cases a simple phone call to the clerk of the course will be sufficient to change this "and" to "or." Other tracks require a faxed request or a personal visit and signature to change this document. Once the document has been changed, the clerk of the course will notify the paymaster's office, and the ownership information will be changed in the accounting system. All future checks for this partnership will then be issued in that way.

A cautionary note to partnerships: At the end of the year, the paymaster will generally issue Form 1099 to one partner, the one who has given his or her social security number or federal tax identification number or the one whose name appears alphabetically first. To avoid this individual partner's being taxed on large amounts of income that he or she ultimately does not receive, he or she should report the entire amount and then deduct the amount paid out to his or her partners as a sales return. He or she should then prepare Form 1099's for the other partners who receive a portion of the purse income.

Remember that after collecting your purse earnings, you will still owe the trainer his or her share as a commission. The jockey will already have received his or her share — it is automatically deducted by the paymaster and deposited into the jockey's account. The trainer will add the proper commission to your monthly training bill – pay it promptly. Your trainer depends upon these amounts for his livelihood. He's earned it and should not have to wait 30, 60, or 90 days to receive the commission.

14

State-Bred Incentive Programs

To increase demand for their horses, many states have devised incentive programs for owners and breeders who choose to raise and race horses within their borders. Having a healthy local Thoroughbred industry is key to filling fields at many racetracks and equally or more importantly, helps the industry have clout in the state legislature. A thriving Thoroughbred breeding industry contributes significantly to a state's economy and preserves green space.

You would be wise to investigate your state, or a surrounding one's, state-bred incentive program, as many times lucrative bonuses or special racing opportunities are offered that can help boost your stable's profits. Carefully consider such programs as you plan your stable's composition and its future.

Your state's breeders' association is worthy of investigation, too. Many publish informative magazines, hold educational seminars, and provide a chance to network with other local owners and breeders. Below is a listing of states that have a breeders organization and a brief description of the state's breed incentive program. Rules and regulations regarding breed incentive programs can change so please check with the state organization listed to receive the most up-to-date information.

Alabama

Although Alabama does not conduct pari-mutuel Thoroughbred racing, a group of Thoroughbred enthusiasts residing in the state have formed the Alabama Thoroughbred Association. This association works with the Birmingham Racing Commission to offer a handful of races for Alabama-breds at Fair Grounds and Tampa Bay Downs racetracks. An Alabama-bred race at Hoosier Park is being planned.

The group also annually rewards the owners of registered Alabama-breds that have earned the most purses in races throughout the country, excluding purses earned in the races restricted to Alabama-breds.

For more information, contact the Alabama Thoroughbred Association at (205) 877-8510.

Arizona

Owners of winning Arizona-breds receive, on average, an additional 15% of the purse money won at in-state tracks. This award is calculated on wins only and is paid at the end of a race meet. Breeders receive an 8% bonus on average, which is paid at the end of the race meet, along with an additional 15% from the state, which is paid out quarterly.

One race a day must be written for Arizona-breds, giving owners of such horses ample opportunities to run. The state also offers a series of stake races restricted to Arizona-breds, along with the Arizona Breeders' Day in April.

To qualify as an Arizona-bred, a horse must be foaled by a registered mare and live in the state for a minimum of six months during its first year. For more information, contact the Arizona Thoroughbred Breeders Association at (602) 942-1310 or at www.atba.net.

Arkansas

The Oaklawn Jockey Club, in accordance with state legislation, provides Arkansas Racing Commission's Purse and Awards Fund. A designated percentage of Oaklawn Park's handle, during both live and simulcast racing and Instant Racing (an electronic pari-mutuel game based upon previously run races) on Oaklawn's premises, is paid into this fund, which is then distributed to owners and breeders of Arkansas-bred horses as follows.

Two three-year-old stakes, the Rainbow Stakes (for colts and geldings) and the Rainbow Miss Stakes (for fillies), are supplemented annually from the gross Purse and Awards Fund to insure a purse of $50,000 for each race (after crediting $25,000 paid to each by the Oaklawn Jockey Club).

After subtracting these two purse supplements from the total monies available in the fund, 10% of the remaining money is designated as owners' awards, 70% as breeders' awards, and 20% as stallion awards.

Owner awards are paid to the owner of a registered Arkansas-bred in proportion to the horse's earnings during Oaklawn Park's live meet the previous calendar year.

Breeder and stallion awards are paid to mare and stallion owners in proportion to the earnings of their progeny the previous calendar year. These awards are paid on total progeny earnings in the United States and Canada and are not limited to earnings at Oaklawn Park.

All awards are paid annually by the end of March of the following year in which they were earned.

An Arkansas-bred horse is one that has been foaled in the state and whose sire and dam are registered with the Arkansas Thoroughbred Breeder and Horsemen's Association (ATBHA). If a foal is by an out-of-state sire, it must have been foaled in Arkansas and its dam bred back to a registered Arkansas stallion on the next breeding to qualify for awards.

Contact the ATBHA at (501) 624-6328 or at atbha@direclynx.net for more information.

California

California has a rich, albeit complex, incentive program for its state-bred horses, with more than $30 million devoted to both bonus incentives and purses for races restricted to Cal-breds. The incentive awards are divided into three categories: those paid to owners, those to breeders, and those to stallion owners.

Owner awards are paid only to Cal-breds running in open races (those not restricted to Cal-breds) and are further divided into those given to Cal-breds competing in allowance, non-claiming, and overnight stake races; and those given to Cal-breds competing in upper-level claiming races. Both programs' monies are paid directly to the owner through the track's paymaster and are considered a part of purse earnings.

Owners of Cal-breds competing in an open allowance, overnight stake, or non-claiming maiden race are paid an additional 30% of their share of the purse for first- through fifth-place finishes. This program is jointly administered by the Thoroughbred Owners of California (TOC) and the California Thoroughbred Breeders' Association (CTBA).

Those owners who race Cal-breds in upper-level qualifying open claiming and starter allowance races (as long as the purse is greater than $15,000) receive a bonus equaling 20% of the winner's share of the purse. This bonus is paid to winners only. Qualifying races are those open claiming races with a purse greater than a specified minimum, which varies from race meet to race meet but is usually greater than $20,000. The CTBA is the sole provider of funds for this program.

The Cal-bred Race Fund, which receives nearly $1.35 million annually from the incentive awards program, is used to boost purses of selected Cal-bred stakes. Nearly 50% of the $1.275 million offered in purses on Cal-Cup Day is supplemented from this race fund.

Owners of Cal-breds can also take advantage of the races written for Cal-breds, as state law mandates that at least one race a day at each California track be restricted to state-breds. State law also requires that California's tracks allocate at least 10% of their total stakes money to Cal-bred restricted stakes. Currently this equates to more than 60 stakes statewide, with total purses of $6.4 million.

Unlike owners' awards, which are paid as part of purse earnings, breeders' awards are paid semi-annually. Stallion awards are paid once a year. At the end of the year, after amounts paid to both the owners' awards and Cal-bred Race Fund are deducted from California's incentive fund, 75% is directed to breeders' awards and 25% to stallion awards. Individual breeder and stallion awards are then figured based upon the proportion of an individual Cal-bred's qualifying earnings to the total amount available in the fund. These payments are distributed by March 31 of the following year in which they were earned.

For a horse to be registered as a Cal-bred, it must either be conceived by a California-based stallion and foaled in the state or if conceived by an out-of-state stallion, it must be foaled in California and its dam be bred back to a California stallion. Contact the CTBA at (626) 445-7800 or at www.ctba.com.

Colorado

Registered Colorado-breds are eligible to share in Colorado's Breeders' Awards and the Supplemental Purse Fund, which is accumulated annually from a percentage of the pari-mutuel handle (both on and off-track).

The breeders' award money is split with 30% going to owners, 60% to breeders, and 10% to stallion owners. Awards are paid annually using a point system based on annual earnings from first-, second-, and third-place finishes at Colorado tracks to determine the percentage paid to each eligible owner, breeder, or stallion owner.

The Supplemental Purse Fund supports a series of stakes races for Colorado-breds, each with a minimum purse of $30,000.

A Colorado-bred is one that has been foaled in Colorado by a mare registered with the Colorado Thoroughbred Breeders' Association that was in Colorado by December 31 preceding the year the foal was dropped. For more information, contact the Colorado Thoroughbred Breeders' Association at (303) 294-0260 or at www.colo-ctba.com.

Florida

Breeders and owners of Florida-bred foals registered with the Florida Thoroughbred Breeders' and Owners' Association (FTBOA) are eligible for more than $15 million in incentives.

The owner of a Florida-bred foal that wins a maiden, claiming, or allowance race is eligible for a Florida Owners' Award, which is paid by the participating tracks as a supplement to the purse.

The owner of a Florida-bred racing in Florida is also eligible for more than 50 stakes races annually. Purses for these stakes are either restricted, preferred, and/or supplemented by the FTBOA Stakes Fund and range in value from $50,000 to $100,000.

Foals by stallions standing in Florida that are registered with the FTBOA and nominated to the Florida Stallion Stakes are eligible for more than $1 million in the Florida Stallion Stakes races for two-year-olds.

The breeder of a Florida-bred that wins a race at a Florida track is eligible for a breeders' award of 15% of the gross purse. There is a $15,000 limit on any single award.

The owner of a stallion (currently standing in Florida) that sires a Florida-bred foal that wins a stakes race at a Florida track is eligible for a stallion owners' award of 20% of the gross value of the stakes race. There is also a $15,000 limit on any single award.

To be eligible for these awards, a foal or stallion must be registered with the FTBOA. Babies must be foaled in Florida by a dam normally domiciled in the state. If foaled by a dam that normally resides elsewhere, the baby can still be registered as long as the mare is bred back to a Florida stallion.

For more specifics, contact the FTBOA at (352) 629-2160 or at www.ftboa.com.

Georgia

Even though Georgia does not have pari-mutuel racing, the state does have its own Georgia Thoroughbred Owners and Breeders Association (GTOBA), which organizes a series of stakes for Georgia-breds that are run in Florida. GTOBA is negotiating to expand the series to some Midwest tracks.

To be eligible for these stakes, which generally have purses between $50,000 and $75,000, a horse must be by a stallion that has had a season donated to the association's annual charity event. The horse need not be the result of a mating from this season. To see whether a horse's sire has ever had a season donated to the auction, which would make it eligible for these stakes, visit GTOBA's website at www.gtoba.com or call them at (770) 451-0409.

Illinois

The Illinois Thoroughbred Breeders Fund, which is generated by revenues from the state's racing programs, provides owner, breeder, and stallion awards, along with stakes and overnight races restricted to Illinois-registered Thoroughbreds.

Owners earn awards when their Illinois -registered Thoroughbred (see below) finishes first, second, or third in certain open races, including maiden special weights, allowance races, overnight handicaps, and claiming races with claiming prices of $10,000 or more. This owner's award equals 60% of the earned portion of the purse for an Illinois conceived and foaled thoroughbred (IB), or 40% of the earned portion of the purse for an Illinois foaled thoroughbred (IF). The track's paymaster pays these awards along with the purse.

A breeder's award is earned when an Illinois-registered Thoroughbred wins any race in the state. In open races, this award is 11.5% of the winner's share of the base purse (meaning not including the owner's award). In restricted races, the 11.5% is still based upon the winner's share of the purse, but is divided among the first four finishers, with the winner receiving 60%; second, 20%; third, 15%; and fourth, 5%. Breeder's awards are paid 30 days after a meet's conclusion.

In addition, Illinois-registered Thoroughbreds are offered a minimum of two restricted races each day and close to 30 restricted stakes a year.

To qualify for these awards and races, a foal must be registered as an

Illinois Conceived Foal (ICF) or an Illinois Foaled Only (IF). Foals registered as ICF are foals by Illinois registered sires out of Illinois registered mares and are foaled in state. The Illinois-foaled program has three registration options: the Early Arrival Program, in which mares in foal to out-of-state sires must arrive in Illinois by December 1; the New Purchase Program, which requires mares be in the state by February 1 and is used for mares purchased at auction only; and the Breed-Back Program, which requires that mares in foal to out-of-state sires must arrive by March 1, foal in Illinois, and then be bred back to an Illinois registered sire the same year as foaling in order to have their current foal registered.

For more information on either eligibility or the fund's awards, contact the Illinois Thoroughbred Breeders Fund Program at (217) 782-4231.

Indiana

Indiana-breds can receive substantial rewards, but they must win to do so. The state's Breed Development Fund, generated both by pari-mutuel handle and admissions from riverboat gambling, awards owners, breeders, and stallion owners.

Owner awards in the amount of 25% of the gross (total) purse are paid to winners of all allowance and stakes races run in Indiana, including maiden special weight races. A 15% bonus (again, of the gross purse) is paid to winners of claiming races other than those offered with a claiming price of $5,000 or less.

Breeder awards consist of a 20% bonus of the gross purse for all wins in stakes, allowance, and claiming races run in Indiana, except for claiming races with a price of $5,000 or less. An out-of-state breeder award is also paid to Indiana-breds that win a race in another state or Canada. This award, which equals 10% of the winner's share of the purse, is applicable only in the event that the Indiana Horse Racing Commission approves less than 75 days of live Thoroughbred racing during a calendar year and only when a live Thoroughbred meet is not in progress in Indiana.

Indiana's Thoroughbred Advisory Committee sets forth a stakes schedule and purse supplement schedule to races restricted to Indiana-breds.

To register as an Indiana-bred, a horse must be foaled in Indiana from an Indiana-registered mare that was in the state by December 1 of the year prior to foaling. The mare must remain in the state until foaling. If a mare enters the state after December 1, her foal will still be eligible (as long as it is foaled in Indiana) for registration as long as she is bred back to an Indiana-registered sire.

For more information, contact the state's Thoroughbred Development Advisory Committee at (317) 233-0187 or www.state.in.us/ihrc or contact the Indiana Thoroughbred Owners and Breeders Association at (317) 462-0046 or at www.itoba.com.

Iowa

Owners are offered a minimum of one race a day for their Iowa-breds, along with a series of restricted stakes races. Purse supplements in the form of owner bonuses are also offered, with owners of Iowa-breds that finish first through fourth in open company receiving a purse supplement that is greater than the bonus given to owners of state-breds finishing first through fourth in restricted races. Iowa's Breeders Fund directs 25% of its monies to these purse supplements, which range from 20% of the purse upward. Both awards won in open and restricted races are paid to horses finishing first through fourth place. They are paid through the horseman's bookkeeper and are distributed along with the purse.

Breeder awards are also paid – awards equaling 12% of the purse won by an Iowa-bred racing in the state are paid annually through the Iowa breeders fund. Stallions earn points based on their progeny's wins in various categories of races. Total points are divided by the total dollars available for stallion awards to determine the dollars awarded per point.

To register as an Iowa-bred, a horse must be foaled in the state by a mare registered with Iowa's Department of Agriculture, which must also inspect the foal. The sire can be in or out of state as long as the mare is in Iowa by January 1 of the year foaling. If the mare returns to Iowa after January 1, she must be bred back to an Iowa stallion in order for her current foal to be registered.

Contact the Iowa Thoroughbred Breeders and Owners Association at (800) 577-1097 or at www.iowathoroughbred.com for further details.

Kansas

The Kansas Horsemen's Association administers the Kansas-bred program, which is funded from breakage, the spare change retained by the track on payoffs, which is usually paid in 10-cent increments and outs (uncashed pari-mutuel tickets) generated by the state's pari-mutuel system. A 35% purse supplement is paid to owners of Kansas-breds running first through third in open company, with first place receiving 60% of the supplement, second place receiving 25%, and third place 15%. A 25% purse supplement is paid to Kansas-breds running one, two, or three in restricted races, with 60% of the supplement paid to winners, 25% to second, and 15% to third. These awards are issued by the state and are paid about three weeks after being earned.

Kansas-breds can also compete in races restricted to state-breds and can earn additional purse supplements on specified stakes races.

The state's eligibility requirements are easy – the horse simply must be foaled in the state.

For more information, contact the Kansas Horsemen's Association at (785) 368-6563.

Kentucky

Kentucky has a lucrative program worth more than $10 million for owners of Kentucky-sired and foaled horses. Three-quarters of 1% of all money wagered at the state's Thoroughbred tracks is deposited in the Kentucky Thoroughbred Development Fund (KTDF), along with 2% of all money wagered on Thoroughbred races through inter-track and whole-card simulcasting.

This KTDF fund pays a bonus equaling 25% of the purse to owners running in the state's non-claiming maiden, allowance, handicap, and stake races with a purse up to $100,000. (Some exceptions are made to include stakes of greater value, including the Kentucky Cup stakes run at Turfway Park in September.) The bonus, which is paid along with the purse, is divided among the first four finishers in a race, with 65% going to the winner, 20% to second, 10% to third, and 5% to fourth. Bonus money is considered a part of a horse's earnings.

To be eligible for KTDF money, a horse must be both sired by a stallion standing in Kentucky the entire season in which the horse was conceived and be foaled in the state. For more information, contact the Kentucky Thoroughbred Association/Kentucky Thoroughbred Owners and Breeders Inc. at (859) 259-1643 or at www.kta-ktob.com.

Louisiana

While Louisiana doesn't offer owner awards, owners of Louisiana-breds are offered ample purse supplements. The supplements are added to the three races restricted to Louisiana-breds that are written daily at each track, including one maiden race. Louisiana-bred horses can also compete in seven stakes races on Louisiana Champions Day, which is usually held in December at Fair Grounds racetrack, and in eight stakes races offered at the Louisiana Breeders Festival of Racing at Louisiana Downs, usually held in October.

Breeders of Louisiana-bred horses receive bonuses for first-, second-, or third-place finishes in any race in the state; or first, second, or third in any stakes race with a purse of at least $25,000 outside of Louisiana. For the top-three finishers in any race in Louisiana, the bonus equals 10% of the purse. Restricted race awards are paid within 60 days of the race. Non-restricted race awards are paid within 30 days after the meet's conclusion.

Stallion owners receive a bonus if their stallion's progeny finish first, second, or third in an open or restricted stake, handicap, or allowance race in Louisiana or first, second, or third in a stake race outside the state. Stallion awards are paid once a year with calculations based on earnings from July 1 to June 30 of the preceding year.

To be registered as an accredited Louisiana-bred, a foal must be produced by a mare that permanently resides in the state. The mare may, after foaling, be shipped out-of-state to be bred, provided she is returned to Louisiana no later than August 1.

Contact the Louisiana Thoroughbred Breeders Association at (800) 772-1195 for further details.

Maryland

Maryland was the first state to initiate a fund for its homebred horses. The primary focus of the Maryland Fund, created by its General Assembly in 1962, is to encourage the production of horses that are competitive in open company rather than races restricted to state-breds. It is supported by a small percentage of the track's mutuel handle and breakage, with 55% designated for purse money and owner awards and 45% to breeder and stallion awards.

Money from the fund is distributed as purses for Maryland-bred stakes races, owner awards for wins, breeder and stallion awards for wins and stakes placings, and bonus awards for the four highest-earning two- and three-year-olds shown at the annual Maryland Horse Breeders Association's yearling show. This fund also supports the purses paid on Maryland Million Day, which showcases horses by Maryland stallions.

Owner awards are paid when a Maryland-bred horse wins any race other than stakes, starter race, or claiming race in which the winner runs for a claiming price of less than $25,000 (or $20,000 at Timonium). These awards amount to approximately 17% of the winner's share of the purse and are paid within 30 days of the close of each meet.

Breeders and stallion awards are paid to breeders of Maryland-breds that win or that finish first through fourth in stakes races and range from 10% to 20% of the earned share of the purse for breeders awards and 5% to 10% for stallion awards.

In order for the horse to be registered as a Maryland-bred, the breeder must be a Maryland resident. If the breeder is not a resident but keeps horses in Maryland year-round, a letter attesting to that fact must be on file with the breeders' organization to eliminate further requirements. If the breeder does not qualify under either of these, then the sire of the foal must be a Maryland stallion, or the mare, if in foal to an out-of-state stallion, must be covered by a Maryland stallion following the birth of that foal.

For more information, contact the Maryland Horse Breeders Association at (410) 252-2100 or at www.mdhorsebreeders.com.

Massachusetts

Massachusetts-breds are offered a series of restricted stakes races and can earn bonuses for their owners and breeders. Income for these programs is generated from the Massachusetts Breeders' Fund, which receives 1% of wagers made on live races at Suffolk Downs and .5% of simulcast handle.

Owners receive an additional 30%, breeders receive 25%, and stallion owners receive 15% of the purse when their registered Massachusetts-bred finishes first, second, or third at Massachusetts tracks. The fund also offers a series of stakes races with purses of $30,000 for state-bred horses.

To be registered as a Massachusetts-bred, a horse must be foaled in the state and its dam must reside in the state from October through foaling or must be bred back to a registered Massachusetts stallion.

For further information, contact the Massachusetts Thoroughbred Breeders Association at (617) 492-7217 or at www.massbreds.com.

Michigan

Michigan offers owners' awards, breeders' awards, stallion awards, and purse supplements for races restricted to Michigan-breds. The state also offers 20 stakes races restricted to Michigan-breds with purses totaling nearly $2 million. Owners of state-bred horses are offered many opportunities to run, as by law the state's racetracks are required to write at least two races a day restricted to Michigan-breds and run one of them. Additionally, the Michigan Sire Stakes series offers six stakes with purses of more than $100,000 each to encourage the breeding and purchasing of Michigan-sired horses.

Owners' awards are paid to Michigan-bred horses finishing first through third in an open company race. Owners who race Michigan-sired horses receive an additional award when their horse wins in open company. Both owner awards and the Michigan-sired owner awards are paid annually by the Michigan Thoroughbred Owners and Breeders Association (MTOBA).

Breeders' awards are paid when a Michigan-bred horse wins any race at a licensed pari-mutuel track within the state. Award amounts equal 10% of the gross purse and are paid by Michigan's Department of Agriculture. Stallion awards are paid to the owner of a Michigan stallion whose offspring win a race at a licensed Michigan pari-mutuel track – these awards are administered by MTOBA and are paid annually.

To be eligible for these awards, a horse must be a Michigan-bred or sired horse and must be registered with the MTOBA. A Michigan-bred is defined as a Thoroughbred foaled in the state whose dam has remained a minimum of seven months of the foaling year within the state.

For further information, contact MTOBA at (231) 798-7721 or at www.mtoba.com.

Minnesota

Minnesota's Breeders' Fund, income for which is derived from a small percentage of handle, encourages the production of state-bred horses through purse supplements and breeder and stallion awards.

Purse supplements receive 62% of the fund and are used to boost purses paid to Minnesota-breds in open and restricted overnight races and in restricted stakes. Supplements vary from 20% to 40% of the purse, depending upon the quality of the race. Horses running in lower-level claiming races receive the lower end of the bonus range, while those competitive in higher quality races receive more. These awards are paid to the first three finishers in a race, with the winner receiving 60% of the supplement; second, 18% to 20% (depending upon the race's field size); and third, 10% to 12%. The track's horsemen's bookkeeper distributes these supplements along with the purse.

Breeders receive 31% of the fund, while stallion owners receive the fund's remaining 7%. Both receive awards for horses that finish in the top three of a race, either restricted or open. These awards are paid within 45 days of the end of a meet and are based on horse's earnings compared to the total earnings of all Minnesota-breds during that live meet.

To be registered as a Minnesota-bred, and thus eligible for awards, a horse must simply be foaled in the state by a resident mare or by a mare that entered the state previous to foaling or no later than March 15. To receive stallion awards, the stallion must be in Minnesota and registered prior to January 1 of the breeding year and remain in the state for the entire season.

For more information, contact Minnesota's State Racing Commission at (952) 496-7950.

Mississippi

Although Mississippi does not offer pari-mutuel racing, some dedicated Thoroughbred owners have banded together to form the Mississippi Breeders and Owners Association, which offers the Mississippi Futurity for Mississippi-owned horses. This futurity is annually held at Fair Grounds racetrack in New Orleans and offers a purse of about $30,000. For more information, contact the Mississippi Breeders and Owners Association at (601) 856-8293.

Nebraska

Nebraska supplements both its state-bred and open races through its Nebraska Thoroughbred Breeders' Development Fund (NTBDF), which is funded through the takeout. Races restricted to Nebraska-breds receive a 15% purse supplement, while owners of Nebraska-breds running first through third in open company receive an 8% purse bonus, which is divided among them, with the first-place finisher receiving 60%; second-place, 30%; and third-place, 10%.

Breeders and stallion awards are also distributed. Breeders of Nebraska foaled and sired horses receive an additional 12% of the earned purse for horses finishing first through third in all Nebraska races, while breeders of Nebraska-foaled, but not -sired, horses receive a 5% bonus.

After these distributions, any funds remaining in the NTBDF at the end of a race meet are distributed to owners, breeders, and stallion own-ers of Nebraska-breds in the form of bonus money. These bonuses can be substantial.

To be registered as a Nebraska-bred, a horse must be foaled in the state by a registered Nebraska mare that has resided in the state 90 days con-tinuously prior to foaling. This 90-day period may be reduced if a mare is purchased at a nationally recognized Thoroughbred auction and arrives and remains in Nebraska for at least 30 days immediately prior to foaling.

For more information, contact the Nebraska Thoroughbred Breeders Association Inc. at (308) 384-4683.

New Jersey

Owners of New Jersey-breds can receive an additional 10% of their earned purse for first- through third-place finishes in open races, provid-ed that the open race was not already supplemented by the state's Thoroughbred fund. New Jersey-breds also have ample opportunities to run because the state mandates one race a day be written for state-breds (usually two races each day fill with New Jersey-breds). They can also compete in more than 13 restricted stakes.

Breeders receive a 35% breeders' award for horses finishing first through third in races restricted to state-breds if their New Jersey-bred is by a registered New Jersey stallion. If the horse is by an out-of-state sire, a 25% award is given. These percentages are based on the horse's earned share of the purse, with a maximum bonus of $5,000 for wins and $3,000 for sec-ond- and third-place finishes. Stallion owners receive a 10% purse bonus for their stallion's progeny's earnings at New Jersey tracks.

All bonuses are calculated and paid at the end of each race meet.

A horse must be registered as a New Jersey-bred to be eligible for these awards. To be registered, a horse must be foaled in the state and its breeder be a resident of the state or maintain a breeding farm there. If the breeder is a non-resident, the horse may still be registered provided it is by a registered New Jersey stallion or if conceived outside of the state, the mare must return by September 1 of that year and remain in New Jersey until she foals.

For more information, contact the Thoroughbred Breeders' Association of New Jersey at (732) 870-9718 or at www.njbreds.com.

New Mexico

Aided by a rule that directs 20% of the net take from gaming at New Mexico's tracks to purses, the New Mexico Horseman's Association offers purse supplements and breeders awards to its state-bred horses. Approximately 81% of this gaming revenue is directed to the general purse fund, with the remaining 19% going to the New Mexico Horse Breeders Association's Gaming Fund. This gaming fund is then divided evenly among the Incentive Award Fund, the New Mexico Stakes Fund, and the Overnight Purse Fund.

An owner's award is paid to any New Mexico-bred finishing first, second, or third in any race held within New Mexico. These awards are paid annually in November and are distributed based upon race quality, with the top-three finishers in stakes and allowance races receiving more than claiming races.

Breeders and stallion owners receive an award based upon wins only. Breeders are awarded an additional 10% of the winner's share of the purse. This 10% is paid within a month by the track at which the horse has won.

A minimum of one race a day must be written for New Mexico-breds. This, coupled with a series of stakes for state-bred horses, allows owners of New Mexico breds ample opportunities to earn purses.

To be registered as a New Mexico-bred, a horse must be foaled in the state by a registered New Mexico dam that remained in the state during her entire pregnancy and must be sired by an active registered New Mexico stallion standing in the state.

For more information, contact the New Mexico Horse Breeders' Association at (505) 262-0224 or at www.nmhorsebreeders.com.

New York

New York-breds compete for lucrative awards. Program incentives distributed by the New York State Thoroughbred Breeding and Development Fund Corporation, along with purses earmarked for New York-breds, exceed $35 million annually for breeders, owners, and stallion owners. The state program consists of more than 43 stake races exclusively for New York-breds with purses exceeding $3.5 million and almost 900 overnight races annually for state-bred horses.

In addition to the generous purses offered on these restricted races, New York distributes breeder and stallion owner awards on these in-state races. Breeders receive 20% of the earned purse as an award for horses finishing first through fourth in any open or restricted race, and if the horse is by a New York sire, the stallion owner receives a 7% award. If the horse is by a non-New York sire, the breeders' award is 10% of the earned purse. There is an award cap of $10,000 per horse per race.

If a New York-bred competes in open company races (with a minimum claiming price of $30,000 through stakes races) at a New York racetrack, in addition to the breeder and stallion owner awards, the owner of the horse receives 20% of the earned purse (first through fourth place) if by a New York sire and 10% if by a non-New York sire. There is an award cap of $20,000 per horse per race.

A small percentage of Thoroughbred racing pari-mutuel wagers in New York is returned to support this incentive program.

Included in the stake schedule is Showcase Day, seven New York-bred restricted stake races held at Belmont Park each fall with more than $1 million in purses.

There is also the annual N.Y. Stallion Stake Series for New York-sired horses. Consisting of eight races at Aqueduct Racetrack, the series' total purses are in excess of $1.25 million.

The newest series for New York-breds is the Big Apple Triple, which comprises three races for three-year-olds, with a $250,000 bonus if a horse wins all three. This series is worth $625,000.

To be considered a New York-bred, a horse must be registered by the

New York Breeding and Development Fund. To qualify for registration, the dam of a foal must either be continuously in residence in the state of New York no later than 90 days after her last cover in the year of conception and remain in residence until foaling in New York or she must foal in the state and be bred back to a registered New York stallion and thereafter remain in New York for 90 consecutive days after giving birth to such foal.

For more information, contact the New York Thoroughbred Breeders Inc. at (518) 587-0777 or at www.nybreds.com.

North Carolina

Although North Carolina does not have pari-mutuel Thoroughbred racing, the state does have the North Carolina Breeders Association. This association, which was formed more than 30 years ago, hosts an annual awards dinner honoring its members' horses, educational seminars, and socials, including a day at the races at Virginia's Colonial Downs racetrack. Members also received a subscription to the Mid-Atlantic Thoroughbred magazine. Contact the association's secretary Teo Zanchelli at (800) 957-3490 or at diamondzcary@aol.com for more information.

Ohio

Like many incentive funds, the Ohio Thoroughbred Race Fund Program was developed to foster growth in the state's Thoroughbred industry and to upgrade the quality of its state-bred horses.

Ohio's Thoroughbreds must have at least one race a day written for them in the condition book. They are eligible to compete in more than 30 state-bred stakes and receive purse supplements ranging from $3,500 to $6,000 (depending upon the type of race) for winning an open race.

Ohio breeders receive awards of 10% of the purse for winning races other than claiming or starter allowance. These races receive 5% of the winner's share of the purse. Stallion owners receive 5% and 3%, respectively, in these races.

To be considered an accredited Ohio Thoroughbred Horse, a horse must be produced by a mare domiciled in the state and by a stallion standing in Ohio. A horse by an out-of-state sire may be registered as an Ohio-bred if the mare enters the state by July 15 of the year she conceives and then remains in the state until she foals. If a mare ships into the state after July 31, her foal can also be registered as long as she remains in the state one year after foaling or until foaling to the cover of an Ohio stallion, whichever comes sooner.

For more information, contact the Ohio Thoroughbred Breeders and Owners at (513) 574-0440 or at www.otbo.com.

Oklahoma

The Oklahoma Breeding Development Fund Special Account for Thoroughbreds, income for which is generated by breakage and unclaimed pari-mutuel ticket revenue, rewards owners through purse supplements and races restricted to state-bred horses.

Fifty percent of the Thoroughbred fund is directed to purse supplements for owners of Oklahoma-breds, 34% is directed to breeders as broodmare awards, and 16% of the fund is directed to the owners of the sires as stallion awards.

These awards are paid to the owner, breeder, and stallion owner of the first three finishers in any race, except for stakes, with first place receiving 50% of the listed award amount, second place receiving 30%, and third-place finishers receiving 20%. These awards are paid by the Oklahoma Horse Racing Commission after post-race drug tests clear (about ten days after the race).

Oklahoma-breds are also offered a minimum of two restricted races each day, along with a series of Oklahoma-bred stakes races (including the Oklahoma-Bred Classics Day Races).

For a racehorse to be registered as an accredited Oklahoma-bred, and thus be eligible for purse supplements and owner awards, it must foaled in Oklahoma from an accredited Oklahoma-bred mare. Breeding stock must be entered into the Oklahoma-bred registry to become eligible for broodmare and stallion awards.

For more information, contact the Oklahoma Horse Racing Commission at (405) 943-6472.

Oregon

Oregon offers an owner bonus program, breeder awards, purse supplements for restricted Oregon-bred races, and a stakes program for state-breds.

Owners of Oregon-bred horses with purse earnings (first through fifth in any race) from a race run at a commercial meet receive an owner bonus after the end of the race meet. A commercial meet is one that is simulcasted – currently this only includes Portland Meadows. Funding for the owner bonus is provided for by law. One percent of the total pari-mutuel handle wagered during the meet (live or simulcast is set aside for that purpose. The percentage paid to each owner as a bonus is calculated by dividing the total 1% pool by total Oregon-bred purse earnings during the entire race meet.

Breeder awards are paid to breeders of Oregon-bred Thoroughbreds that win a race at a recognized race meet in the state. The breeder award is paid on winning efforts at a current rate of 10% of the winner's share of the purse.

Both owner and breeder awards are paid after the conclusion of each recognized race meet.

One race restricted to Oregon-breds is offered each race day during a commercial race meet. The Portland Meadows' race meet usually offers ten stakes races restricted to Oregon-breds.

To be registered as an Oregon-bred, a horse must be foaled in the state.

For more information, contact the Oregon Thoroughbred Breeders Association at (503) 285-0658 or by e-mail at otba@mindspring.com.

Pennsylvania

Owners of Pennsylvania-breds can earn purse bonuses that are paid along with purse earnings and are directly deposited into their accounts at the track. These owner bonuses are funded by the Pennsylvania Breeding Fund, which also provides breeder and stallion awards, and funds Pennsylvania-bred stakes races. The fund is financed by 1% of the state's total Thoroughbred pari-mutuel handle.

The owner bonus program rewards owners of Pennsylvania-breds finishing first, second, or third in all overnight races at Penn National and Philadelphia Park racetracks. It pays the owner an additional 40% of his or her share of the purse and is considered part of a horse's official earnings. In stakes races, a winning Pennsylvania-bred generates an owner award amounting to 10% of the purse share.

Pennsylvania-breds also have preferred starter status in most overnight races at Penn National and Philadelphia Park. The state also offers a stakes program (with approximately 25 stakes) for its state-breds.

Breeders receive an award whenever a Pennsylvania-bred finishes first, second, or third in any pari-mutuel race in the state. For horses sired by registered Pennsylvania stallions, this award amounts to 30% of the purse share earned. For those sired by out-of-state stallions, the award is 20%. Stallion awards are paid to registered Pennsylvania stallions whose state-bred offspring finish first, second, or third in any race in the state. They equal 15% of the purse share. Both breeders and stallion awards are paid monthly.

To be registered as a Pennsylvania-bred, a horse must be born in Pennsylvania and then either it or its dam must reside in the state for at least 90 days during the year of foaling. The 90 days need not be consecutive. Returning the foal or mare to Pennsylvania after weaning may satisfy this requirement. For more information, contact the Pennsylvania Horse Breeders Association at (610) 444-1050 or at www.pabred.com.

South Carolina

South Carolina does not have an incentive program as the state does not offer pari-mutuel wagering, but it does have a Thoroughbred organization. The South Carolina Thoroughbred Owners and Breeders Association holds an annual meeting and awards banquet and issues a quarterly newsletter. Contact the association at (803) 957-6336.

Texas

Texas offers the Accredited Texas-bred (ATB) Program, which is an incentive program that pays awards to owners and eligible breeders and stallion owners of accredited Texas-breds finishing first, second, or third in any race in Texas. Funds for the ATB program come from breakage and a percentage of exotic handle at that meet. Beginning in 2002, there is an owner bonus fund set aside for accredited Texas-bred horses placing first, second, or third in any open company race in the state. The fund is off the top of available ATB money for that meet. In 2002, this equates to 10%, increasing annually by 2.5% to a maximum 25% in 2008. The remainder of the ATB funds for that meet is distributed as follows: 40% to owners, 40% to eligible breeders, and 20% to eligible owners of accredited Texas sires of those finishers. The awards are paid by the Texas Thoroughbred Association at the end of each race meet.

Texas tracks are required to write two races a day restricted to accredited Texas-breds. In addition, each of the tracks now have a full day of races restricted to either Texas-bred or connected horses: Stars of Texas Day at Lone Star Park, Texas Hall of Fame Day at Retama Park, and Texas Champions Day at Sam Houston Race Park.

To be eligible to become an accredited Texas-bred racehorse, a horse must be foaled in Texas and be out of an accredited Texas broodmare. The sire can be any registered Thoroughbred. The mare must be returned to Texas by August 15 of the year bred and remain in the state. Any breeder who breeds his mare to an accredited Texas stallion at least every other breeding is eligible (if the resulting foals are accredited) for full breeders' awards. Breeders choosing to breed to other than accredited Texas stallions year after year will be eligible for 50% of breeders' awards (the other 50% will revert to the fund for redistribution in the same meet). Texas has implemented these rules to encourage all Texas owners and breeders to support the program while improving the quality of Texas-breds.

For more information, contact the Texas Thoroughbred Association at (512) 458-6133 or at www.texasthoroughbred.com.

Virginia

Virginia is the only program that rewards its state-breds running in three different states: Virginia, Maryland, and West Virginia. Special purses for Virginia-breds are also offered in Delaware. Awards are paid through the Virginia Breeders' Fund, income for which is generated through 1% of pari-mutuel handle.

Owner awards and restricted races receive 50% of the Breeders' Fund monies. Owner awards are paid to Virginia-bred or -sired horses racing not only in Virginia, but also Maryland and West Virginia. Virginia-breds running in non-restricted races at Virginia's Colonial Downs receive a 40% purse bonus that is paid along with the purse to first- through sixth-place finishers. An annual owner bonus is also paid to Virginia-bred or sired horses racing in West Virginia and Maryland. The amount of this bonus varies annually as it is dependent upon the amount remaining after bonuses are paid on Virginia races.

A Virginia-sired program also exists that rewards horses conceived in Virginia but foaled in another state. Thus an owner could take advantage of two state's programs, as a horse sired by a registered Virginia stallion could be foaled in and registered with a different state's program but still receive awards from the Virginia-sired program. Owners of Virginia-sired horses earn money when their horse wins a race in West Virginia and Maryland, although a $10,000 cap per award applies.

Virginia also offers races restricted to state-breds, along with a series of Virginia-bred or sired stakes races, some of which are run in Delaware and West Virginia.

Breeder and stallion awards are paid for Virginia-bred and/or Virginia-sired horses running in Virginia, Maryland, and West Virginia. Breeders receive 35% and stallion owners 15% of the Virginia Breeders Fund monies. Awards are earned when a Virginia-bred or sired horse wins any race and are usually about 15% of the purse. A $25,000 cap per award is placed on horses earning awards through the Virginia-sired program. Both breeder and stallion awards are paid annually.

All award recipients must have a Form W-9 on file with the Virginia Thoroughbred Association (VTA) before awards will be paid.

A horse must be registered as a Virginia-bred or -sired horse in order to be eligible for these awards. To be registered as a Virginia-bred horse, a horse must be foaled in Virginia and be sired by a Virginia stallion or its dam must be bred back to a Virginia stallion or the dam must remain in Virginia continuously from September 1 to the date of foaling. To be a Virginia-sired horse, a horse must be by a Virginia stallion registered with the fund.

For more information, contact the VTA at (540) 347-4313 or at www.vabred.org.

Washington

One percent of Washington's pari-mutuel handle (excluding revenues generated from the sale of Emerald Downs' signal to other tracks) is funneled into the northwestern state's Owner Bonus Program, while 1% of handle from exotic wagers (again, excluding revenues from the sale of Emerald Downs' signal) funds Washington's breeder awards program. However, a portion of both of these award programs is redirected to the state's major track, Emerald Downs (to the benefit of more than $1 million a year), to help keep the track afloat.

Owner awards are paid by Washington's racing commission and are based on a horse's earned portion of the purse for first- through fourth-place finishes in any pari-mutuel race in the state. Award amounts are determined on the basis of the funds available in the Owner Bonus Program versus the total amount earned by all Washington-breds (from first- to fourth-place finishes) to determine a factor. An individual owner's purse winnings (again, from first- to fourth-place finishes) are multiplied to this factor to come up with his or her bonus amount. Owner bonuses are calculated at the end of the year and are paid annually.

Breeder awards are distributed annually by the Washington Thoroughbred Breeders Association (WTBA). Although a horse must win to earn its breeder an award, all pari-mutuel races a horse competes in are eligible. Award amounts are also calculated by dividing the total breeder awards available by the total purses earned by winning Washington-breds. The resulting factor is then used to determine individual awards by multiplying it by the amounts an individual state-bred horse has made from wins to determine its breeder's award amount.

Washington's tracks must also offer at least one race a day for its state-bred horses.

To be considered a Washington-bred, a horse must simply be foaled in the state.

For more information, contact the Washington Thoroughbred Breeders Association at (253) 288-7878.

West Virginia

West Virginia's Thoroughbred Development Fund promotes the breeding of Thoroughbreds by providing breeder awards, purse supplements, and stakes races that are restricted to state-breds. In addition, West Virginia's participating racetracks must offer at least one race that is restricted to state-breds for every two days of racing.

Twenty-five percent of the Thoroughbred Development Fund is directed to owners' awards. Individual awards are based upon the ratio of a horse's earnings to the total amount earned by all West Virginia-breds. However, owners may not be awarded in excess of 35% of the horse's earnings in that year.

Breeders of West Virginia-breds receive 60% of the fund. Individual breeder awards are calculated in the same manner as owner awards, although a breeder cannot receive more from the fund than the horse earned in purses. Stallion owners receive 15% of the fund, and no individual stallion owner can receive from the fund an amount in excess of 35% of the stallion's offspring's earnings.

Owner, breeder, and stallion owner awards are only calculated on the first $100,000 of a race's purse. All awards are paid annually on February 15 for a horse's achievements the previous year.

To be considered a West Virginia-bred, a horse must be foaled in the state by a West Virginia resident. If not a resident, the horse may qualify if the breeder keeps his or her stock in the state year-round. If the breeder does not qualify under these provisions, a foal may still be considered a West Virginia-bred if its sire is a registered West Virginia stallion or its dam is bred back to a West Virginia stallion.

Contact the West Virginia Racing Commission at (304) 558-2150 for more information.

15

Breeding Your Own What Will It Cost?

So you've fallen in love with Thoroughbred racing and find the business of racing a fascinating, challenging endeavor. It is easy to see why. Thoroughbreds are beautiful animals, and owning one opens a new world full of excitement, along with a chance for financial rewards.

But you want to breed your own racehorse. You want the satisfaction of watching a horse produced from a mating that you planned, raised at a farm of your choice, and developed by your trainer, make it to the winner's circle. Some equate it to the rewards of raising a successful child, without the headaches of the teenage years.

Breeding your own racehorses has many rewarding aspects.

While the primary focus of this handbook is to provide an overview of owning racing horses (the subject of breeding racehorses deserves a guidebook of its own), we can give you an idea of the costs of raising your very own racehorse, from in utero to its first race. Once you have an idea of the time (you'll need to give yourself four years to see the fruits of your labor) and money involved (again, four years of boarding and training bills), you will know better whether developing a foal into a full-grown racehorse is for you.

Although generalizations in the complex world of Thoroughbred racing are difficult to make, we will illustrate the costs of breeding and raising one's own racehorse through a specific example of a horse bred, raised, and raced in Kentucky. As mentioned before in this book, costs vary from state to state, and your actual costs may differ from this example.

Mares and Stud Fees

To produce your own racehorse, you will need a broodmare. Enlist the services of a professional, reputable adviser when selecting your first mare, for she is going to be the foundation of your future racing stock. The breeding stock sales in the fall of the year offer many good mares, many of which are already in foal. Or, you could find a well-bred filly at the track that might turn into a quality broodmare once her racing days are over, if she has a good pedigree with a race record to match. (Many owners become involved with breeding this way when they retire their favorite race filly and decide to raise her foals.) Whatever your acquisition method, let us say that you have obtained a broodmare that is valued at $50,000.

What stallion do you breed her to? Once again, we encourage you to enlist the services of a professional to help you decide whom to breed to. If you board your mare at a reputable Thoroughbred farm, many times the farm manager can help you plan your mating and find a stud, especially the popular ones whose services are difficult to obtain. But how much should you spend? Stud fees widely vary, with fees ranging from a few hundred to several hundreds of thousands of dollars (or more!). An old rule of thumb in the Thoroughbred business is that the stud fee should cost anywhere from 25% to 35% of the value of the mare. If your mare is valued at $50,000, figure on spending about $12,500 to $15,000 for a suitable stud.

First Year Costs — Foal In Utero

For the first year, not counting the capital cost of the mare, you will need between $12,500 and $15,000 for the services of a stud. In this example, you have purchased a guaranteed live foal stud fee, which means that if your mare aborts or fails to produce a live foal, your stud fee will be refunded. The payment date of live foal stud fees varies, with some being due on September 1, some on November 1, and some due when the foal stands and nurses. In this example, your payment is due on September 1.

No-guarantee stud fees are also available and are less expensive than a guaranteed live foal fee, but if your mare fails to produce a live foal, you will be out your no-guarantee fee. However, if you do decide to purchase a no-guarantee stud fee, you can protect your investment by purchasing barrenness insurance. Barrenness insurance will cost about 25 percent of the stud fee, although it may be difficult to obtain.

Year One

Mare-in-Foal Costs

Stud Fee (Guaranteed Live Foal)	$15,000
Mare's Board	$9,125
Mare's Insurance	$2,500
Mare's Vet Care	$1,000
Mare's Farrier	$180
Mare's Dental	$60
Vanning (to and from stud)	$250

If you choose a guaranteed live foal stud fee, you will not have to add the cost of prospective foal insurance to your ledger. But you might want to insure the mare, especially if she represents a sizeable portion of your net worth. Figure insurance to run about 5% of the mare's value, or $2,500 in this case.

You will need to board your mare, which in this instance is being kept at a solid Kentucky farm at a cost of $25/day. While mares don't usually require the veterinary upkeep of a horse in training, they will need some routine prenatal care. Your mare may need shots to help her cycle and become in heat. She may not "take," or become pregnant, when first bred and have to be bred again. Even if she becomes in foal on her first cover, she will need to be palpated and scanned periodically to make sure that she is still carrying the foal. She also needs to be kept up-to-date with vaccines,

Coggins, and other routine vet work. Estimate an annual veterinary cost for your pregnant mare of about $1,000.

Her feet will also need to be trimmed (she's carrying excess weight, and like humans, her feet do spread) every 30-45 days, $20 each time. Her teeth will need to be floated once a year, which will cost about $60.

Finally, do not forget to figure the cost to van your mare back and forth to her date with your future foal's father. In Central Kentucky, this cost averages $125, and she may need to make the trip twice before becoming pregnant. If you are shipping your mare out-of-state to be bred, increase this figure substantially.

As your dreams for your future foal expand along with the size of your mare, be prepared to spend about $13,000 plus the stud fee during your first year of "foal growing," excluding the cost of the mare.

Year Two — A Foal Arrives

Your patience as a breeder is rewarded in year two by the arrival of a healthy foal. In this example, your mare was bred last year in May and produces a gorgeous chestnut filly the beginning of April. Thankfully, foaling costs are much less than hospital costs for human births – they average only about $100, assuming no complications. Let us assume you wish to insure your new filly. Insurance rates vary for foals, depending upon whether the foal is insured after 24 hours, after 30 days, or after 90 days. Being this is your first foal, and you wish to protect your investment, you decide to insure her as soon as you can – or 24 hours after birth. Such insurance will cost about 5% of the baby's value. In this instance, we've valued this filly foal based upon the stud fee to produce it, or $15,000, so an insurance policy to cover her first year will cost $750.

You will still be paying the $25/day board for the

Year Two	
Keeping a Baby	
Mare Board ($25/day)	$9,125
Mare Insurance	$2,500
Mare Care (Vet, Farrier, Dental)	$1,240
Foaling Cost	$100
Foal Board (April-Aug., $6/day)	$900
Weanling Board (Sept.-Dec., $25/day)	$3,000
Foal Insurance	$750
Weanling Care (Vet & Farrier)	$370
Total	**$17,985**

mare, plus an extra $6 a day for your filly. For now, mare and foal live a simple life on the farm, enjoying the company of other mares and babies, warm sunshine, and plenty of space to kick up their heels. About five (or six) months later, about September 1, the foals are weaned from their mothers and are turned out with other weanlings. The cost to board a weanling is the same as to board a mare, about $25 day – now you are paying to board two horses.

Like all horses, weanlings need some routine vet care, including a series of vaccines to immunize them from disease. You've been blessed with a healthy filly, one that remains free from respiratory infections and the dreaded foal scours (diarrhea). This good fortune is reflected in your vet bill, which only amounts to $250 annually. Your weanling's feet will need to be trimmed regularly for an annual cost of about $120.

In this example we will continue to figure the cost of keeping the mare throughout year two, but will not in years three and four as we are illustrating the costs to raise one foal. If you think you like the breeding business and want to continue producing foals, you then need to add another stud fee and related costs in year two.

Year Three — Your First Yearling

On January 1, the universal birthday for all Thoroughbred racehorses, your foal turns one. She is now officially a yearling, although her first birthday will not occur for three more months.

The yearling year can test the patience of owners used to the action of the racetrack. Board bills of $25/day continue to mount. You continue to outlay cash with no opportunities for income on the horizon, unless you decide that breeding to race is not for you, and you choose to enter your yearling in one of the summer or fall sales.

But if you decide not to sell your young horse, you will soon be able to witness (if you choose) your youngster receiving its first lessons under saddle in autumn. Most yearlings are "broken" (a misnomer, most sessions are a cooperative venture between rider and horse) sometime between August and October, when they learn to accept a saddle, bridle, and rider. These early lessons can be done at a farm or training center, depending upon if your farm has the facilities and personnel for such work. Either way, figure that such schooling will add an extra $15 to your daily board bill, as the rates to break a yearling average about $40/day.

About November, after learning how to behave with a rider aboard, your yearling will be released from school to enjoy the last two months of the year turned out in pastures. Your board bill will drop

> **Year Three**
> **Yearling Costs**
> Yearling Board, Jan.-Aug. ($25/day)........ $6,000
> Yearling Breaking & Training $2,400
>   (Sept.-Oct., $40/day)
> Yearling Board, Nov.-Dec. ($25/day) $1,500
> Insurance $428
> Routine Vet Work $250
> Routine Farrier Work $180
> **Total .... $ 10,758**

back down to $25/day (just in time for your holiday shopping), although you will need to prepare for your horse's serious training, which will begin after the first of the year.

As a yearling, your filly will still need routine veterinary care and farrier work throughout the year. And you may wish to continue insurance coverage to protect your investment. Thankfully, insurance rates for yearlings drop to about 2.85% of their estimated value.

Year Four — Off to the Track

In your fourth year of raising a racehorse, your patience is rewarded by seeing a horse that you bred and raised finally make it to the races.

But that is six months away.

Once again, in January, your horse will celebrate a birthday – you are now the proud owner of a two-year-old. This is the year you will have the pleasure of watching your youngster grow into a racehorse.

After one final month of frolic on the farm, you ship your filly to a nearby training center in February to begin school again. The training center is where the horse will learn how to gallop on the racetrack, how to train with other youngsters, how to work at speed, and how to break from the gate. Her fitness will gradually increase as she learns these lessons, and she will start to become accustomed to the daily rhythms of being in training. Although not as expensive as life at the track, life at the training center will cost about $50/day.

Now that your filly is in training, she will need regular farrier and veterinary care. Figure on your horse being shod every month for about $100 each time. Barring any prolonged injury or illness, your horse should only need routine vet work, at an approximate cost of $150/month.

After about 60 days at the training center, your filly is sufficiently "legged up" to try life at the track. So in May, you make arrangements for your two-year-old to join the racing world and ship her off to your trainer at the track. Do not forget to figure in the cost of shipping. We've allocated $250 in this example, but this figure can vary depending upon how far your horse is traveling to the track.

Young horses need time to adjust to real race training, for they are now experiencing life in the bustling big city. Hundreds of horses make their daily pilgrimage to the track, while a constant stream of horses whiz past as they backtrack along the outside rail in preparation for their daily exercise. It is confusing, exciting, and somewhat intimidating to a young horse, and it needs time to adjust. It also needs time to increase its fitness in preparation for its first start.

Training, vet, and farrier costs continue. As your filly is now in training at the track, her daily upkeep will increase to $65/day. Vet costs vary, depending upon your horse's health and your trainer's philosophy. As young horses are more susceptible to colds and coughs, we've now budgeted $250 a month for vet costs while at the track. Allocate about $125 every month now to shoe your horse. Your horse's teeth will also need to now be floated about twice a year, for an annual cost of $120. And you'll probably want to continue your insurance coverage, although you should discuss with your insurance agent what value to place on your filly. If you

---

Year Four

Two-Year-Old Costs

Farm Board (Jan., $25/day)	$750
Training Center Board (Feb.-March, $50/day)	$3000
Vet Care (Feb.-March, $150/month)	$300
Farrier (Feb.-March, $100/month)	$200
Vanning to Training Center	$100
Training Costs at the Track (April-Dec., $65/day	$17,550
Vet Costs @ the Track ($250/mo)	$2,250
Farrier Costs @ the Track ($125/mo)	$1,125
Vanning to Racetrack	$250
Insurance	$1,063
Total	**$26,588**

want to cover some of the training expenses you've invested in her, you could probably increase the filly's insured value to $25,000. As rates for fillies in race training average around 4.25 percent of their estimated value, your annual premium will cost about $1,063.

While you may eagerly point out an upcoming two-year-old race in the condition book, do not pressure your trainer into running your youngster before she is ready. Although the prospect of a purse is surely enticing (especially in light of the $65-plus/day training fee), don't get impatient now. You have spent more than three years getting to this point, so take the time needed to make sure your horse is ready for its first race, both mentally and physically.

If all goes well, and your horse doesn't buck shins, develop a cold, or pop a splint, she may be ready to make her first start in late spring or early summer. In this example, your trainer has spotted a race for your filly in June that will be run at the same track where she has been training. Do not plan on using any purse money from this first race to pay your training bill, though. Many times a horse needs a race under its girth before performing at its best. But if all goes well and your horse comes out of the

Total Cost From In Utero to In Training	
Year One	$28,115
Year Two	$17,985
Year Three	$10,758
Year Four	$26,588
Total Cost	**$83,446**

race sound and healthy, you may get four or five starts out of her before the end of the year and begin to recoup some of the thousands you've invested.

In the example we have outlined in these pages, more than $80,000 was spent over four years to take a horse from conception to the track. This was for a horse that remained free from illness and injury. Over $56,000 was spent in the first three years, while the opportunity to recoup some of this money occurred only in the last six months of the fourth year. Granted, years five, six, and seven could be quite profitable if the filly has talent and stays sound, but as you can see, to breed one's own racehorse takes lots of patience, not to mention a healthy pocketbook.

However, the excitement of watching a horse that you bred and developed make it to the races and run is indescribable, especially when you run to greet her in the winner's circle. There is nothing in this world quite like it – and it can make all those years of check writing quite worthwhile.

16

The Final Owner

In the relatively short history of the Thoroughbred (a little more than 300 years), only 40 to 50 generations of racehorses have been produced. The alchemy of creating the classic horse is an imperfect science with many excuses for failure and an equal number of theories about how to succeed. The fact is the racehorse has changed little, if we measure success by stopwatch timings. They have improved only marginally over the past 70 years, and some of that improvement is coming from more accurate timing devices.

The wonder of Thoroughbred racehorses, and the quality that draws us to them, is their genetic need to run as far and as fast as they can. Like all great athletes, they are prone to injury – in fact, especially prone. When they are competing, more than 1,000 pounds of muscle and bone land jarringly on spindly front legs 120 times every quarter of a mile. They tell us about their injuries by the manner in which they eat, walk, gallop, and respond to human handling.

So the owner must be a vigilant monitor of the horse's condition. Once the physical signs of deterioration show up, decisive action must be taken. The question the owner must now face when, sadly, the horse's career is threatened by serious injury is: what do we do? It is particularly difficult when the horse is unfit for breeding. Experienced owners often have people willing to give the horse a home where it may be used as a riding or pleasure horse after six months or so of recuperation and retraining.

For those who own farms as well as Thoroughbreds, the question of maintaining an injured horse is the decision to provide food and pasture. A large majority of owners do not have that luxury. A minimum fee for care at a boarding farm is between $12 and $20 a day. Given a life expectancy of 15 to 20 more years after its brief racing career, a retired racehorse becomes a major expense.

An alternative is to donate your horse to one of the non-profit organizations that will either retrain and place it with a new owner or board it for the remainder of its life. Please visit www.toba.org for a state-by-state lising of adoption agenices. As an owner you have a responsibility to find a good home for your horse once its racing career is done.

An important note: There is an unexpected black market in retired racehorses. It can happen that the horse you think you have retired and given or sold to a private individual is resold, either for slaughter, for a cruel practice known as "hormone milking" (in the case of broodmares) for Premarin, or, strangely enough, for continued racing at tracks elsewhere. If you do not personally know the individual to whom you are transferring your horse, check him or her out. In the case of continued racing black market, there is a prescribed and workable solution: If you know your horse is no longer fit for racing or race breeding and want to ensure that it *is* retired, return the horse's Certificate of Foal Registration to The Jockey Club with an accompanying notation that the horse was transferred, or sold, "without pedigree" (Thoroughbreds cannot be raced or bred to produce foals without their pedigree papers). This notation must state the date the horse was transferred and must be signed by the owner or the owner's authorized agent. For a Report of Sold Without Pedigree form, contact The Jockey Club at (800) 444-8521.

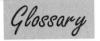

Glossary

action: 1) A horse's manner of moving or way of going. 2) A term meaning wagering: "The horse had a lot of action."

added money: Money added to the purse of a race either by the racing association, a breeding or other type fund, or by the amount paid by owners in nomination, eligibility, entry, and starting fees.

age: All Thoroughbreds are deemed a year older on January 1 of every year.

agent: An individual authorized to 1) transact business for a stable owner, trainer, jockey, etc.; or 2) to sell or buy horses on behalf of another.

allowance race: A race, other than claiming or stakes, for which entry is limited to those horses that satisfy specific conditions established by the racing secretary.

also-eligible: A horse officially entered for a race but not permitted to start unless the field is reduced in size by a scratch to below a specified number, usually that number considered safe to compete.

also ran: A horse who finishes out of the top three places.

anhydrosis: The inability to sweat in response to work output or increases in body temperature; a "non-sweater."

apprentice: A new jockey or one who has not ridden a specified number of winners within an established period of time. Also known as a "bug," referring to the asterisk following the jockey's name or weight.

apprentice allowance: A weight concession given to an apprentice rider. Usually the allowance is five pounds.

arthroscope: A device used for viewing structures inside a joint. The device is used to perform arthroscopic surgery and eliminates the need to open the joint with a large incision.

back at the knee: A leg that looks like it has a backward arc, with the center of the arc at the knee when viewed from the side.

backside: The areas of a racetrack where the stable area, dormitories, track kitchen, chapel, and recreation area for stable employees are generally located. Also known as "backstretch."

backstretch: 1) Straight portion of the far side of the racing surface between the turns; or, 2) See "backside."

bandages: Wrappings used on a horse's legs to protect them from injury or to provide support to the legs.

barren: Used to describe a filly or mare that was bred but did not conceive during a stated breeding season.

bar shoe: A horseshoe closed at the back to help support the frog and heel of the foot. It is often worn by horses with quarter cracks or bruised feet.

bay: A term to describe the color of a horse that varies from a yellow-tan to a dark brown. The mane, tail, and lower portion of the legs are always black, unless white markings are present.

bearing in/out: Deviating from a straight course, in relationship to the rail, often due to fatigue, inexperience, physical distress, or fault of the jockey.

bit: A stainless steel, rubber, or aluminum bar attached to the bridle which fits in the horse's mouth, providing one of the means by which a jockey exerts guidance and control.

black: A term to describe the color of a horse. The entire coat is black, including the muzzle, the flanks, mane, tail, and legs, unless white markings are present.

black type: Boldface type used in sales catalogs to distinguish horses that have won (upper case) or placed in a stakes race. In accordance with the International Cataloguing Standards Committee, all black-type races are stakes races, but not all stakes races qualify for black type.

blanket finish: Horses finishing so closely together a single blanket could cover them.

bleeder: The term commonly used to describe exercise-induced pulmonary hemorrhage (EIPH). A horse that bleeds internally or through the nostrils during or after a workout or race due to ruptured blood vessels. The condition is often evidenced by the horse stopping or slowing suddenly.

blinkers: A cup-shaped device designed to restrict a horse's lateral vision to prevent swerving or erratic running.

blister: A counter-irritant administered to ease pain or to treat an ailment.

bloodstock agent: A person who advises and/or represents the buyer or seller of Thoroughbreds at public auction or private sale.

blood-typing: A means to verify a horse's parentage. Blood-typing is usually completed within the first year of a horse's life and is required before The Jockey Club will issue registration papers.

blow-out: A short, timed workout, usually three-eighths or a half-mile in distance, given a day or two before a race to sharpen a horse's speed.

bobble: A bad step away from the starting gate, usually caused by the track surface breaking away under a horse's hooves, causing the horse to duck its head or nearly go to its knees.

bog spavin: A condition marked by puffy swelling on the inside and slightly in front of the hock, usually caused by overwork or strain.

bolt: The sudden veering from a straight course, usually toward the outside rail.

book: 1) The group of mares bred to a stallion in a given year. If a stallion attracts the maximum number of mares allowed by the farm manager, he is said to have a "full book." 2) A term used to describe a jockey's riding commitments with his agent: "An agent handles a jockey's book."

bottom line: A Thoroughbred's breeding or pedigree on the female side; the lower half of an extended pedigree diagram.

bowed tendon: A type of tendonitis. The most common injury to the tendon is a strain or "bowed" tendon, so named because of the appearance of a bow shape due to swelling.

brace (or bracer): Rubdown liniment used on a horse after a race or workout.

break: 1) To train a young horse, usually beginning late in its yearling year, to wear a bridle and saddle, carry a rider, and to respond to a rider's commands. 2) To leave from the starting gate.

breakdown: When a horse suffers a potentially career-ending injury, usually to the leg: "The horse suffered a breakdown." "The horse broke down."

bred: A horse is considered to have been bred in the state or country of its birth: "Secretariat was a Virginia-bred."

breeze (breezing): To work a horse at a moderate speed.

bridle: A piece of equipment, usually made of leather or nylon, which fits on a horse's head and to which the bit and reins are attached.

broodmare: A filly or mare that has been bred or has produced foals.

bucked shins: Painful inflammation of the front of the cannon bones to which young horses are particularly susceptible, usually due to stress.

bug boy: An apprentice rider; see "apprentice."

bullet (work): The best workout time for a particular distance on a given day at a track. Also known as a "black-letter" work in some places.

bursa: A sac of lubricant fluid that pads, cushions, and facilitates motion between soft tissue and bones, often where tendons and bones meet.

bursitis: Inflammation of the bursa due to excess fluid.

bute: Short for phenylbutazone, a non-steroidal anti-inflammatory medication that is legal in many racing jurisdictions.

buy-back: A horse put through a public auction that did not reach a minimum (reserve) price set by the consignor and so was retained by the consignor. Often referred to as RNA (reserve not attained).

calk (caulk): A projection on the heels of a horseshoe, similar to a cleat, on the rear shoes of a horse to prevent slipping, especially on a wet track. Also known as a "sticker." See "mud calks."

cannon bone: The largest bone between the knee and ankle joints in the front of the leg.

capped hock/elbow: Inflammation of the bursa often due to hitting the area. If at the elbow, also referred to as a "shoe boil."

cast: To have rolled into a wall or fence in such a way as to prevent the horse from getting up.

chalk: Wagering favorite in a race.

chart: A statistical picture of a race (from which past performances are compiled), that shows the position and margin of each horse at designated points of call (depending on the distance of the race), as well as the horse's age, weight carried, owner, trainer, jockey, and the race's purse, conditions, payoff prices, odds, time, and other data.

check(ed): When a jockey slows a horse and changes its stride due to other horses impeding its progress.

chestnut: 1) A term to describe the color of a horse that varies from a red-yellow to golden yellow. The mane, tail, and legs are usually variations of coat color, unless white markings are present. 2) Horn-like, irregular growths found on the inside of the legs. On the forelegs, they are just above the knees. On the hind legs, they are just below the hocks. No two horses have been found to have the same chestnuts, so they may be used for identification. Also called "night eyes."

chute: Extension of backstretch or homestretch to permit a straight running start in a race as opposed to starting on or near a turn.

claiming: Process by which a licensed person may purchase a horse entered in a designated race for predetermined price. When a horse has been claimed, its new owner usually assumes title after the starting gate opens, although the former owner is entitled to all purse money earned in that race. Claiming rules vary from state to state.

claim box: Box in which claims are deposited before the race.

claiming race: A race in which each horse entered is eligible to be purchased at a set price. Claims must be made before the race and only by licensed owners or their agents who have a horse registered to race at that meeting or who have received a claim certificate from the stewards.

classic: 1) A race of traditional importance. 2) Used to describe a distance: The American classic distance is currently 1 1/4 miles; the European classic distance is 1 1/2 miles.

clerk of scales: An official whose chief duty is to weigh the riders before and after a race to ensure proper weight has been carried.

climbing: When a horse lifts its front legs abnormally high as it gallops, causing it to run inefficiently.

clocker: One who times workouts and races.

closed knees: A condition in which the cartilaginous growth plate above the knee (distal radial physis) has turned to bone. Indicates completion of long bone growth and is one sign of maturity.

clubhouse turn: Generally the turn on a racing oval that is closest to the clubhouse facility; usually the first turn after the finish line.

colic: Abdominal pain. It can range from mild stomach upset to more severe cases, such as a twisted intestine, that require surgery.

colt: An ungelded (entire) male horse 4 years old or younger.

condition book(s): A series of booklets issued by a racing secretary that set forth conditions of races to be run at a particular racetrack.

conditions: The requirements of a particular race. This may include age, sex, money or races won, weight carried, and the distance of the race.

cooling out: Restoring a horse to normal temperature, usually by walking, after a race or other exercise.

cover: A single breeding of a stallion to a mare: "He covered 70 mares." Referred to as "last service date" in sales catalogues.

cow hocks: Abnormal conformation in which the points of the hock turn in.

cribber: An undesirable behavior describing a horse that clings to objects with its teeth and sucks air into its stomach; can be controlled. Also known as a "wind sucker."

crop: 1) The number of foals by a sire in a given year. 2) A group of horses born in the same year: "An average crop of 3-year-olds." 3) A jockey's whip.

cuppy (track): A dry and loose racing surface that breaks into clods and shows distinct hoofprints.

curbs: The swelling and thickening of the ligament or tendon at the lower part of the hock.

cushion: The loose, top portion of the racing surface on a dirt track.

dam: The female parent of a foal.

dam's sire (broodmare sire): The sire of a broodmare. Used in reference to the maternal grandsire of a foal.

dark bay or brown: A term to describe the color of a horse that ranges from brown (with areas of tan on the shoulders, head, and flanks) to a dark brown (with tan areas seen only in the flanks and/or muzzle). The mane, tail, and lower portions of the legs are always black, unless white markings are present.

dead track: Racing surface lacking resiliency.

declare: See "scratch."

deep: A racing surface recently harrowed or to which extra topsoil has been added, increasing holding qualities.

Derby: A stakes event for 3-year-olds.

distaffer: A female horse.

distanced: Well-beaten; finishing a great distance behind the winner.

dogs: Rubber traffic cones (or a wooden barrier) placed at certain distances out from the inner rail when the track is wet, muddy, soft, yielding, or heavy to prevent horses during the workout period from churning the footing along the rail. Used in the phrase: "The dogs are up," or simply, "dogs up."

driving: A horse that is all out to win and under strong urging from its jockey.

drop(ped) down: A horse meeting a lower class of competitors than it had been running against in previous races.

eased: A horse that is gently pulled up during a race. The jockey decides that his horse is hopelessly beaten and allows the horse to gallop to the finish under no pressure.

Eclipse Award: Thoroughbred racing's year-end awards honoring the top horses and people in several categories. They honor the great 18th century racehorse and sire Eclipse, who was undefeated in 18 career starts and sired the winners of 344 races. Any Eclipse Award winner is referred to as a "champion."

endoscope: An instrument used for direct visual inspection of a hollow organ or body cavity such as the upper airway or stomach. A fiberoptic endoscope is a long, flexible tube that has a series of lenses and light at the end to allow the veterinarian to view and photograph the respiratory system through the airway. Other internal organs may be viewed through a tiny surgical opening. A video endoscope has a small camera at the tip of the instrument.

entry fee: Money paid by an owner to enter a horse in a stakes race or sale.

exercise rider: Rider who is licensed to exercise a horse during its morning training session.

far turn: The turn located to the race viewer's left that horses enter from the backstretch.

far side: The right side of the horse. Also called the "offside."

farrier: Horseshoer, blacksmith. Also called a "plater."

fast (track): Racing surface of a dirt track that is dry, even, and resilient.

fetlock (joint): Joint between the cannon bone and the long pastern bone. Also referred to as the "ankle."

field: The horses in a race or a betting combination.

filly: Female horse 4 years old or younger.

firing: See "pin firing."

firm (track): The condition of a turf course corresponding to fast on a dirt track. A firm, resilient surface.

flag: Signal manually held a short distance in front of the gate at the exact starting point of a race. Official timing starts when flag is dropped by the "flagman" to denote proper start.

flatten out: A very tired horse that slows considerably, dropping its head on a straight line with its body. Some horses, however, like to run with their heads lowered.

float: 1) An equine dental procedure in which sharp points of the teeth are filed down. 2) The instrument with which the aforementioned procedure is performed.

foal(ed): 1) A horse of either sex in its first year of life. 2) As a verb, to give birth; also known as "dropped." 3) Can also denote the offspring of either a male or female parent: "She is the last foal by Secretariat."

founder: See "laminitis."

free handicap: A race in which no nomination fee is required. More recently and commonly, a ranking of horses by weight for a theoretical race.

frog: The V-shaped, pliable support structure on the bottom of the foot.

frozen: A track surface that is frozen as a result of sustained low temperatures.

furlong: One-eighth of a mile; 220 yards; 660 feet.

furosemide: A medication used in the treatment of bleeders, commonly known under the trade name Salix® (formerly Lasix), which acts as a diuretic, reducing pressure on the capillaries.

futurity: A race for 2-year-olds in which the owners make a continuous series of payments over a period of time to keep their horses eligible. Purses for these races vary, but can be considerable.

gallop: A morning workout during which the horse is running at a pace that ranges from slow to moderately fast. Less strenuous than a work.

gap: An opening in the rail where horses enter and leave the racecourse.

gate card: A card, issued by the starter, stating that a horse is properly schooled in starting gate procedures.

gelding: A male horse of any age that has been neutered by having both testicles removed (gelded).

girth: An elastic and leather band, sometimes covered with sheepskin, which passes under a horse's belly and is connected to both sides of the saddle to keep the saddle in place.

good (track): A dirt track that is almost fast.

graded race: Established in 1973, a classification of select stakes races, denoted by Roman numerals I, II, and III with grade I being the highest quality. These races must meet certain criteria and are graded based upon quality by the American Graded Stakes Committee. Capitalized when used in race title (the Grade I Kentucky Derby). See "group race."

gravel: Infection of the hoof resulting from a crack or bruise in the sole usually requiring rest.

gray: A term to describe the color of a horse whose coat is primarily a mixture of black and white hairs. The mane, tail, and legs may be either black or gray, unless white markings are present. Starting with foals of 1993, the color classifications gray and roan were combined as "roan or gray." See "roan."

groom: A person who cares for a horse in a stable. Known as a "lad" or "girl" in Britain.

group race: Established in 1971 by racing organizations in Britain, France, Germany, and Italy to classify select stakes races outside North America. Collectively called "pattern races." Equivalent to American graded races. Always denoted with Arabic numerals 1, 2, or 3. Capitalized when used in race title (the Group 1 Epsom Derby). See "graded race."

half brother, half sister: Horses out of the same dam, but by different sires. Horses with the same sire and different dams are not considered half siblings in Thoroughbred racing.

halter: 1) Like a bridle, but lacking a bit. Used in handling horses around the stable and when they are not being ridden. 2) As a verb, "to halter": generic term meaning to claim a horse.

hand: Four inches. A horse's height is measured in hands and inches from the top of the shoulder (withers) to the ground, e.g., 15.2 hands is 15 hands, 2 inches. Thoroughbreds typically range from 15 to 17 hands.

hand ride: Urging a horse with the hands and not using the whip.

handicap: 1) Race for which the racing secretary assigns the weights to be carried based upon an assessment of the horse's past performances. 2) To make selections on the basis of past performances.

handily: 1) In a workout, when a horse is being asked for speed by his rider. 2) In reference to a race, when the winner is well in command through the final furlong.

hard (track): A condition of a turf course in which there is no resiliency to the surface.

heavy (track): Wettest possible condition of a turf course; not usually found in North America.

high weight: Highest weight assigned or carried in a race.

hock: The large joint above the shinbone in the rear leg. Corresponds to the knee in the front leg.

horse: When reference is made to gender, a "horse" is an ungelded male 5 years old or older.

horsing: Behavior of a mare in heat (in season).

hot walker: Person who walks horses to cool them out after a workout or race.

hung: A horse that does not advance its position in a race when urged by its jockey.

icing: When a horse is stood in a tub of ice or ice packs are applied to the legs to reduce inflammation and/or swelling.

impaction: A type of colic caused by a blockage of the intestines by ingested materials (constipation).

in hand: Running under moderate control, at less than top speed.

irons: Slang for stirrups.

jail: Refers to the period of time following a claim when the claimed horse, which next runs in a claiming race, must run for a price higher than the price at which it was claimed. Commonly used in the phrase: "The horse is in (out of) jail."

jog: Slow, easy gait.

juvenile: 2-year-old horse.

lame: A deviation from a normal gait due to pain in a limb or its supporting structures.

laminitis: An inflammation of the sensitive laminae, which connect the inside of the foot to the hoof wall. Many factors are involved and many events can cause laminitis, including ingesting toxic levels of grain, eating lush grass, high temperature, excessive weight-bearing that occurs when the opposite limb in injured, and the administration of some drugs. Laminitis usually manifests itself in the front feet, develops rapidly, and is life-threatening. Also referred to as "founder."

Lasix: See "furosemide."

lead [LED]: Lead weights carried in pockets on both sides of the saddle, used to make up the difference between the actual weight of the jockey and the weight the horse has been assigned to carry during the race.

lead [LEED]: 1) See "shank." 2) The front leg that is last to hit the ground during a gallop or canter. A horse usually leads with its inside leg around a turn and with its outside leg on straightaways.

leg up: 1) To help a jockey mount a horse. 2) A jockey having a mount.

length: A measurement approximating the length of a horse (eight to 10 feet) used to denote a distance between horses in a race.

listed race: A stakes race just below a graded or group race in quality.

lug (in or out): See "bearing in (out)."

lunge: 1) A horse rearing and plunging. 2) A method of exercising a horse by working it in a circle on a long line.

maiden: 1) A horse or rider that has not won a race. 2) A female that has never been bred.

maiden race: A race for non-winners.

maiden special weight race: A race for horses that have never won. Most horses begin their careers competing in this type of race.

mare: Female horse 5 years old or older.

mash: Soft, moist mixture, either hot or cold, of grains and other feeds that are easily digested.

medication list: A list kept by the track veterinarian and published by the track and *Daily Racing Form* (when provided by track officials) showing which horses have been treated with legally prescribed medications.

middle distance: Broadly, from one mile to 1 1/8 miles.

morning glory: Horse that performs well in morning workouts, but fails to reproduce that form in races.

mud calks (caulks): Horseshoes with cleats or "stickers" to provide better traction on sloppy or muddy tracks.

muddy (track): A condition of a racetrack that is wet, whose base has been permeated by moisture, but has no standing water.

muzzle: 1) Nose and lips of a horse. 2) A guard placed over a horse's mouth to prevent it from biting or eating.

navicular disease: A disease of the navicular bone of the front feet. In most cases, it ends a racing career.

near side: The left side of the horse. Side on which the rider mounts the horse. Opposite of "far side."

neurectomy: A surgical procedure in which the nerve supply to the navicular area is removed. The toe and remainder of the foot have feeling. Also referred to as "posterior digital neurectomy" or "heel nerve." Also known as "nerving."

night eyes: See "chestnuts."

non-sweater: See "anhydrosis."

nose: Smallest advantage by which a horse can win. Called a "short head" in Britain.

nose band: A leather strap that goes over the bridge of a horse's nose to help secure the bridle. A "figure eight" nose band goes over the bridge of the nose and under the rings of the bit to help keep the horse's mouth closed. This keeps the tongue from sliding up over the bit, providing more control, and is used on horses that do not like having a tongue tie used.

Oaks: A stakes event for 3-year-old fillies (females).

OCD lesion: A cartilaginous or bony lesion that is the result of a failure in development.

on the bit: When a horse is eager to run. Also known as "in the bridle."

open knee: Reverse condition of closed knee, often found in young horses, indicating an immature knee. See "closed knee."

osselet: Bony growth on the fetlock or ankle joint, initially due to increased joint fluid, which causes the joint capsule to swell, later resulting in calcium deposits at this joint.

over at the knee: A leg that when viewed from the side looks like it has a forward arc with its center at the knee.

overgirth: An elastic band that goes completely around a horse, over the saddle, to keep the saddle from slipping.

overnight: A sheet published by the racing secretary's office listing the entries for an upcoming racing card.

overnight race: A race in which entries close a specific number of hours before running (such as 48 hours), as opposed to a stakes race for which nominations close weeks and sometimes months in advance.

paddock: The area where horses are saddled and paraded before being taken onto the track for a race. Also used on a farm for "schooling."

paddock judge: The racing official responsible for overseeing pre-race activities in the paddock.

Glossary

past performances: A horse's racing record, earnings, bloodlines, and other data presented in composite form.

pastern (bones): Denotes the area between the fetlock joint and the hoof.

patrol judge(s): An assistant to the stewards. This official observes the progress of a race from various vantage points around the track to watch for infractions and fouls.

pill: Small numbered ball used in a blind draw to decide post positions.

pin firing: Applying a searing instrument, hot iron or electric needle, to an injured portion of the leg to promote healing of the injury or problem.

pinhooker: A person who buys a horse, usually a weanling or yearling, with the specific intention of re-selling it for a profit.

place: Second position at finish.

placing judge: An official who posts the order of finish in a race.

plate(s): A generic term for lightweight, (usually) aluminum horseshoes used during a race.

plater: A generic term for a claiming horse.

pole(s): Markers at measured distances around the track designating the distance from the finish. The quarter pole, for instance, is a quarter of a mile from the finish, not from the start.

poll: The top of the head between the ears.

post: 1) Starting point for a race. 2) An abbreviated version of post position: "He drew post four." 3) As a verb, to record a win: "He's posted 10 wins in 14 starts."

post time: Designated time for a race to start.

preferred list: A list of horses with prior rights to starting in a race, usually because they have previously been entered in races that have not filled with the minimum number of starters.

purse: The total money distributed after a race to the owners of the entrants who have finished in the (usually) top four or five positions.

quarter crack: A crack in the hoof between the toe and heel, usually extending into the coronary band.

quarter pole: A marker one quarter of a mile from the finish.

rabbit: A speed horse running as an entry with another, usually a come-from-behind horse. The rabbit is expected to set a fast pace to help the chances of its stablemate.

racing secretary: An official who drafts conditions of races and assigns weights for handicap events.

rank: A term to describe a horse that refuses to settle under a jockey's handling in a race, running in a headstrong manner without respect to pace.

receiving barn: Structure used by horses shipping in for a race who do not have a stall at the racetrack.

refuse: When a horse will not break from the gate.

reserve: A minimum price, set by the consignor, for a horse in a public auction: "The horse did not reach its reserve."

ridden out: A term to describe a horse that finishes a race under mild urging; not as severe as driving.

ridgling: A horse in which one or both testicles are undescended.

roan: A term to describe the color of a horse whose coat is mostly a mixture of red and white or brown and white hairs. The mane, tail, and legs may be black, chestnut, or roan, unless white markings are present. Starting with foals of 1993, the color classifications roan and gray were combined as "roan or gray." See "gray."

roaring (laryngeal hemiplegia): A whistling sound made by a horse during inhalation while exercising.

rogue: An ill-tempered horse.

route: Broadly, a race distance of longer than 1 1/8 miles.

run-downs: Abrasions of the fetlocks. The result of weak hind pasterns, causing a horse to hit and scrape its fetlocks during a race or workout.

run-down bandages: Bandages on the hind legs, often with pads, to prevent run-downs.

run-out bit: A special type of bit to prevent a horse from bearing out (or in).

scale of weights: Fixed weights to be carried by horses according to their age, sex, race distance, and time of year.

schooling: Process of familiarizing a horse with the starting gate and teaching it racing practices. A horse may also be schooled in the paddock. In steeple-chasing, to teach a horse to jump.

scratch: To withdraw a horse from a race before it starts. Trainers usually scratch horses due to adverse track conditions or a horse's poor health. A veterinarian can scratch a horse at any time.

second call: A secondary mount of a jockey in a race in the event his primary mount is scratched.

sesamoid bones: Two small bones (medial and lateral sesamoids) located above and at the back of the fetlock joint.

sesamoid fracture: Fractures of the sesamoid bone ranging from small chips to the entire bone. Surgical repair is often arthroscopic.

set: A group of horses being exercised together.

set down: 1) A suspension: "The jockey was set down five days for careless riding." 2) When a jockey assumes a lower position in the saddle while urging the horse to pick up speed: "The horse was set down for the drive to the wire."

sex allowance: Female horses (fillies and mares), according to their age and the time of year, are allowed to carry three to five pounds less when meeting males.

shadow roll: A roll, usually of sheepskin, that is secured over the bridge of a horse's nose to keep it from seeing shadows on the track and shying from or jumping them.

shank: A rope or strap attached to a halter or bridle by which a horse is led.

shed row: The stable area. A row of barns.

short: A horse in need of more work or racing to reach winning form.

show: Third position at the finish.

silks: The distinct colored jacket and cap jockeys wear in a race designating the owner of the horse.

sire: 1) The male parent. 2) To beget foals.

slipped: A mare that has aborted a fetus after being pronounced in-foal.

sloppy (track): A racing strip that is saturated with water; standing water is visible; however, the base is still solid.

slow (track): A racing strip that is wet on both the surface and base and is beginning to dry out.

soft (track): Condition of a turf course with a large amount of moisture. Horses sink very deeply into it, causing flying divots.

sound: A term to describe a horse that is free from injury. Opposite of lame.

speedy cut: Injury to the inside of the knee or hock caused by a strike from another foot.

spit box: A generic term for test barn. See "test barn."

spit the bit: A term referring to a tired horse that begins to run less aggressively, backing off on the "pull" a rider normally feels on the reins from an eager horse.

splint: 1) Either of the two small bones that lie along the sides of the cannon bone. 2) The condition where calcification occurs on the splint bone causing a bump. This can result from a fracture or other irritation to the splint bone. A common injury is a popped splint.

stakes race: A race in which the owner usually must pay a fee to run a horse. The fees can be for nominating, maintaining eligibility, entering and starting, to which the track adds more money to make up the total purse. Some stakes races are by invitation and require no payment or fee.

stakes-placed: Finished second or third in a stakes race.

stakes-horse: A horse whose level of competition includes mostly stakes races.

stallion/stud: A male horse used for breeding.

stallion season: The right to breed one mare to a particular stallion during one breeding season.

stallion share: A percentage of ownership, which entitles the owner a lifetime breeding right to a stallion, one mare per season per share.

stall walker: A horse that moves about its stall constantly and frets rather than rests.

star: 1) A type of credit a horse receives from the racing secretary if it is excluded from an over-filled race, giving it priority in entering future races. 2) A white marking on the forehead of a horse.

starter race: An allowance or handicap race restricted to horses that have started for a specific claiming price or less.

stayer: A horse that can race long distances.

steadied: A horse being taken in hand by its rider, usually because of being in close quarters, often resulting in being thrown off stride momentarily.

step up: A horse moving up in class to meet better competition.

stewards: Officials of the race meeting responsible for enforcing the rules of racing.

(home) stretch: Final straight; portion of the racetrack to the finish.

stride: Distance covered between successive imprints of the same hoof. Also, manner of going.

subscription: Fee paid by owner to nominate a horse or maintain eligibility for a stakes race.

substitute race: Alternate race used to replace a regularly scheduled race that does not fill or is canceled.

suckling: A foal that is still nursing.

suspensory ligament: A ligament that originates at the back of the knee (front leg) and the back of the top part of the cannon bone (hind leg), attaching to the sesamoid bones. The lower portion of the ligament attaches the lower part of the sesamoid bones to the pastern bones. Its function is to support the fetlock. The lower ligaments that attach the sesamoid bone to the pastern bones are the distal sesamoidean ligaments.

swayback: Horse with a prominent concave shape of the backbone, usually just behind the withers (saddle area).

tack: 1) Rider's racing equipment. Also applied to stable gear. 2) As a verb, a jockey, including his/her equipment, as in: "He tacks 112 pounds."

taken up: A horse pulled up sharply by its rider because of being in close quarters. It generally causes a horse to alter its stride and lose ground.

tattoo: A permanent, indelible mark on the inside of the upper lip used to identify the horse.

teaser: A male horse used at breeding farms to determine whether a mare is ready to receive a stallion.

test barn: The structure where horses are taken for post-race testing. Tests may include saliva, urine, and/or blood.

Thoroughbred: A Thoroughbred is a horse whose parentage traces back to any of the three founding sires: the Byerly Turk, Darley Arabain, and Godolophin Barb, who has satisfied the rules and requirements of The Jockey Club, and is registered in The American Stud Book or in a foreign stud book recognized by The Jockey Club and the International Stud Book Committee. Any other horse, no matter what its parentage, is not considered a Thoroughbred for racing and/or breeding purposes.

tight: Ready to race.

tightener: 1) A race used to give a horse a level of fitness that cannot be obtained through morning exercises alone. 2) A leg brace.

toe in: A conformation flaw in which the front of the foot faces in and looks pigeon-toed, often causing the leg to swing outward during locomotion (paddling).

toe out: A conformation flaw in which the front of the foot faces out, often causing the leg to swing inward during locomotion (winging).

tongue strap/tie: Strip of cloth-type material used to stabilize a horse's tongue to prevent it from swallowing or "choking down" in a race or workout, or to keep the tongue from sliding up over the bit, rendering the horse uncontrollable.

top line: A Thoroughbred's breeding on its sire side.

track bias: A racing surface that favors a particular running style or position. For example, a track bias can favor either front-runners or closers or horses running on the inside or outside.

track condition: Condition of the racetrack surface. See "fast," "good," "muddy," "sloppy," and "frozen" for dirt surfaces; "hard," "firm," "soft," "yielding," and "heavy" for turf courses.

trip: An individual horse's race, specifically the difficulty or lack thereof during the race.

turn down(s): Rear shoe that is turned down a half to 1 inch at the ends to provide better traction on an off-track. Illegal at many tracks.

twitch: A restraining device usually consisting of a stick with a loop of rope or chain at one end, which is placed around a horse's upper lip and twisted, releasing endorphins that relax a horse and curb its fractiousness while it is being handled.

tying up (acute rhabdomyolysis): A form of muscle cramps that ranges in severity from mild stiffness to a life-threatening disease.

under wraps: Horse under stout restraint in a race or workout to keep it from pulling away from the competition by too large a margin.

valet: A person employed by a racing association to clean and care for a jockey's tack and other riding equipment.

walkover: A race in which only one horse competes.

washed out: The presence of noticeable, often lathery, sweat on a horse, usually indicating pre-race nervousness.

weanling: A foal that is less than one year old that has been separated from its dam.

weigh in (out): The certification, by the clerk of scales, of a rider's weight before (after) a race. A jockey weighs in fully dressed with all equipment except for his/her helmet, whip, and (in many jurisdictions) flak jacket.

weight-for-age: An allowance condition in which each entrant is assigned a weight according to its age. Females usually receive a "sex allowance" as well. (Compare with a handicap race.)

wobbler syndrome: Neurological disease associated with incoordination and weakness; can be caused by injury or by malformation.

work: To exercise a horse by galloping, usually in the morning, a pre-determined distance.

workout: A timed morning work. The official time is recorded by the clockers and published in the program.

yearling: A horse in its second calendar year of life, beginning January 1 of the year following its birth.

yielding: Condition of a turf course with a great deal of moisture. Horses' hooves sink in and dig up the course, and times are slower.

Licensing Requirements

(1)   Arizona licenses are issued on a three-year cycle. The cost is pro-rated depending upon the year licensed.

(2)   In California, corporation register fee is waived for California corporations.

(3)   In Florida, a contact person must be appointed if there are more than 10 shareholders in a horse.

(4)   In Indiana, if under 16, the parents or legal guardians must also be licensed as owners.

(5)   In Kentucky and Michigan, if under 18, the parents or legal guardians must also be licensed as owners.

(6)   Kentucky and New York only licenses individuals. While a stable name may be used, an individuals name is listed with it.

(7)   In Maryland, a contribution to the Jockey Injury Compensation Fund must be made before becoming licensed. This fee runs between $75 and $100.

(8)   In Maryland, an owner must be in the process of obtaining an annual license while using their temporary license.

(9)   In New Jersey there is no fee to register a two-person partnership.

(10)   In New York, horses with 35 or less owners, all must be licensed. If 35 or more owners, each person having a 3% interest or greater must be licensed.

(11)   In Ohio, a partnership of six or more must use a stable name.

(12)   In Virginia, proof of workers' compensation must be shown if a stable has three or more employees.

(13)   In Washington, a $30 owners license is available for those owners running in race meets of less than 10 days.

Appendix

State-by-State Claiming Rules

	Arizona	Arkansas	California	Colorado	Delaware	Florida (Calder)	Florida (Tampa)	Florida (Gulfstream)
Non-owners may claim if issued claiming authorization certificate.	x	x	x	x	x	x	x	x
Claiming authorization must be submitted _ days before the race.	7	NS	NS	NS	NS	NS	NS	NS
Claiming authorization certificate valid for ? or first claim, whichever comes first.	6 months	calendar year	two years	30 days	30 days	NS	meet	meet
Authorized agent of owner may claim.	x	x	x	x	x	x	x	x
Maximum number of horses that one owner can claim from a race.	NS	1	1	NS	1	1	1	1
If a stable consists of horses owned by more than one person that are trained by the same trainer, not more than one claim may be entered on behalf of such stable in any one race.	x	x	x	NS	x	NS	x	x
Claims must be deposited at least _ minutes prior to post.	10	15	15	10	10	15	15	15
Claim is effective when horse _.	Starts	Starts	Starts	Steps on track	Starts	Starts	Starts	Starts
For _ days after being claimed, a horse may not start in a race unless entered for a claiming price at least 25% greater than the amount for which it was claimed.	30	30	25	No such rule	30*	30*	No such rule	30
No horse claimed shall be sold or transferred within _ days after the day it was claimed, unless in another claiming race.	30	30	30	30	30	30	30	30
A claimed horse shall not race elsewhere until the meet from which it was claimed ends, or ? days, whichever is less. (Stakes excluded, with Stewards' approval.)	60 days, or until meet ends	until meet ends	until meet ends	30 days, or until meet ends	60 days, or until meet ends	90 days	In-state, immediately out-of-state, not until meet ends	90 days, or until meet ends
Engagements of a claimed horse pass automatically with the horse to the claimant.	x	x	x	x	x	x	x	x

(NS means not stated in the rules.)

* In Delaware, Florida (Calder & Gulfstream Park), and Oklahoma, a horse must simply race for a price greater than which it was claimed for the 30 days after being claimed.

** In Iowa, only winners must race for a price greater than which they were claimed for the next 30 days.

State-by-State Claiming Rules

	Illinois	Indiana	Iowa	Kansas	Kentucky	Louisiana	Maryland	Massachusetts
Non-owners may claim if issued claiming authorization certificate.	x	x	x	x	x	x	x	x
Claiming authorization must be submitted _ days before the race.	NS	NS	NS	NS	15 days	NS	NS	NS
Claiming authorization certificate valid for ? or first claim, whichever comes first.	calendar year	30 days	NS	30 days	calendar year	30 days	calendar year	calendar year
Authorized agent of owner may claim.	x	x	x	x	x	x	x	x
Maximum number of horses that one owner can claim from a race.	1	1	NS	1	3	1	1	1
If a stable consists of horses owned by more than one person that are trained by the same trainer, not more than one claim may be entered on behalf of such stable in any one race.	NS	x	x	NS	NS	x	NS	x
Claims must be deposited at least _ minutes prior to post.	10	15	10	10	15	15	10	10
Claim is effective when horse _.	Starts	Starts	Starts	Steps on track	Starts	leaves paddock	Starts	Starts
For _ days after being claimed, a horse may not start in a race unless entered for a claiming price at least 25% greater than the amount for which it was claimed.	No such rule	No such rule	30**	30	30	30	No such rule	No such rule
No horse claimed shall be sold or transferred within _ days after the day it was claimed, unless in another claiming race.	30	30	30	30	30	30	30	30
A claimed horse shall not race elsewhere until the meet from which it was claimed ends, or ? days, whichever is less. (Stakes excluded, with Stewards' approval.)	60 days, or until meet ends	until meet ends	until meet ends	30 days	until meet ends	60 days, or until meet ends	60 days	60 days, or until meet ends
Engagements of a claimed horse pass automatically with the horse to the claimant.	x	x	x	x	x	x	x	x

* In Delaware, Florida (Calder & Gulfstream Park), and Oklahoma, a horse must simply race for a price greater than which it was claimed for the 30 days after being claimed.

** In Iowa, only winners must race for a price greater than which they were claimed for the next 30 days.

State-by-State Claiming Rules

	Michigan	Minnesota	Nebraska	New Hampshire	New Jersey	New Mexico	New York	Ohio
■ Non-owners may claim if issued claiming authorization certificate.	x	x	x	x	x	x	x	x
■ Claiming authorization must be submitted _ days before the race.	10 days	10 days	NS	NS	NS	NS	NS	15 days
■ Claiming authorization certificate valid for ? or first claim, whichever comes first.	6 months	calendar year	two years	30 days	30 days	NS	meet	meet
■ Authorized agent of owner may claim.	x	x	x	x	x	x	x	x
■ Maximum number of horses that one owner can claim from a race.	1	1	1	NS	1	NS	1	1
■ If a stable consists of horses owned by more than one person that are trained by the same trainer, not more than one claim may be entered on behalf of such stable in any one race.	x	NS	x	x	x	NS	x	x
■ Claims must be deposited at least _ minutes prior to post.	15	15	10	15	10	10	10	10
■ Claim is effective when horse _ .	Starts	Starts	Starts	Steps on track	Starts	Steps on track	Starts	Starts
■ For _ days after being claimed, a horse may not start in a race unless entered for a claiming price at least 25% greater than the amount for which it was claimed.	No such rule	No such rule	30	No such rule	30	No such rule	30	No such rule
■ No horse claimed shall be sold or transferred within _ days after the day it was claimed, unless in another claiming race.	30	30	30	30	30	30	30	30
■ A claimed horse shall not race elsewhere until the meet from which it was claimed ends, or ? days, whichever is less. (Stakes excluded, with Stewards' approval.)	30 days, or until meet ends	60 days or until meet ends	until meet ends	60 days, or until meet ends	until meet ends	NS	until meet ends	30 days
■ Engagements of a claimed horse pass automatically with the horse to the claimant.	NS	x	NS	x	x	x	NS	NS

* In Delaware, Florida (Calder & Gulfstream Park), and Oklahoma, a horse must simply race for a price greater than which it was claimed for the 30 days after being claimed.

** In Iowa, only winners must race for a price greater than which they were claimed for the next 30 days.

State-by-State Claiming Rules

	Oklahoma	Oregon	Pennsylvania	Texas	Virginia	Washington	West Virginia
■ Non-owners may claim if issued claiming authorization certificate.	x	x	x	x	x	x	x
■ Claiming authorization must be submitted _ days before the race.	NS	NS	NS	NS	NS	NS	5
■ Claiming authorization certificate valid for ? or first claim, whichever comes first.	NS	NS	30	NS	calendar year	end of meet	calendar year
■ Authorized agent of owner may claim.	x	x	x	x	x	x	x
■ Maximum number of horses that one owner can claim from a race.	1	1 or more	1	1	1	1	1
■ If a stable consists of horses owned by more than one person that are trained by the same trainer; not more than one claim may be entered on behalf of such stable in any one race.	x 1 per owner		x	NS	x	x	x
■ Claims must be deposited at least _ minutes prior to post.	10	15	10	15	15	15	10
■ Claim is effective when horse _.	Starts	Starts	Starts	Steps on track	Starts	Starts	Starts
■ For _ days after being claimed, a horse may not start in a race unless entered for a claiming price at least 25% greater than the amount for which it was claimed.	30*	NS	x	NS	30	30	No such rule
■ No horse claimed shall be sold or transferred within _ days after the day it was claimed, unless in another claiming race.	30	30	30	30	30	30	30
■ A claimed horse shall not race elsewhere until the meet from which it was claimed ends, or _ days, whichever is less. (Stakes excluded, with Stewards' approval.)	30 days, or until meet ends	NS	60 days	until meet ends	30 days, or until meet ends	NS	60 days
■ Engagements of a claimed horse pass automatically with the horse to the claimant.	x	x	x	x	NS	NS	NS

* In Delaware, Florida (Calder & Gulfstream Park), and Oklahoma, a horse must simply race for a price greater than which it was claimed for the 30 days after being claimed.

** In Iowa, only winners must race for a price greater than which they were claimed for the next 30 days.

Appendix

Average 2002 Operating Costs

	Arizona	Arkansas	California (Northern)	California (Southern)	Colorado	Delaware	Florida	Illinois	Indiana
■ Day Rate	$30-$35	$50-65	$50-60	$65-90	$20-35	$55	$50 (Calder) $75-90 (Gulfstream)	$50-65	$40-45
■ Farrier	$65	$80-125	$100	$110-120	$60-70	$80	$80 (Calder) $100-125 (Gulfstream)	$100	$60-70
■ Equine Dentist	$40	$50-60	$75	$40-65	$40	$35	$35-40	$45-50	$30-35
■ Race Day Pony to Post	$12	$10	$25	$25	$12	$15-20	$15	$15	$20
■ Race Day Lasix	$20	$15	$25	$25	$20	$20	$12	$20	$15
■ Pre Race Bute	$12	$15-20	$15	$15	$12	$10-12	$12	$15	$10-12
■ Farm Lay-Up	$8-10	$10-25	$15	$10-25	$10	$15-25	$10-25	$18	$10-15
■ Tax on Claimed Horses	None	Sales + City	Sales	Sales	None	None	**Sales	None	None
■ Other Racehorse Tax	None	None	None	*L.A. Co. Racehorse Tax	None	None	None	None	None

	Iowa	Kansas	Kentucky	Louisiana	Maryland	Massachusetts	Michigan	Minnesota	New Hampshire
■ Day Rate	$40-$45	$25-35	$65	$40-45	$50-55	$40-45	$35	$35-40	$40-45
■ Farrier	$80-85	$70	$100	$75-100	$80	$85	$80	$70-75	$85
■ Equine Dentist	$45	$25	$45-50	$60-75	$35	$40	$40	$40	$40
■ Race Day Pony to Post	$20	$12	$20-25	$15	$20	$12	$10	$15	$12
■ Race Day Lasix	$16	$15	$15	$15	$10-12	$10-15	$17	$20	$10-15
■ Pre Race Bute	$10	$15	$15	$15	$10-12	$12	$11	$12	$12
■ Farm Lay-Up	$12-15	$15	$17-25	$10-20	$15-25	$15	$11	$10-15	$15
■ Tax on Claimed Horses	Sales	None	Sales	Sales	Sales	Sales	None	None	None
■ Other Racehorse Tax	None	None	None	None	***"Gate" Fee	None	None	None	None

Average 2002 Operating Costs

	New Jersey	New Mexico	New York	Ohio	Oklahoma	Oregon	Pennsylvania	Texas	Virginia
■ Day Rate	$60-65	$30	$70-90	$30-40	$40	$20	$30 (Penn Nat'l) $40-50 (Phil. Park)	$45-55	$50
■ Farrier	$90-110	$65	$125-150	$75	$65	$65	$70-80	$70-90	$80
■ Equine Dentist	$40-50	$35	$45-60	$20-40	$45	$55	$35-45	$50	$35
■ Race Day Pony to Post	$17	$15	$20	$20	$15	$12	$12-17	$15	$15-20
■ Race Day Lasix	$15	$25	$15	$15-20	$15	$17	$15-20	$15-20	$20
■ Pre Race Bute	$15	$15	$10	$5-15	$15	$15	$15	$15-20	$10-12
■ Farm Lay-Up	$15-20	$10-12	$20	$12	$10-15	$8	$12-15	$15-25	$15-25
■ Tax on Claimed Horses	****Sales	None	None	None	None	None	None	None	None
■ Other Racehorse Tax	None	None	None	None	None	None	None	None	None

	Washington	West Virginia
■ Day Rate	$40-50	$35-40
■ Farrier	$90	$65-75
■ Equine Dentist	$60	$25-40
■ Race Day Pony to Post	$20	$15-20
■ Race Day Lasix	$25	$10-15
■ Pre Race Bute	$15-20	$10-15
■ Farm Lay-Up	$12-15	$10-14
■ Tax on Claimed Horses	Sales	Sales
■ Other Racehorse Tax	None	None

* Los Angeles County charges a nominal ($20-150) tax on racehorses based upon a horse's earnings.

** In Florida, sales tax is not charged if a horse is claimed from its breeder.

*** While not a tax, Maryland's tracks charge a "Gate" fee of $15.00 per start to help fund the Horsemen's Assistance Program for backstretch workers.

**** In New Jersey, sales tax is only charged the first time a horse is claimed in a year. However, if a horse is subsequently claimed in the same year for a higher price, sales tax is charged on the incremental difference in claiming price.

Appendix

Conformation

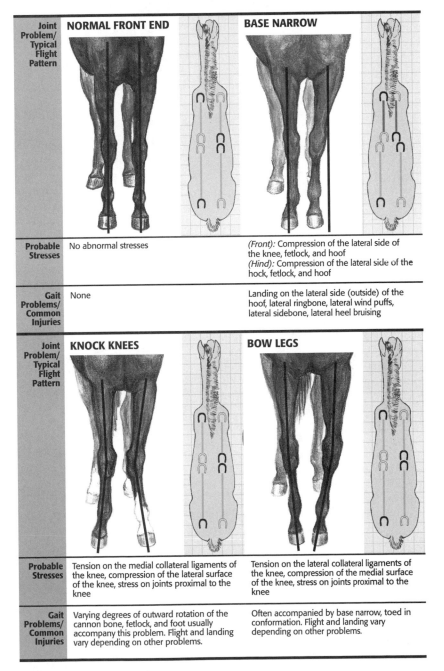

	NORMAL FRONT END	BASE NARROW
Joint Problem/ Typical Flight Pattern		
Probable Stresses	No abnormal stresses	*(Front):* Compression of the lateral side of the knee, fetlock, and hoof *(Hind):* Compression of the lateral side of the hock, fetlock, and hoof
Gait Problems/ Common Injuries	None	Landing on the lateral side (outside) of the hoof, lateral ringbone, lateral wind puffs, lateral sidebone, lateral heel bruising
	KNOCK KNEES	BOW LEGS
Joint Problem/ Typical Flight Pattern		
Probable Stresses	Tension on the medial collateral ligaments of the knee, compression of the lateral surface of the knee, stress on joints proximal to the knee	Tension on the lateral collateral ligaments of the knee, compression of the medial surface of the knee, stress on joints proximal to the knee
Gait Problems/ Common Injuries	Varying degrees of outward rotation of the cannon bone, fetlock, and foot usually accompany this problem. Flight and landing vary depending on other problems.	Often accompanied by base narrow, toed in conformation. Flight and landing vary depending on other problems.

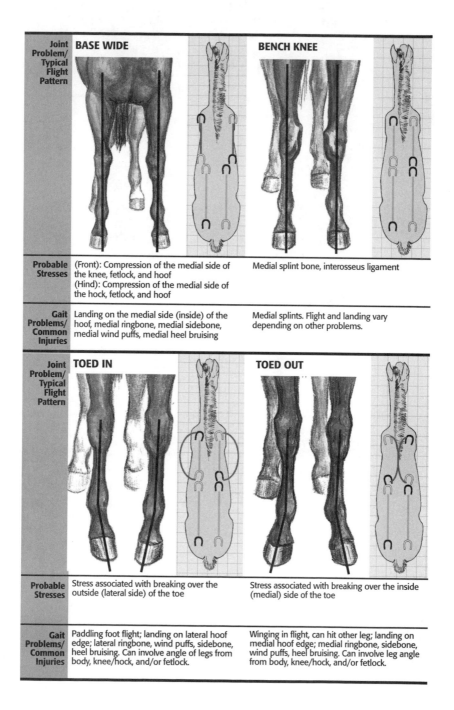

Joint Problem/ Typical Flight Pattern	**BASE WIDE**	**BENCH KNEE**
Probable Stresses	(Front): Compression of the medial side of the knee, fetlock, and hoof (Hind): Compression of the medial side of the hock, fetlock, and hoof	Medial splint bone, interosseus ligament
Gait Problems/ Common Injuries	Landing on the medial side (inside) of the hoof, medial ringbone, medial sidebone, medial wind puffs, medial heel bruising	Medial splints. Flight and landing vary depending on other problems.
Joint Problem/ Typical Flight Pattern	**TOED IN**	**TOED OUT**
Probable Stresses	Stress associated with breaking over the outside (lateral side) of the toe	Stress associated with breaking over the inside (medial) side of the toe
Gait Problems/ Common Injuries	Paddling foot flight; landing on lateral hoof edge; lateral ringbone, wind puffs, sidebone, heel bruising. Can involve angle of legs from body, knee/hock, and/or fetlock.	Winging in flight, can hit other leg; landing on medial hoof edge; medial ringbone, sidebone, wind puffs, heel bruising. Can involve leg angle from body, knee/hock, and/or fetlock.

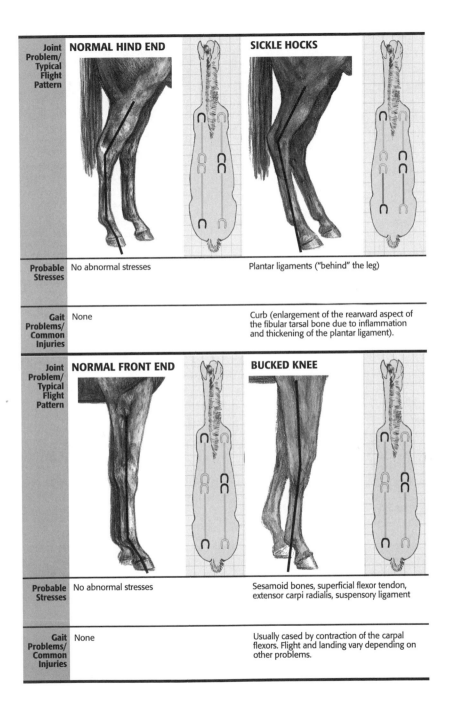

	NORMAL HIND END	SICKLE HOCKS
Joint Problem/ Typical Flight Pattern		
Probable Stresses	No abnormal stresses	Plantar ligaments ("behind" the leg)
Gait Problems/ Common Injuries	None	Curb (enlargement of the rearward aspect of the fibular tarsal bone due to inflammation and thickening of the plantar ligament).

	NORMAL FRONT END	BUCKED KNEE
Joint Problem/ Typical Flight Pattern		
Probable Stresses	No abnormal stresses	Sesamoid bones, superficial flexor tendon, extensor carpi radialis, suspensory ligament
Gait Problems/ Common Injuries	None	Usually cased by contraction of the carpal flexors. Flight and landing vary depending on other problems.

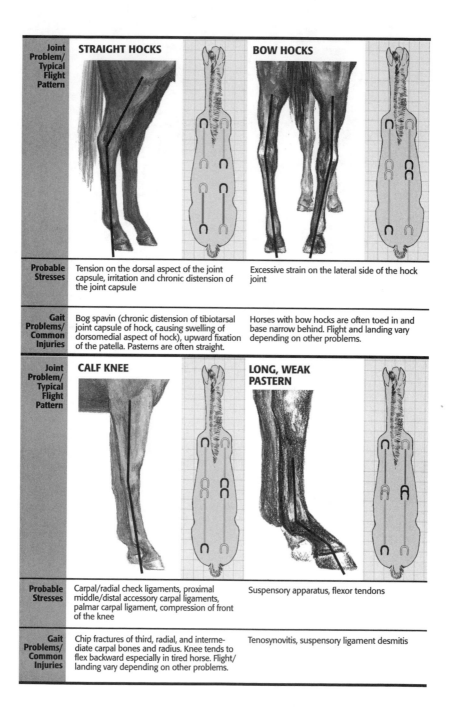

	STRAIGHT HOCKS	BOW HOCKS
Joint Problem/ Typical Flight Pattern		
Probable Stresses	Tension on the dorsal aspect of the joint capsule, irritation and chronic distension of the joint capsule	Excessive strain on the lateral side of the hock joint
Gait Problems/ Common Injuries	Bog spavin (chronic distension of tibiotarsal joint capsule of hock, causing swelling of dorsomedial aspect of hock), upward fixation of the patella. Pasterns are often straight.	Horses with bow hocks are often toed in and base narrow behind. Flight and landing vary depending on other problems.

	CALF KNEE	LONG, WEAK PASTERN
Joint Problem/ Typical Flight Pattern		
Probable Stresses	Carpal/radial check ligaments, proximal middle/distal accessory carpal ligaments, palmar carpal ligament, compression of front of the knee	Suspensory apparatus, flexor tendons
Gait Problems/ Common Injuries	Chip fractures of third, radial, and intermediate carpal bones and radius. Knee tends to flex backward especially in tired horse. Flight/ landing vary depending on other problems.	Tenosynovitis, suspensory ligament desmitis

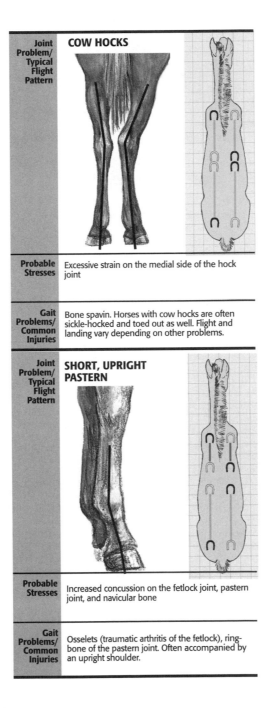

Joint Problem/ Typical Flight Pattern	**COW HOCKS**
Probable Stresses	Excessive strain on the medial side of the hock joint
Gait Problems/ Common Injuries	Bone spavin. Horses with cow hocks are often sickle-hocked and toed out as well. Flight and landing vary depending on other problems.
Joint Problem/ Typical Flight Pattern	**SHORT, UPRIGHT PASTERN**
Probable Stresses	Increased concussion on the fetlock joint, pastern joint, and navicular bone
Gait Problems/ Common Injuries	Osselets (traumatic arthritis of the fetlock), ringbone of the pastern joint. Often accompanied by an upright shoulder.

Illustrations courtesy of Robin Peterson

Acknowledgments

This *Owners' Handbook* was first published by the Thoroughbred Owners of California (TOC) in 1996 and was written by **Paula Deats** and **Alan Landsburg**.

The text was expanded, revised, and updated by **Laura Proctor** for TOBA in 2002 and edited and produced by **Eclipse Press**, the book division of Blood-Horse Publications. A special thanks is extended to the following individuals for their assistance, insight, and advice with this guide.

John Amerman, Thoroughbred owner
Ed Anthony, Pedigree Consultant, Three Chimneys Farm
Rick Arthur, DVM
Kyle Baze, Farrier
Rogers Beasley, Director of Racing, Keeneland Association
Pam Blatz-Murff, Senior Vice-President, Breeders' Cup
Steve Conboy, DVM
Robert Courtney Jr., principal, Crestfield Farm
Richard Craigo, equine attorney
Gene Davis, Weaver & Associates Insurance Agency
Allison DeLuca, Assistant Racing Secretary, Churchill Downs
Mark Dewey, Farrier, B. Walter Services, Inc.
Kevin Dunlavy, DVM
Robert Hill, CPA, Crowe Chizek & Co.
Bob Hubbard, President, Bob Hubbard Horse Transportation, Inc.
Robert Keck, Pedigree Consultant, Crestwood Farm
Dan Kenny, Dan Kenny Bloodstock Agency
Lucinda Mandella, Owners' Liaison, Thoroughbred Owners of California
Jim Miller, Paymaster of Purses, Hollywood Park
Steve Obrekaitis, Steward, Ellis Park
Ed O'Rourke, Jerry Parks Insurance Group
John Oxley, Thoroughbred owner
Jerry Parks, Jerry Parks Insurance Group
Hap Proctor, General Manager, Glen Hill Farm
Ken Reed, DVM
Geoffrey Russell, Director of Sales, Keeneland Association
John Russell, racing consultant and former trainer
Scott D. Stanley, PhD, UC Davis Equine Analytical Chemistry Laboratory
Nancy Tripp, Consultant, Colombo Bloodstock Agency
Scot Waterman, DVM, NTRA Drug-Testing Task Force
Sue Winter, Assistant Paymaster of Purses, Hollywood Park

Finally, special thanks is given to Thoroughbred Owners of California President **John Van de Kamp,** who generously allowed TOBA use of TOC's original Handbook for Thoroughbred Owners of California as a basis for this book.